JOHN WESLEY'S CONCEPTION AND USE OF SCRIPTURE

JOHN WESLEY'S CONCEPTION
AND USE OF SCRIPTURE

Scott J. Jones

KINGSWOOD BOOKS

An Imprint of Abingdon Press
Nashville, Tennessee

JOHN WESLEY'S CONCEPTION AND USE OF SCRIPTURE

95 96 97 98 99 00 01 02 03 04—10 9 8 7 6 5 4 3 2 1

Library of Congress Cataloging-in-Publication Data

Jones, Scott J.
  John Wesley's conception and use of scripture / Scott J. Jones.
    p. cm.
  Revision of the author's thesis (doctoral)—Southern Methodist Univ.
  Includes bibliographical references and index.
  ISBN 0-687-20466-6 (alk. paper)
    1. Wesley, John, 1703–1791. 2. Bible—Criticism, interpretation, etc.—History—
18th century. 3. Bible—Evidences, authority, etc.—History of doctrines—18th century.
I. Title.
BX8495.W5J58   1995
220'.092—dc20   95-20420
                                                                              CIP

Except for brief paraphrases or unless otherwise noted, scripture quotations are from the Authorized (AV) or King James Version of the Bible.

Printed in the United States of America on recycled, acid-free paper.

To Mary Lou,
my partner in serving God

Contents

Acknowledgments

To paraphrase Isaac Newton, however far I have seen, it is because I have stood on the shoulders of others. This study is indebted to a number of persons who have shared their knowledge of John Wesley and the history of biblical interpretation with me. Some of them are acknowledged in the notes and bibliography. This book is a revision of my doctoral dissertation at Southern Methodist University. The members of my dissertation committee, Professors John Deschner, Richard Heitzenrater, and William Babcock, have been my teachers; I am especially grateful to them for their guidance during the past eighteen years. In addition, the late Albert Outler started me on this research and gave a great deal of helpful advice in its early stages.

The members of Prosper United Methodist Church, Prosper, Texas, were more than patient with me during the years of my pastorate there. More recently, the people of First United Methodist Church in Howe, Texas, have helped me finish my work. Specifically, Jamie Middleton helped check the accuracy of references in the notes. The support of both these churches for this project of academic research has been genuine and timely.

The support of my family has been instrumental in completing the project, which took far longer than originally intended. To Mary Lou and my children, Jameson, Arthur, and Marynell, I say thank you.

Scott J. Jones
Howe, Texas
March 1995

Introduction

Questions about the authority and proper use of Scripture have been at the center of theological inquiry in Western Christianity since 1518, if not longer.[1] Martin Luther's appeal to the Bible as an authority to counter the Papacy began a long process of inquiry and questioning which gave birth to modern Western theology in all its forms. Since that time many new developments in theology have been accompanied by corresponding developments in the conception and interpretation of the Bible. These developments have led to a wide diversity of views about the Bible and occasionally to bitter debates and divisions within the Christian church. To remedy the divisions and make progress in the debates, it is desirable for Christian theology to articulate a coherent, credible, and widely accepted conception of Scripture.

Further progress toward such a conception would be helped in two ways by a more complete understanding of the history of biblical interpretation. First, it would clarify the present situation. By illuminating how we arrived at the present range of views held by Christian theologians, it would help to explain many of the differences within that range. Underlying problems and possibilities could become more clear if placed within a larger context. Second, there may be resources in the past that could serve as guides for the future. Historical theology is in part the research that seeks help from the past for addressing today's problems. Without guaranteeing that such help exists, historical theologians can examine the past for ideas and approaches that could conceivably open up new avenues of research for constructive theology in the future.

Purpose

This study of John Wesley's conception and use of Scripture seeks to contribute to a fresh understanding of the interpretation of Scripture in both of these ways. First, it will add a segment to the history of biblical interpretation by describing the work of a key figure in eighteenth-century Christianity. While a complete history of biblical interpretation even in this one century is not yet possible, this study might contribute to that larger project. Studies of key figures like Wesley are a necessary prerequisite to a coherent historical view of that crucial period of transition. Second, this study asks if Wesley has any contribution to make to the resolution of theological problems facing us today. While anachronism must be avoided, it is still possible that the past, properly interpreted, can inform the present. A third purpose of this study is to contribute to the field of Wesley Studies by describing Wesley's theological method. Richard Heitzenrater has usefully surveyed the history of research in this field. At the level of "specialist studies," he says there is a need for studies of Wesley that take into account a broader range of factors than has been considered before.[2] By building on previous research and improvements in method, scholarly appraisals of John Wesley can be brought to a much higher level of accuracy. We must rigorously ask the questions that will allow us to understand his own life and thought.[3]

Method

This study is primarily descriptive in nature, seeking critically to describe and analyze Wesley's relation to the Bible. A fully critical description requires three stages of research: comprehensive examination of Wesley's writings, thorough description of both his conception and his use of Scripture, and broad description of Wesley's relation to his historical context. This study seeks to accomplish the first two of those tasks. Attention to Wesley's context will be given at certain key points, but to fully discuss his relation to the history of eighteenth-century biblical interpretation is beyond the scope of this study.

Comprehensiveness

A comprehensive description of Wesley's conception of Scripture must carefully consider all of Wesley's relevant statements.[4] While partial studies of Wesley's writings have been done, they suffer from the possibility that they have overlooked a crucial component of Wesley's thought. Wesley's writings are not systematic in structure. Albert Outler argues that their eclectic style was deliberately chosen by Wesley because theology ought to be conceived as "coherent reflection upon Christian living, with all its natural divagations."[5] They are occasional in nature, written for specific audiences on specific topics. Some of his most important themes, such as Christian perfection, are treated numerous times as the primary subject of discussion in the corpus. Others, such as his doctrine of God, are treated only in short sections as a secondary topic or presupposition of the main point. Thus, it is impossible to claim that a small group of Wesley's writings provides an adequate basis for determining Wesley's position on a given subject. To understand Wesley fully, a comprehensive review of his writings must be carried out. For this study all of Wesley's original writings have been searched, and some 1,230 references to Scripture and theological method have been compiled. These references form the database from which conclusions about Wesley's views are drawn.

With two exceptions, only Wesley's original writings have been used. Abridged and edited works, such as *The Christian Library*, pose methodological problems for an investigation that aims to discover Wesley's own views. Not only did he not compose the original words, he sometimes explicitly disclaimed responsibility for every detail of the finished product.[6] In cases where Wesley includes borrowed material in the middle of an otherwise original work,[7] the borrowed portions have been ignored.

The two exceptions to this are the two works of abridgment for which Wesley took special responsibility: *The Explanatory Notes upon the New Testament* and the "Articles of Religion." Although the *Notes* were borrowed largely from Bengel, with additional material from Doddridge, Guyse, and Heylyn,[8] they do contain significant contributions from Wesley himself. The main reason for including this material is that Wesley himself took responsibility for this work as a measure of Methodist preaching. Along with the "four volumes of 'Sermons,'" the *Notes* were the standards for Methodist preaching enshrined in the Model Deed.[9] Frank Baker notes that Wesley carefully revised and enlarged the third edition of the work and quotes the *Journal* for December 12, 1759, where Wesley says that he, his brother, and others were "correcting and enlarging the notes as we saw occasion."[10] All of this work will be treated as if it were Wesley's own.

The "Articles of Religion" also felt Wesley's formulating hand, but in a different way. Here, Wesley took the Thirty-nine Articles of the

13

Church of England and revised them down to twenty-four. While he added very little new material, his omissions are significant. Wesley also took special responsibility for this editorial work since the Articles were to form the standard of doctrine for the new Methodist Episcopal Church in America. Although this work cannot be treated as Wesley's own, his editorial work can yield significant conclusions if handled carefully.

With regard to Wesley's use of Scripture, comprehensiveness is best served by intensive analysis of a representative body of material. Appendix 1 gives a complete list of the works used for this purpose. It was selected to be representative of the different types of his work as well as the different periods of his life. The generally reliable "Index of Scriptural References"[11] in the Bicentennial Edition of Wesley's sermons has been used to draw statistical conclusions about his use of Scripture in that body of material.

Conception and Use

For the study of any Christian theologian's relation to Scripture, it is of fundamental importance to compare and contrast that person's *conception* of Scripture with his or her *use* of Scripture. Whether or not all theologians must work with some conception of written revelation is not at issue here. This methodological argument concerns the proper study of Christian theologians for whom the issue of scriptural authority is inescapable. By "conception" I mean explicit statements about Scripture, whether systematically formulated or not. By "use" I mean an analysis of how scriptural citations and allusions actually perform in the relevant texts.

This distinction is similar to that between words and deeds. What a person *says* about Scripture is one thing. What that same person *does* with Scripture is a separate matter. It is not enough simply to quote any theologian's words about Scripture without asking whether his or her use is congruent with those stated views. The words about Scripture are called the "conception," and what is actually done with Scripture is called its "use."

To the extent that a theologian has addressed basic issues of religious authority and theological method, his or her conception will include treatments of a number of familiar topics about Scripture. One would expect to find statements about Scripture's authority, its inspiration, hermeneutical rules, and the relationship between the Old and New Testaments. A full treatment of theological method would certainly include discussions of each of these.

For each of these topics, an analogue can be isolated in the person's use of Scripture. With regard to the authority of Scripture, a critical analysis can ask in what relation does Scripture actually stand to other warrants for theological conclusions. In Wesley's doctrine of authority, Scripture is given first place, but some role is given to reason, Christian antiquity, experience, and the Church of England. An analysis of use should ask if Scripture really has primacy as a norm in his theology and what are the precise roles played by the other norms he uses. Similarly, explicit statements about biblical inspiration need to be compared with the differences between interpretations of the Bible and texts considered to be noninspired. Hermeneutical rules need to be compared with the actual exegesis employed. Any theory about the relationship between the two testaments must be compared with how texts from both are used to explain, refute, or support one another.

Only by carefully examining both conception and use can a theologian's relation to Scripture be fully understood. For example, it is possible to make strong claims about the authority of Scripture and then to do theology in a way that rarely relies on that authority at all. Conversely, it is possible to have a broad understanding of multiple authorities, but in practice to rely on Scripture to the near exclusion of all competing authorities. To consider only one side, either the conception or the use, runs the risk of misunderstanding the subject by ignoring significant data.

As with any comparison between theory and practice, one can expect to find both consistency and inconsistency. What becomes interesting is the way in which the differences between the conception and use of Scripture illuminate each other. The stated conception of Scripture may show why Scripture is being used in a certain way, and the various uses of Scripture may show what was really intended by the conception.

A critical description of Wesley's conception of Scripture must allow Wesley to speak for himself in an organized manner. Wesley was not, however, a systematic theologian; he did not write a treatise on the Bible or on theological method. Rather, he addressed topics that were needed for the preaching of the Gospel and the maintenance of the Revival. His explicit statements about Scripture are scattered throughout his writings. Thus, one must find an appropriate way to organize the material. The goal of this investigation is in part to construct a unified view of Scripture that is authentically Wesley's. This approach assumes that Wesley had a coherent doctrine of scriptural authority. If he did, the historian's task is to state that position and account for the apparently contradictory formulations in the Wesley corpus. If he did not, that will be apparent at the end of the study.

In short, a statement of Wesley's conception of Scripture should allow him to articulate his own position clearly. Such a statement should then be compared with an analysis of his use. This procedure will yield a more complete understanding of Wesley's theological method than would an examination of either conception or use alone.

PART ONE

JOHN WESLEY'S CONCEPTION OF SCRIPTURE

CHAPTER 1

The Authority of Scripture Alone

John Wesley conceives of Scripture alone as the authority for Christian faith and practice. Paradoxically, he also acknowledges the roles other authorities play in religious matters. This apparent contradiction between Scripture as sole authority and the roles of reason, Christian antiquity, experience, and the Church of England will be explored later in this study, but an accurate description of Wesley's conception must begin with his understanding of the authority of Scripture alone.

The categories which form the sections for this and the following chapter arise in part out of the corpus of Wesley's writings and in part out of the larger Christian tradition. Albert Outler's annotations of Wesley's *Sermons* have demonstrated his wide knowledge of that tradition. Thus, it is appropriate to use traditional theological categories as analytical tools to structure Wesley's own words on the relevant topics and show the systematic connections between different aspects of his conception of Scripture.

For example, Wesley does not give significant attention to the clarity of Scripture, and yet in this study it is treated as a distinct topic. There are two reasons for this. First, there is a prior history of the topic within Protestant theology, and Wesley was aware of that history. It is a helpful principle in interpreting Wesley to assume that he has the larger Christian tradition in mind even while writing "plain truth for plain people."[1] Second, isolating Wesley's views on this topic will help formulate his overall conception of Scripture. He presupposes the clarity of Scripture, and his views are succinctly stated in several places. By examining those views and showing their connections to the other aspects of Wesley's understanding of Scripture, one can gain a more complete and systematic account of his position. It is helpful to begin with the topic of revelation to show how Wesley understands the origins of the biblical writings. That understanding then sets the stage for a discussion of the inspiration of Scripture as a property of the text. Scripture's authority and infallibility can then be examined, and its sufficiency, clarity, wholeness, and canonicity considered.

Revelation

Wesley's understanding of revelation involves a communication of the divine message from God to God's chosen messengers—prophets, evangelists, and apostles. While recognizing that there are both divine and human elements in the process, he minimizes the human element and emphasizes the faithfulness with which the message is transcribed. Wesley's clearest statements about revelation are found in the *Explanatory Notes upon the New Testament*. In its Preface he says:

> Concerning the Scriptures in general, it may be observed, the word of the living God, which directed the first Patriarchs also, was, in the time of Moses, committed to writing. To this were added, in several succeeding generations, the inspired writings of the other Prophets. Afterwards, what the Son of God preached, and the Holy Ghost spake by the Apostles, the Apostles and Evangelists wrote.[2]

This description minimizes the human element in the process of revelation as much as possible. The "word of the living God" was written down. In the New Testament it was the words of Jesus and the Holy Ghost that the apostles and evangelists wrote down. Revelation is thus a faithful rendering of the message God gave to human beings. The messengers faithfully transmit what they were given and act as conduits of the divine message.

Wesley comes closest to an explicit statement of a dictation theory of revelation in his comments on the book of Revelation. Wesley notes that "all the books of the New Testament were written by the will of God, but none were so expressly commanded to be written."[3]

John's function was to write down what was spoken, and this became chapter 1. "What was contained in the second and third chapters was dictated to him in like manner."[4] By minimizing the participation of the recipients of revelation, the account at first appears to be a type of dictation. Even the human language employed was "the language which God Himself used."[5] An understanding of Wesley's view of inspiration must take into account these places where it appears that the process was like God dictating to the "penmen."

However, this is not the whole of Wesley's position; in other places his terms are more carefully nuanced. The note on 1 Thessalonians 4:15 identifies "the word of the Lord" as a "particular revelation." The same qualifier is used at 1 Corinthians 7:25:

> *I have no commandment from the Lord*—By a particular revelation. Nor was it necessary he should; for the apostles wrote nothing which was not divinely inspired: but with this difference,—sometimes they had a particular revelation, and a special commandment; at other times they wrote from the divine light which abode with them, the standing treasure of the Spirit of God. And this, also, was not their private opinion, but a divine rule of faith and practice.[6]

Thus, there are different types of revelation. A particular revelation is one where the specific words are given to the person. Indeed, the opening chapters of the Apocalypse of John contain such a revelation because specific words were commanded to be written down. Other parts of Scripture are explicitly noted as *not* being particular revelations but nevertheless inspired.

This distinction is crucial to a balanced account of Wesley's understanding of revelation. Wesley does not intend a mechanical dictation theory of inspiration. All Scripture is revealed from God, but only part of it was dictated by particular revelation. Most Scripture originated in a more general inspiration, "the divine light which abode with them, the standing treasure of the Spirit of God." This allows much more human participation in the process.

Wesley refers to at least three ways in which the prophets and apostles participated in the writing of Scripture. First, there is the possibility of other sources used for Scripture. Three possible sources are noted for Jude's claim that Enoch had foretold the second coming of Christ. "St. Jude might know this either from some ancient book, or tradition, or immediate revelation."[7] Discovering truths in ancient books or from traditional sources is outside the mechanical understanding of revelation where the Holy Spirit is understood to have told the inspired writers precisely what to put down.[8]

Second, revelation operates in such a way that normal human processes are left intact. In his comment on 1 Corinthians 14:32, he writes:

> The impulses of the Holy Spirit, even in men really inspired, so suit themselves to their rational faculties, as not to divest them of the government of themselves, like the heathen priests under their diabolical possession. Evil spirits threw their prophets into such ungovernable ecstacies, as forced them to speak and act like madmen. But the Spirit of God left his prophets the clear use of their judgment, when, and how long, it was fit for them to speak, and never hurried them into any improprieties either as to the matter, manner, or time of their speaking.[9]

Clearly, on this view, the prophets were participating in the process by using their judgment about how the message was best communicated. Although their judgment did not affect the content of what was said, the manner of speaking, and by implication, of writing also was a matter of judgment on the part of the individual who received the revelation. This view is strengthened by Wesley's contention that the apostles were left ignorant of some things and thus had "room to exercise faith and patience."[10] Concerning the Council of Jerusalem described in Acts 15, Wesley is puzzled that these men could be so confused about an issue so basic to the Christian faith. On verse 7 he comments, "For how really soever they were inspired, we need not suppose their inspiration was always so instantaneous and express, as to supersede any deliberation in their own minds, or any consultation with each other."[11] He sees that the apostles, while having God's spirit as a standing treasure, still must work through human processes of consultation to discover what is the right course of action. Nevertheless, they were protected from making a mistake in that process.

Third, the motivations of the apostles can be determinative in the content of an epistle. In discussing why Paul would write to Timothy, it is to Paul's motivations that Wesley turns. Although Paul had instructed Timothy privately, Wesley says that these letters were written "to fix things more upon his mind, and to give him an opportunity of having recourse to them afterward, and of communicating them to others, as there might be occasion, as also to leave divine directions in writing, for the use of the church and its ministers, in all ages."[12]

These motivations are directly attributed to Paul as reasons for writing the letters to his "son in the faith." They could be conceived as divine reasons for revealing these things to Paul, but they are not discussed in that way at all. Instead, the motivations are explained from a human point of view.

Thus, the process of revelation is seen by Wesley as a divine-human collaboration where the message of God is accurately communicated, but in a way that does not override human faculties, judgments, and motivations. This allows for ignorance on the part of the writers of Scripture, as well as confusion about some basic points. Most of the Scripture comes from the "standing treasure of the Spirit of God," which was with the inspired men all of the time. Some parts of Scripture, however, originate in "particular" revelations where the precise words are commanded to be written and are faithfully transcribed.

The Inspiration of Scripture

The process of revelation resulted in a set of writings which are described as "inspired." Despite the human participation in its writing, God is understood to be its author. The Preface to the *Notes* says:

> In the language of the sacred writings, we may observe the utmost depth, together with the utmost ease. All the elegancies of human composures sink into nothing before it: God speaks not as man, but as God. His thoughts are very deep; and thence his words are of inexhaustible virtue. And the language of his messengers, also, is exact in the highest degree: for the words which were given them accurately answered for the impression made upon their minds: And hence Luther says, "Divinity is nothing but a grammar of the language of the Holy Ghost."[13]

While human beings may shape the way the message is delivered, God is the author of the text. The Bible is the product of a divine-human collaboration, but the divine contribution far predominates the other side.

One of Wesley's strongest arguments for the inspiration of Scripture appears in "A Clear and Concise Demonstration of the Divine Inspiration of the Holy Scriptures." Here Wesley makes four basic arguments for inspiration: "miracles, prophecies, the goodness of the doctrine, and the moral character of the penmen." He then elaborates a version of the fourth argument:

> The Bible must be the invention either of good men or angels, bad men or devils, or of God.
>
> 1. It could not be the invention of good men or angels; for they neither would nor could make a book, and tell lies all the time they were writing it, saying, "Thus saith the Lord," when it was their own invention.
>
> 2. It could not be the invention of bad men or devils; for they would not make a book which commands all duty, forbids all sin, and condemns their souls to hell to all eternity.
>
> 3. Therefore, I draw this conclusion, that the Bible must be given by divine inspiration.[14]

Several points should be emphasized with reference to the content of this argument. First, Wesley makes a brief appeal to the fulfillment of prophecies and the miracles in the New Testament as evidence of Scripture's divine authorship. These arguments were standard ones for Scripture in his day and bore the brunt of the attacks made by the Deists. Anthony Collins' *Scheme of Literal Prophecy* attacked the credibility of the first, while Thomas Woolston and David Hume attacked the second.[15] Wesley shows no sign of replying to such attacks, but assumes that the conventional arguments need only to be referred to by name.

Second, there is a complete lack of historical perspective in the logical alternatives Wesley sets up. He assumes that the biblical writers shared his eighteenth-century understanding of divine revelation and especially of particular revelation. Wesley does not investigate any alternative understandings of what the biblical writers were doing. In his mind, the line between divine speech and human speech is sharply drawn. The recipient of a revelation could not fail to distinguish between God's words and his or her own thoughts. Thus, only a liar would write "thus saith the Lord" when the words were not genuinely given by God. How this sharp dichotomy compares with the broader view of revelation as "the divine light which abode with them" is unclear. Wesley would clearly say that a prophet should preface a particular revelation with "thus saith the Lord." Should such a preface be given to all inspired writings? How can prophets or apostles distinguish God's words from their own judgments and ways of expressing the message? Wesley does not answer these questions. In part, this is because the inspiration of Scripture is not a topic which he has investigated and on which he has arrived at an independent conclusion. Rather, the doctrine is only considered as a way to bolster his assertion of Scripture's authority.

Third, Wesley uses simplistic categories for grouping people based on their character. Good men would not lie about an important matter, and bad men would not act against their own interests.

Fourth, the logic of the argument is impeccable. For Wesley, there can be no doubt that God is the author of Scripture. Once the terms of the argument have been accepted, no other alternative makes sense. While Wesley's understanding of revelation allows for a human component, the text itself is inspired. The human part of its composition in no way obstructs the divine authorship of the text. The Bible is best understood as the written testimony of God. Wesley acknowledges that the human factors in the composition of Scripture play a role, but God's message gets through in a way that makes the written word truly divine.

The Infallibility of Scripture

An important corollary of Wesley's doctrines of revelation and inspiration is the claim that Scripture is free from error. Frequently, the inspiration and infallibility of the Scriptures are intertwined. Typically, Wesley seeks to understand what the Scripture said about a disputed question and then argues that the Scripture's position has to be right since God could not be a liar.[16]

The point about faith due to the testimony of God is a long-standing position which Wesley takes. Rex Matthews has noted that Wesley uses three different definitions of "faith," one of which is the idea of assent.[17] A clear example occurs in a letter to his mother written in 1725:

Faith is a species of belief, and belief is defined, an assent to a proposition upon rational grounds. Without rational grounds there is therefore no belief, and consequently no faith. . . .

I call faith an assent upon rational grounds because I hold divine testimony to be the most reasonable of all evidence whatever. Faith must necessarily at length be resolved into reason. God is true, therefore what he says is true. *He* hath said this; therefore this is true. When anyone can bring me more reasonable propositions than these, I am ready to assent to them. Till then it will be highly unreasonable to change my opinion.[18]

While Matthews and George Croft Cell argue that this notion of faith was dominant in Wesley prior to 1738,[19] he used it as late as 1750 in his *Compendium of Logic*.[20]

Recall the evidence just presented that Wesley often understands Scripture as God's testimony. He distinguishes between divine faith, which is assent to God's testimony, and human faith, which is assent to human testimony. Thus, the logic of Wesley's argument appears to be as follows:

1. The Scriptures are God's testimony.
2. God's nature is such that he cannot be ignorant and he cannot lie.
3. The Scriptures are therefore without mistake.

To Wesley, it is inconceivable that any rational person would deny that Scripture is revealed truth. To him the Deists and *philosophes* are not "rational" persons.[21] The claim that Scripture is not "of divine original" is literally absurd in the sense that no right-thinking person would ever support such a position. If Wesley can reduce his opponents to that point, he shows that their position is untenable.

Wesley holds the traditional Protestant view, arguing that God inspired the Scriptures and therefore they are infallible. Because of their infallibility, they are trustworthy, and ought to serve as the sole authority for Christian faith and practice. Wesley's statements on this point are unambiguous and frequent. In two places he refers to the Bible as "an infallible test."[22] In two other places he is even more clear about there being no mistakes in the Bible. In the *Journal* for August 24, 1776, he writes:

I read Mr. Jenyns's admired tract on the *Internal Evidence of the Christian Religion*. He is undoubtedly a fine writer, but whether he is a Christian, Deist, or Atheist I cannot tell. If he is a Christian, he betrays his own cause by averring that "all Scripture is not given by inspiration of God, but the writers of it were sometimes left to themselves, and consequently made some mistakes." Nay, if there be any mistakes in the Bible, there may as well be a thousand. If there be one falsehood in that book, it did not come from the God of truth.[23]

The same point is made in a 1756 letter to William Law.[24] Wesley makes the same point again when he says that the one who "follows hard" after perfection will find it because "the Scripture cannot be broken."[25] That phrase appears as the justification for the difficulties of Christian discipleship in the sermon "On Riches": "O how hard a saying is this to those that are at ease 'in the midst of their possessions'! Yet the Scripture cannot be broken."[26]

God's authorship thus provides a negative guarantee that the Scripture is free from error. But at the same time it provides a positive guarantee that the Scripture is unquestionably true, perfect, and consistent. At the same time, it lays upon ministers of the gospel an obligation to be faithful to the Scripture because it is God's word to his people. This extends even to using the words God had chosen, such as "perfect."[27] In an early sermon, "On Corrupting the Word of God," Wesley makes a similar point as he talks about those who are sincere in preaching the gospel.

> They must publish, as proper occasions offer, all that is contained in the oracles of God: whether smooth or otherwise it matters nothing, since 'tis unquestionably true, and useful too. For "all Scripture given by inspiration of God is profitable either for doctrine, or reproof, or correction, or instruction in righteousness;" either to teach us what we are to believe or practise; or for conviction of error or reformation of vice. They know that there is nothing superfluous in it, relating either to faith or practice; and therefore they preach all parts of it, though those more frequently and particularly which are more particularly wanted where they are.[28]

Nowhere does Wesley explicitly say that the Bible has errors in it. On this point he is quite consistent. However, two qualifiers to this conception of infallibility will be noted later. First, it is possible that some parts of Scripture may imply an absurdity or contradiction.

This calls for a special hermeneutical rule; namely, a nonliteral method of interpretation must be employed. This matter will be dealt with in conjunction with Wesley's rules for interpretation. Second, there is always the possibility that human beings will misinterpret the Scripture. While Scripture itself is error-free, one is not always certain that one's interpretation has the same accuracy. This issue will be treated in the section on Scripture's clarity.

The doctrine of inspiration is not primarily a historical account of how the books actually came to be written. Nor is the doctrine of infallibility the result of a careful inductive analysis of the text, at the end of which he pronounces that there are no errors. Rather, both doctrines are theological constructs that serve certain functions in the network of arguments for Christianity. It will be noted, however, that all of these are very much intertwined. Rarely does Wesley speak of God's being the author of Scripture without talking about infallibility, because the function of·the doctrine is preeminently to secure Scripture's reliability as a warrant for doctrine.

Wesley does not directly address the arguments of the Deists and Hume that pose such a challenge to traditional Christian thinking about Scripture. In his arguments for inspiration and infallibility, he is highly conservative and repeats arguments that were common before 1700. Nevertheless, Wesley is part of a significant transition in Western culture—the emergence of a modern worldview in the fields of philosophy, science, history, and theology. The problem of certainty held center stage in many fields of human knowledge during the sixteenth and seventeenth centuries. During this time a great transition took place which fundamentally changed the complexion of Western European thought, including the fundamental assumptions and methods in these disciplines. What occurred during this time has been called a "cultural process" by Klaus Scholder, whereby most aspects of the society were slowly transformed.[29] This was "the age of reason" where old authorities were challenged and a new role for reason based on observation was proposed. Barbara Shapiro has argued that in both natural philosophy and religion, this turn to a more empirical methodology was accompanied by a new view of how certain any human knowledge can be. For the Latitudinarians and the followers of the new science (and many persons belonged to both groups), most human knowledge fell in the categories of opinion and moral certainty at best.[30] This understanding of human knowledge as "probabilistic" in nature was both an antidote to the dogmatism of former times, and a foundation for future research based on facts.

Within the English situation, the change marks the emergence of the modern period in religious thought. As Gerald Cragg points out, "Richard Hooker and Launcelot Andrewes belong to one period, John Locke and Isaac Newton clearly belong to another."[31] These changes meant that the authority of the Bible was questioned as never before, and that even those who accepted its authority viewed it in a manner different from earlier periods. Hans Frei, in his *Eclipse of Biblical Narrative*, argues that this transition is best characterized as the loss of the narrative sense of Scripture.[32] This new way of looking at the world no longer used the lenses of Scripture to see, but viewed Scripture itself as one more object to be investigated. The automatic certainty and authority of the sacred writings was no longer assumed, but had to be demonstrated in new ways.

An example of this uncertainty is seen when Wesley refers to the truth of the Bible as the protasis of a conditional sentence. Examples abound from throughout Wesley's life in all types of writing. In the *Journal* for January 29, 1738, he writes:

> If the oracles of God are true, if we are still to abide by "the law and the testimony," all these things, though when ennobled by faith in Christ they are holy, and just, and good, yet without it are "dung and dross," meet only to be purged away by "the fire that never shall be quenched."[33]

In "The End of Christ's Coming," written in 1781, he writes about the basic truths of real religion, "And yet, if we believe the Bible, who can deny it? Who can doubt of it?"[34] The same conditional use of belief in the Bible comes in the reference to "those who believe in the Scriptures." In "The Signs of the Times," written in 1787, he says:

> What excuse then have any that believe the Scriptures to be the Word of God for not discerning the signs of these times, as preparatory to the general call of the heathens? What could God have done which he hath not done to convince you that the day is coming, that the time is at hand, when he will fulfil his glorious promises; when he will arise to maintain his own cause, and to set up his kingdom over all the earth?[35]

Two conclusions can be drawn from these conditional references to an acceptance of Scripture's authority. First, it is clear that these are rhetorical moves on Wesley's part. He is not genuinely offering arguments about whether the Scripture is true, or whether one ought to accept it as the word of God. The answer which is presumed to be obvious is the truth of Scripture. Consider the following characterization of those who agree with him and those who do not:

> What shall we say to these things [the brothers' steps]? Why, to Atheists, or Infidels of any kind, I would not say one word about them. For "if they hear not Moses and the Prophets," they will not regard anything of this kind. But to men of candour, who believe the Bible to be of God, I would say, Is not this an astonishing instance, held forth to all the inhabitants of London, of the justice and power of God? Does not the curse he has denounced upon this ground bear some little resemblance to that of our Lord on the barren figtree, "Henceforth let no fruit grow upon thee for ever?" I see no reason or pretence for any rational man to doubt of the truth of the story; since it has been confirmed by these open, visible tokens for more than a hundred years successively.[36]

Clearly, the alternatives posed here are, on the one side, atheism and infidelity, and on the other side, candor, rationality, and belief in the Scriptures. Wesley has difficulty conceiving of any Christian faith that has questions about the authority and veracity of the Bible.

Second, it is significant that Wesley uses the conditional language at all. If the authority of Scripture were as clear to all thinking persons as he thinks it is, then there would be no need to raise the issue. When something is universally presupposed it is not generally a matter of discussion or argument. The fact that Wesley has to qualify his statements by saying "for those who believe the Bible to be of God" is a recognition that there are those for whom this is not true.

Wesley never spends much time on issues that he regards as being settled or of little importance to the salvation of plain people. For these reasons, he does not write an extended treatise on the authority of Scripture. However, the problems related to its status were not wholly unfamiliar to him. Wesley is aware of some of the basic issues about which he and the Deists differ. There are times when he states them clearly:

Thus almost all men of letters, both in England, France, Germany, yea, and all the civilized countries of Europe, extol "humanity" to the skies, as the very essence of religion. To this the great triumvirate, Rousseau, Voltaire, and David Hume, have contributed all their labours, sparing no pains to establish a religion which should stand on its own foundation, independent of any revelation whatever, yea, not supposing even the being of a God. So leaving him, if he has any being, to himself, they have found out both a religion and a happiness which have no relation at all to God, nor any dependence upon him.

It is no wonder that this religion should grow fashionable, and spread far and wide in the world. But call it "humanity," "virtue," "morality," or what you please, it is neither better nor worse than atheism.[37]

Conditional statements about the authority of Scripture are a nod in the direction of John Toland, Collins, Hume, and others who do not share the same basic presuppositions Wesley does.

One of the most basic presuppositions on which Wesley and the Deists differ is the claim that the Scriptures are God's testimony. Nowhere does Wesley discuss at length the problems raised by his opponents. While it is not clear why this is so, three explanations are possible. Conceivably, Wesley could have viewed these questions as speculative and not worth the time it would take to deal with them. Alternatively, he could have assumed that the numerous responses already made had sufficiently dealt with the matter. Both of these probably play some role in Wesley's attitude here. However, a more likely explanation rests on the disdain he felt for all those who did not believe God to be the author of Scripture. People who disbelieved the Bible had opened the possibility of believing anything. He writes in 1774: "I cannot but repeat the observation, wherein experience confirms me more and more, that they who disbelieve the Bible will believe anything. They may believe *Voltaire!* They may believe the *Shastah!* They may believe a man can put himself into a quart bottle!"[38]

The irony in this quotation is rich. It is precisely to achieve the freedom "to believe anything" that the Deists attacked scriptural authority. On their view, only the limits of reason should be allowed to determine the credibility of any claim at all. Wesley failed to understand the Deists' program and to anticipate the drive for freedom from authority that characterized Enlightenment thought generally. Without consciously attempting to do so, Wesley provided another path for this same drive for freedom by focusing on the religious experience of the individual as the goal of true religion.

This disdain is similar to the simple logic of the "Clear and Concise Demonstration." The argument given there eliminates what Wesley sees as the only options competing with divine authorship. He has no conception of an alternative view whereby Scripture could be the product of human factors and still retain its divine authority. Whenever the topic of scriptural authority is discussed, Wesley emphasizes its divine authorship.

Wesley is part of the cultural process described by Scholder in the sense that his own position exemplifies the transition from a traditional, unquestioning view of Scripture as God's written word to a view that at least raises the questions of human participation in creating the Scriptures. On the one hand, Wesley does not fully belong to the critical period, because he still is disdainful of those who take the questions seriously. He views the Deist critique as *prima facie* unreasonable, and never seriously addresses the problems they raise.

For example, the Deist Anthony Collins treats Scripture like any other book.[39] To it he applies "the common rules of grammar and logick."[40] He places the Bible alongside other sacred books, and treats them all as instances of establishing revealed religions.[41] He asks why Josephus and other historians know nothing about the slaughter of the innocents described in Matthew 2, and suggests that this account may have been added to the Gospel at a later date.[42] Hans Frei says Collins "identified literal sense with historical reference in a new way." He continues:

> In effect Collins' identification of literal and historical statements involved that he first break up their previous identity and then reintegrate them by subsuming literal meaning under the dominance of an independent criterion for deciding whether or not a statement is historical. A proposition is literal if it describes and refers to a state of affairs known or assumed on independent probable grounds to agree or disagree with the stated proposition.[43]

The key point here is "independent criterion." The narrative value of Scripture, which Frei holds to have dominated biblical interpretation before Collins, has been lost to "the single, external reference of the words."[44] Wesley still holds the view of Scripture as authoritatively determining the shape of the world.

On the other hand, Wesley adopts a methodological approach that provides an opening for the Deist critique. Even when used in a rhetorical manner, conditional sentences about the authority of Scripture acknowledge the possibility of the Bible's position as subject to the judgment of reason. As we shall see, Wesley holds a high view of the authority of reason in relation to Scripture. In addition, a reliance upon experience as a source of knowledge opens the possibility that the experience of others may not always confirm what the Scripture teaches. In these ways, Wesley is part of the transition to the modern approach to Scripture.

The Authority of Scripture Alone

The obvious corollary of Wesley's understanding of revelation, inspiration, and infallibility is that Scripture is authoritative for Christians in all matters of faith and practice. Though other authorities are acknowledged as well,[45] Wesley frequently states that Scripture *alone* ought to determine Christian teaching. This is summarized by several well-known self-designations. He calls himself *homo unius libri* in 1746,[46] and asserts the same is still true of Methodists in 1787.

> From the very beginning, from the time that four young men united together, each of them was *homo unius libri*—a man of one book. God taught them all to make his "Word a lantern unto their feet, and a light in all their paths." They had one, and only one rule of judgment with regard to all their tempers, words, and actions, namely, the oracles of God. They were one and all determined to be *Bible-Christians.* They were continually reproached for this very thing; some terming them in derision *Bible-bigots;* others *Bible-moths*—feeding, they said, upon the Bible as moths do upon cloth. And indeed unto this day it is their constant endeavour to think and speak as the oracles of God.[47]

Note here his emphasis on "one, and only one rule of judgment," which was the Bible. When people derisively accused him of being a "Bible-bigot," he adopted the term and used it with pride.[48] Such self-characterizations illustrate Wesley's conviction that the authority of Scripture must be taken very seriously. He believes in the authority of the Bible, and sees the mistakes of others to be consequences of their failure to believe as he did at this point.

The authority of Scripture can logically be divided into two functions, authority as source of truth and as norm for truth. Wesley sees the Bible as both. First, he frequently refers to particular Bible passages as the sources for particular views. In a letter to Henry Venn, he writes that the Bible is the source from which all his ideas flow: "I believe all the Bible as far as I understand it, and am ready to be convinced. If I am an heretic, I became such by reading the Bible. All my notions I drew from thence; and with little help from men, unless in the single point of Justification by Faith."[49]

In another way of talking about the Bible as a source of doctrine, Wesley names "Searching the Scriptures" as one of the principal means of grace. It is included in the list given in *The General Rules*[50] and treated in some depth in "The Means of Grace," where he lists as the three chief means: "prayer," "searching the Scriptures [which implies reading, hearing, and meditating thereon]," and "receiving the Lord's Supper."[51] In that sermon he describes a typical order in which grace comes to a "stupid, senseless wretch."[52] Part of the transition from a state of sin to a state of saving faith is hearing, reading, and meditating on the Scriptures. Wesley suggests that the Bible is a means of grace for all persons, mediating prevenient, justifying, and sanctifying grace.

Wesley's view of Scripture as a source of doctrine is not simply a market from which one can select whatever one wishes. Rather, he frequently talks about the minister as a messenger who is obligated to preach the message given him by the Bible. In "Christian Perfection" he asks:

> But are they [expressions that teach perfection] not found in the oracles of God? If so, by what authority can any messenger of God lay them aside, even though all men should be offended? We have not so learned Christ; neither may we thus give place to the devil. Whatsoever God hath spoken, that will we speak, whether men will hear, or whether they will forbear: knowing that then alone can any minister of Christ be "pure from the blood of all men," when he hath "not shunned to declare unto them all the counsel of God."[53]

In "The Law Established by Faith, II," he makes a similar point in saying that "at the same time that we proclaim all the blessings and privileges which God hath prepared for his children, we are likewise to 'teach all the things whatsoever he hath commanded.'"[54] This understanding is rooted in Wesley's conception of inspiration and the mission of the church. God is the author of the Bible and the giver of the message. The divine authorship means that "the Scripture, therefore, of the Old and New Testament is a most solid and precious system of divine truth. Every part thereof is worthy of God; and all together are one entire body, wherein is no defect, no excess."[55]

This "system of divine truth" is the content of what preachers have been asked to preach and Christians have been asked to live. Faithful service to God means not shirking the duties that have been accepted. The faithful messenger must deliver the entire message, or else be guilty of the spiritual consequences that follow from her or his audience's ignorance. She or he must teach all the scriptural doctrines regardless of how distasteful some may be. The faithful hearer of the message must follow all the behaviors commanded, regardless of how unpleasant they are. Scripture is a source whose teachings must not be ignored.

The second function of Scripture's authority is to serve as a norm for Christian faith. In many places Scripture is referred to as the "whole and sole" rule of Christian faith. In the sermon "On Faith" he describes a Protestant view of Scripture's normative authority:

> The faith of the *Protestants*, in general, embraces only those truths as necessary to salvation which are clearly revealed in the oracles of God. Whatever is plainly declared in the Old and New Testament is the object of their faith. They believe neither more nor less than what is manifestly contained in, and provable by, the Holy Scriptures. The Word of God is "a lantern to their feet, and a light in all their paths." They dare not on any pretence go from it to the right hand or the left. The written Word is the whole and sole rule of their faith, as well as practice. They believe whatsoever God has declared, and profess to do whatsoever he hath commanded. This is the proper faith of Protestants: by this they will abide and no other.[56]

And in *Popery Calmly Considered* he makes the point that "in all cases, the Church is to be judged by the Scripture, not the Scripture by the Church."[57]

While anti-Catholic polemics over the issue of *sola Scriptura* could be expected from an eighteenth-century Anglican, Wesley makes the same point in his controversies with other Anglicans. Between 1745 and 1748 Wesley exchanged twelve letters with an unknown Anglican whom he addressed as "John Smith." In a letter written in May, 1745, "Smith" had argued that if Wesley's "signs and wonders" were indeed true and could be proved as matters of fact, then "no wise and good men will oppose you any longer."[58] On September 28, 1745, Wesley replied:

> I conceive therefore this whole demand, common as it is, of proving our doctrine by miracles, proceeds from a double mistake: (1), a supposition that what we preach is not provable from Scripture (for if it be, what need we further witnesses? To the law and the testimony!); (2), an imagination that a doctrine not provable by Scripture might nevertheless be proved by miracles. I believe not. I receive the written Word as the whole and sole rule of my faith.[59]

This is only one of many places where Wesley makes it clear that for Christian doctrine he cares about only one authority: Scripture. In many places he speaks of bringing a doctrine "to the law and the testimony" as a rhetorical device to insist that only the authority of Scripture is to be considered at that point.[60] In other places, he demands, "Bring me plain, scriptural proof for your assertion, or I cannot allow it."[61] Perhaps even more startling is Wesley's assertion that the Apostles were required to follow the same rule. In the same letter to "John Smith" just quoted, he says the Apostles "were to prove their assertions by the written Word. You and I are to do the same. Without such proof I ought no more to have believed St. Peter himself than St. Peter's (pretended) successor."[62]

Thus, part of Wesley's view is that the Bible is the sole source and sole norm for Christian faith, teaching, and practice. Wesley is clear on this point and insists on it many times and in many ways. This view must be qualified, however. While Wesley says that Scripture is "the whole and sole rule of faith," he also relies on other authorities. Scripture stands in a complex relation to reason, Christian antiquity, Christian experience, and the Church of England. While Scripture is in one sense the only authority, a comprehensive statement of his doctrine must account for these others. Chapter 3 will show the way in which Wesley conceived of all five of these as a unified locus of authority.

It is in this light that we must take his self-proclamation as *homo unius libri*. That phrase and all the others listed in the quotation from "On God's Vineyard" are examples of his hyperbole in the face of criticism. Five paragraphs after one use of *homo unius libri*, he quotes Homer's *Iliad* in Greek.[63] Whatever he means by "man of one book," he cannot mean that one should learn only from the Bible. When the preachers complain about Methodist reading requirements saying, "But I read only the Bible," Wesley puts this response in the *Large Minutes:*

> Then you ought to teach others to read only the Bible, and, by parity of reason, to hear only the Bible: But if so, you need preach no more. Just so said George Bell. And what is the fruit? Why, now he neither reads the Bible, nor anything else. This is rank enthusiasm. If you need no book but the Bible, you are got above St. Paul. He wanted others too. "Bring the books," says he, "but especially the parchments," those wrote on parchment. "But I have no taste for reading." Contract a taste for it by use, or return to your trade.[64]

This opposition to reading "only the Bible" qualifies his statement that he learned all his doctrines from the Bible. At the very least, other books should contribute to one's understanding of Scripture. At most, he will claim one can learn true things from them to supplement Scripture.[65]

Taking such phrases as "Bible-bigot" and *homo unius libri* as hyperbole puts Wesley's view of Scripture's authority in the context of his whole thought. The hyperbole functions well in his roles as controversialist, preacher, and leader of the Methodist Revival. The balanced judgment is that Wesley wants to be a man of one book, among many books. Being a "man of one book" emphasizes his commitment to Scripture, but it should not be construed as being closed to other sources of learning, both sacred and secular.

Conclusion

Wesley's understanding of revelation, inspiration, and the infallibility of Scripture leads to the conclusion that Scripture is the written word of God and as such is authoritative for Christian faith and practice. He frequently insists that it is Scripture *alone* that carries such weight and that no other authorities are necessary to prove a point. His understanding of the authority of Scripture recognizes the role played by the human messengers in its origin, but he steadfastly refuses to admit that this human component of Scripture's composition affects its authority. This leads to his statements about being a "man of one book" and a "Bible-bigot." We have seen how these should be classified as hyperbole to fit a particular situation, and not construed as his complete position. However, these phrases do communicate the intensity with which he regarded Scripture's role as the authority for what was true and right about God and God's commandments for human beings.

In the cultural shift documented by Frei, Scholder, and others, Wesley is best viewed as participating in the shift while resisting and reacting against some of its manifestations. The critique formulated by Collins is outside the realm of rational thought for Wesley. On the issues of Scripture's inspiration and infallibility, Collins and Wesley are very far apart. Wesley does not deign to devote significant attention to him or the other Deists. In the history of biblical interpretation, Wesley should be viewed as providing an alternative route into modernity. William Baird's *History of New Testament Research* treats August Hermann Francke, Johann Albrecht Bengal, and Wesley as Pietists who were concerned primarily with "the practical understanding and application of Scripture." Baird argues that the Pietists' emphasis on religious experience led them to affirm the historical character of revelation, thus showing their accord with the new approaches to Scripture. But like the orthodox, they held to the belief that the Bible is a unified whole and thus resisted a thorough application of the historical principle.[66]

It is simplistic to suggest that Wesley and those aligned with him were reactionaries to the Deist critique of traditional religion. It is much more accurate to see the rise of the Enlightenment as an important tidal change in culture in which Wesley participated in various ways. The questions he raised were in many cases the same ones being dealt with by the Deists. He noted other questions, even if he chose not to answer them. The influence of reason will be shown to be a significant factor in Wesley's theological method; in general, however, Wesley's role in this cultural shift was to maintain some of the newer methodological insights while not giving away the traditional view of inspiration and infallibility.

CHAPTER 2

The Characteristics of Scripture

Wesley's conception of Scripture covers five additional areas that further describe the Bible. Like those considered in the preceding chapter, these categories are not necessarily explicit in Wesley's writings, but they serve to structure Wesley's thoughts in categories with which he was familiar.

The Sufficiency of Scripture

The sufficiency of Scripture for teaching doctrines necessary for salvation is one of the basic tenets of the Reformation and is enshrined in Article VI of the Thirty-nine Articles of Religion. There the Church of England teaches: "Holy Scripture containeth all things necessary to salvation: so that whatsoever is not read therein, nor may be proved thereby, is not to be required of any man, that it should be believed as an article of the Faith, or be thought requisite or necessary to salvation."[1] Wesley edited the Articles for the American Methodists in 1784, and left this sentence intact.[2] He not only subscribed to the article at the time of his ordination, but reaffirmed it by sending it to the Methodists in America.[3]

Much of the discussion in chapter 1 about the sole authority of Scripture bears on this issue. By claiming Scripture as "the whole and sole rule of my faith,"[4] Wesley is, by implication, affirming its sufficiency in matters of faith. Especially in controversial writings against the Roman Catholics, such as *Popery Calmly Considered*, he is clear that Scripture is sufficient: "The Scripture, therefore, being delivered by men divinely inspired, is a rule sufficient of itself: So it neither needs, nor is capable of, any farther addition."[5]

Wesley was following a long line of English polemics against Roman Catholics. John Tillotson had published his *Rule of Faith* in 1666 to counter the Roman Catholic claim that tradition was a coordinate rule with Scripture. John Sergeant's *Sure Footing in Chris-*

tianity, or Rational Discourses on the Rule of Faith urged the Roman Catholic position,[6] and Tillotson was concerned to refute it: "The Opinion then of the Protestants concerning the *Rule of Faith,* is this in general, that those Books which we call the Holy Scriptures, are the Means whereby the Christian Doctrine hath been brought down to us. . . . [and] that the Books of Scripture are sufficiently plain, as to all things necessary to be Believed and Practised."[7] In this matter, Tillotson is simply reiterating a long-standing Protestant tradition whose representatives in England included Jeremy Taylor,[8] Gilbert Burnet,[9] and William Chillingworth,[10] as well as the Thirty-nine Articles.

On one occasion Wesley refuses to use the word "sufficient" because he finds it "ambiguous." Instead, he refers to Scripture as "a complete rule of faith and practice."[11] In this matter, "sufficient" and "complete" are synonyms for Wesley. He prefers the latter to avoid the long history of theological arguments about sufficiency, and seeks to capture the same point in different language. In his sermon "On Faith (Hebrews 11:6)," he writes:

> The faith of the *Protestants,* in general, embraces only those truths as necessary to salvation which are clearly revealed in the oracles of God. Whatever is plainly declared in the Old and New Testament is the object of their faith. They believe neither more nor less than what is manifestly contained in, and provable by, the Holy Scriptures.[12]

Going even further, his comment on Galatians 3:8 reads: "*Foreseeing that God would justify the gentiles* also *by faith, declared before*—So great is the excellency and fulness of the scripture, that all the things which can ever be controverted are therein both foreseen and determined."[13] Here Wesley claims that Scripture's sufficiency extends even to those questions which had not arisen during the time of its composition. Any possible theological question thus has its answer therein. Scripture is therefore able to function alone as the norm for Christian faith and practice.

The question arises whether Scripture is sufficient in areas outside the subjects of Christian doctrine and practice. Wesley never suggests that the Bible contains all we need to know on every subject of human knowledge. In his 1784 sermon "On Charity," he writes that in Scripture "are contained all the depths of divine knowledge and wisdom."[14] Clearly, he does not intend this to be taken as implying all knowledge whatsoever. "Divine" knowledge refers only to knowledge in the area of divinity, the knowledge of God and God's will for human beings. The proof of Wesley's recognition that Scripture's sufficiency is limited to matters of faith and practice is that he acknowledged the contributions that scientific investigations were making in his day, even when they contradicted the literal sense of Scripture. When Wesley abridged John Ray's *Wisdom of God Manifested in the Works of Creation* (1691) and published it as *A Survey of the Wisdom of God in Creation,* he reproduced Ray's scientific arguments concerning the motion of the earth:

> The Earth therefore turns round the Sun. Indeed to suppose the Earth at rest, destroys all the Order and Harmony of the Universe, annulls its Laws, and sets every Part at variance with the others. It renders the Motions of the Planets utterly inexplicable, which are otherwise plain and simple.
>
> Nor is the Motion of the Earth, whatever is vulgarly supposed, contrary to any Part of the Scripture. No other Ideas are to be affixt to the words of Scripture, than such as occur to one who looks at the thing spoken of.[15]

Science during that time sought simplicity of explanation and the harmony of all types of motion. To defend the traditional geocentric view of the universe, which had been thought to be the only biblical view as well, would have denied the tenets of the new empirically based science. Wesley then limits the authority of Scripture in matters of science to what was perceived by the participants. He goes on to discuss that when the Scripture refers to the sun's rising "we are to understand no more, than the Sun's appearing again in the Horizon, after he had been hid below it."[16]

In the sermon "On Divine Providence," Wesley does not doubt that Joshua 10:12-14 is to be taken literally. He believes that God worked a miracle that day.[17] But it is also clear that Wesley does not question the motion of the earth around the sun, and he describes God's act of making the sun stand still as a miracle precisely because it violates the "general laws of nature." On the subject of gravity, Wesley does not argue from Scripture about the reality of attraction proportionate to the quantity of matter. He even says of this new theory, "How clearly do these explain the ways of God!"[18] He then ascribes the power of gravity to "the finger of God." Wesley did not always agree with Newton, however. He agrees with Hutchinson that matter is inert and must be "impelled" by the "ether," with God as the first mover.[19] Thus, Wesley's scientific interests are governed by the empirical method of his time, and not by proofs drawn from Scripture. Wesley adopted John Ray's position on taking Scripture as "accommodated to the common apprehension of mankind," and the rest of his writings show that he did indeed construe Scripture in this way.

Scripture's sufficiency, then, does not extend to matters of science. Wesley stands firmly in the Anglican tradition in asserting its sufficiency only in matters "of faith and practice." Article VI of the Thirty-nine Articles teaches not the inerrancy of Scripture, but its sufficiency for salvation. Anglican theologians such as Hooker, Taylor, and Beveridge had made the same distinction very carefully.[20] However, what is significant in Wesley is the explicit conflict between secular science and the Bible. When such conflicts arise, he abandons the literal sense of the text on the grounds that it was not part of Scripture's intention to teach scientific truth. The message has been accommodated to the limited intellectual capacity of average human beings.

The use of accommodation to explain difficult passages in Scripture has a long history. Farrar's *History of Interpretation* first mentions it with reference to the works of Clement and Origen.[21] Among Reformation writers, Calvin depends on it heavily. He argues that "God's essence is incomprehensible; hence, his divineness far escapes all human perception."[22] When discussing angels, Calvin appeals to the principle of accommodation. He says, "Moses, accommodating himself to the rudeness of the common folk, mentions in the history of the Creation no other works of God than those which show themselves to our own eyes."[23] But Wesley is using the approach of accommodation in a way that is different from Calvin's. Calvin is concerned with places in Scripture that are contradictions and inconsistencies within the Bible, such as why there is no mention of angels in Genesis 1–2. Wesley is concerned with discrepancies between the worldview of Scripture and that of modern science. Here he is prepared to yield Scripture's authority to external authority in a way that was unthinkable to Calvin. In this way, Wesley is clearly part of the transition described by Frei. He is not viewing the world from within the Bible, but viewing the Bible from the perspective of the secular world.

The Clarity of Scripture

The clarity of Scripture is another basic Protestant affirmation with which Wesley agrees. He refers to it in his 1777 sermon "On Laying the Foundation of the New Chapel," saying, "This is the *religion of the Bible*, as no one can deny who reads it with any attention."[24] In "Heavenly Treasure in Earthen Vessels" (1790), he refers to the Scriptures as clarifying basic questions that had been mysteries before: "But what all the wisdom of man was unable to do was in due time done by the wisdom of God. When it pleased God to give an account of the origin of things, and of man in particular, all the darkness vanished away, and the clear light shone."[25] But Wesley's clearest statement of Scripture's character in this matter comes in his sermon "On Divine Providence" (1786): "For only God himself can give a clear, consistent, perfect account (that is, as perfect as our weak understanding can receive in this our infant state of existence; or at least, as is consistent with the designs of his government) of his manner of governing the world."[26]

It is important to note that in two of these texts there is an implicit awareness that Scripture does not always appear clear to everyone. In the quotation from the sermon at the New Chapel, "reading it with any attention" is required of those who want to get its message. In the sermon "On Divine Providence" one must look at the Scripture as "the history of God" to see the clear truth. Wesley qualifies this in a letter to Samuel Sparrow: "I really think that if an hundred or an hundred thousand sincere, honest (I add humble, modest, self-diffident) men were with attention and care to read over the New Testament, uninfluenced by any but the Holy Spirit, nine in ten of them at least, if not every one, would discover that the Son of God was 'adorable' and one God with the Father."[27] This qualification of the clarity of Scripture is minor, but significant. Wesley believes that the vast majority could get the message correctly, and that no more than one in ten who read with care, attention, and objectivity would miss it.

Wesley stands firmly within the Protestant tradition in asserting that Scripture is clear in its main points. The Reformers had argued that the magisterium of the church was not necessary to under-

41

standing the basic message of the Bible. Theologians of the English Church were equally vehement in arguing that Scripture was perspicuous. They typically argued that Scripture is clear in the necessary parts despite the confusion in other areas. The religious controversies of the seventeenth century taught many people on all sides of English Christianity that some doctrinal disputes were not easily resolved. N. H. Keeble suggests that Richard Baxter loved a plain literary style and "was encouraged to maintain it by finding, like many before him, that much of Scripture is *'suited in plainness to the capacity of the simple,'* and is in a style which may well *'seem less polite, than you might think beseemed the Holy Ghost.'*"[28] Keeble also notes that Baxter thought we should not delve into the complexities of doctrine that are beyond our capacity.[29] John Tillotson, in his *Rule of Faith*, made a similar point: "Of the true Sense of plain Texts I hope every one may be certain; and for obscure ones, it is not necessary every one should."[30]

Like both Baxter and Tillotson, Wesley acknowledges the difficulty of understanding the Bible in some places. Wesley responds to Thomas Rutherforth's question: "But 'there are in the Scriptures "things hard to be understood." And is *every unlettered mechanic* able to explain them?' No surely. But may we not likewise ask: is *every clergyman* able to explain them? You will not affirm it."[31] However, the acknowledged problems in understanding the Scripture are minor. He then proceeds to argue that a tradesman who knows the Scripture and works hard to understand it is in fact a "safer" guide to its meaning than many clergymen. It is at most one in ten who cannot get the message about the divinity of Christ. The Scriptures are so clear that almost any unbiased person who reads with attention will get the message.

Wesley is part of a significant transition within Protestant interpretation. For Calvin, Scripture is clear to those who study it and apply the best of human learning to its message. For Baxter, Locke, and Wesley, Scripture is clear to even the most simple human being.[32] For Wesley the clarity of Scripture applies not to its entirety, but only to those points necessary for salvation. Wesley frequently distinguishes between necessary doctrines and matters of opinion. His sermon "Catholic Spirit" argues that Christians ought to be able to disagree on the latter without breaking fellowship. However, necessary doctrines are clear in the Scriptures. In his letter to Conyers

Middleton, Wesley argues, "The Scriptures are a complete rule of faith and practice; and they are clear in all necessary points. And yet their clearness does not prove, that they need not be explained; nor their completeness, that they need not be enforced."[33] In his correspondence with "John Smith," Wesley understands that simply quoting Scripture does not suffice. He refers "Smith" back to "the latter *Appeal,* so great a part of which is employed in this very thing, in fighting my ground, inch by inch, in proving, not that such words are Scripture, but that they must be interpreted in the manner there set down."[34]

In chapter 4 Wesley's rules of interpreting Scripture will be examined. The very existence of such rules, even when informally stated, shows that Wesley recognizes a problem with the clarity of Scripture. Yet, on essential points, he consistently argues that the Scriptures are clear, and according to one of his rules, one then uses the clearer parts to interpret those less clear.

The Wholeness of Scripture

There can be no doubt that Wesley believes Scripture to be a unitary, coherent whole. He makes this clear in his Preface to the *Explanatory Notes upon the New Testament:* "The Scripture, therefore, of the Old and New Testament is a most solid and precious system of divine truth. Every part thereof is worthy of God; and all together are one entire body, wherein is no defect, no excess."[35] Wesley believes that the Bible consistently gives the same message throughout. He appeals to the Methodists to follow the whole of Scripture, "to join together in one scheme of truth and practice what almost all the world put asunder."[36] In his *Farther Thoughts Upon Christian Perfection* he is more emphatic: "At certain seasons, indeed, it may be right to treat of nothing but repentance, or merely of faith, or altogether of holiness; but, in general, our call is to declare the whole counsel of God, and to prophesy according to the analogy of faith."[37]

Throughout his writings he appeals to the entire Bible with phrases such as "the whole Scripture," "the whole tenor of Scripture," and "the general tenor of Scripture." One of the places where several of these appear quite close to one another is in the sermon "Free Grace":

43

And as this doctrine manifestly and directly tends to overthrow the *whole Christian revelation*, so it does the same thing, by plain consequence, in making that revelation contradict itself. For it is grounded on such an interpretation of some texts (more or fewer it matters not) as flatly contradicts all the other texts, and indeed the *whole scope and tenor of Scripture*. For instance: the asserters of this doctrine interpret that text of Scripture, "Jacob have I loved, but Esau have I hated," as implying that God in a literal sense hated Esau and all the reprobated from eternity. Now what can possibly be a more flat contradiction than this, not only to the *whole scope and tenor of Scripture*, but also to all those particular texts which expressly declare, "God is love"?[38]

In the two pages following these sentences, there are five additional references to the wholeness of the Bible. There are at least fifty-seven such references in the Wesley corpus.

Wesley uses "tenor" in reference to many things. He talks about the tenor of someone's behavior,[39] the "whole scope and tenor" of Jesus' discourse,[40] and the "whole tenor" of an argument.[41] One of the most revealing uses of "tenor" comes in the *Remarks on Mr. Hill's "Farrago Double Distilled"*: "Though there are some expressions in my brother's Hymns which I do not use, as being very liable to be misconstrued; yet I am fully satisfied, that, in the whole tenor of them, they thoroughly agree with mine, and with the Bible."[42] It seems clear that, for Wesley, the whole tenor of a text points to the general meaning of that text, which is yet capable of including parts that might be "misconstrued" in another way.

David Kelsey, in *Uses of Scripture in Recent Theology*, distinguishes between the wholeness which analytically is part of a judgment that a book is Scripture, and the quality of being unitary.[43] Wholeness is a pattern within the writings discerned by the theologian. Read in light of that pattern, the whole book functions toward a certain end. Unity, on the other hand, implies both consistency and coherence among the various parts of the book. A theologian must see Scripture as some sort of whole. He or she may or may not see it as unitary. In these terms, Wesley holds Scripture to be both whole and unitary. It not only functions toward a single end, but it is throughout consistent and coherent. This can be seen in his appeal to a "general tenor" of Scripture which should not be violated.

To say that Wesley held the wholeness of Scripture, however, raises the question about what sort of wholeness he sees there. One of the places where he gives an indication of what he means by the "general tenor" of Scripture comes in the *Explanatory Notes upon the New Testament*. In his note to Romans 12:6, he implies that the analogy of faith and the general tenor of Scripture are intimately related. He comments on the phrase "Let us prophesy according to the analogy of faith" saying, "St. Peter expresses it, 'as the oracles of God'; according to the general tenor of them."[44] By exploring Wesley's understanding of this concept, we can gain further insight into his view of the wholeness of Scripture.

"Analogy of faith" is a technical term for Wesley and others in the seventeenth and eighteenth centuries. It should not be understood with reference to contemporary theories of analogy, because the history of the term fixes its meaning in a completely different realm of discourse. It is technical in the sense that in the history of biblical interpretation in the sixteenth through eighteenth centuries, the term carried its own special meaning, which cannot be discovered by a simple grammatical analysis of its three words.

One clue to the technical nature of this term is the fact that those who used it generally started with Romans 12:6. The Greek text for this verse is ἔχοντες δὲ χαρίσματα κατὰ τὴν χάριν τὴν δοθεῖσαν ἡμῖν διάφορα, εἴτε προφητείαν κατὰ τὴν ἀναλογίαν τῆς πίστεως. While those who appealed to this as a rule for hermeneutics translated it as prophesying "according to the analogy of faith," it is significant that no English translation of the Bible available in Wesley's day translates τὴν ἀναλογίαν τῆς πίστεως that way. The Geneva and King James Bibles use "proportion." Tyndale and the Great Bible use "agreeing." The Bishops' Bible uses "measure." Only the Rheims Bible of 1582 gives a hint that there might be a history to the term, translating it as "the rule of faith."[45]

The history of this term is an interesting question whose answer goes beyond the scope of this study. However, a brief outline will show the way in which it came down to Wesley. Prior to the Reformation, it was used by Roman Catholic theologians who appealed to "the rule of faith" as a principle in interpreting Scripture.[46] By the time of the Reformation, the term "analogy of faith" appears. Calvin uses it,[47] and theologians like John Gerhard[48] give it precise definitions similar to Wesley's. William Bucanus says the analogy of faith is "the constant and unchanging sense of Scripture expounded in open passages of Scripture and agreeing with the Apostle's Creed, the Decalogue and the Lord's Prayer."[49] The term also shows up in William Perkins,[50] and John Milton.[51] Daniel Whitby states that ·

> Reason in judging of the sense of Scripture is regulated partly by principles of Faith, partly by Tradition, partly by Catholic maxims of her own.
>
> First, By principles of Faith. For Scripture is to be interpreted *secundum analogiam Fidei;* that is (say we) particular Texts of Scripture, when dubious, are so to be interpreted as not to contradict the Fundamentals of Faith, or any doctrine which evidently and fully stands asserted in the Word of God. And secondly since Scripture cannot contradict itself, when any paragraph of Scripture absolutely considered is ambiguous, that sense must necessarily obtain which is repugnant to no other paragraph, against what may be so; and thus may Scripture regulate me in the sense of Scripture, and what I know of it lead me to the sense of what I do not.[52]

Jeremy Taylor argues against its use because of the subjective nature of its definition.[53] John Locke also rejects its use and says that Romans 12:6 does not authorize it. He suggests "quitting our own Infallibility in that Analogy of Faith which we have made to our selves, or have implicitly adopted from some other."[54] On Romans 12:6 he notes:

> This therefore is far from signifying, that a man in interpreting of Sacred Scripture should explain the sense according to the system of his particular sect, which each party is pleased to call the *analogie of faith.* For this would be to make the Apostle to set that for a rule of interpretation which had not its being till long after, and is the product of fallible men.[55]

This cursory survey suffices to show that the "analogy of faith" was a technical concept used by theological writers in the sixteenth and seventeenth centuries. The various writers generally take it to refer to a system of doctrines which represent the wholeness of Scripture, although they disagree on whether any such system genuinely represents the message of the whole Bible. Thus John Calvin, John Gerhard, William Bucanus, William Perkins, John Milton, and Daniel Whitby refer to it as given, while Jeremy Taylor and John Locke argue that it is a human construct imposed upon the text.

Precisely where Wesley learned the term is not clear. It is possible that he learned it during his studies at Oxford. His mother used it in a letter dated August 18, 1725, as a standard against which one should judge the adequacy of a doctrine: "This is the sum of what I believe concerning predestination, which I think is agreeable to the analogy of faith, since it never derogates from God's free grace, nor impairs the liberty of man."[56] Thirteen months later John used the term in a similar way in his sermon "On Guardian Angels."[57] I have identified a total of eleven places where Wesley uses "analogy of faith."[58] His most extensive explanation of what it means is given in the note on Romans 12:6, where he comments on the phrase "Let us prophesy according to the analogy of faith":

> St. Peter expresses it, "as the oracles of God;" according to the general tenor of them; according to that grand scheme of doctrine which is delivered therein, touching original sin, justification by faith, and present, inward salvation. There is a wonderful analogy between all these; and a close and intimate connexion between the chief heads of that faith "which was once delivered to the saints." Every article therefore concerning which there is any question should be determined by this rule; every doubtful scripture interpreted according to the grand truths which run through the whole.[59]

Five aspects of Wesley's understanding of the term can be gleaned from this text and supported by the other references. First, he believes the Bible is a whole. The analogy of faith is taught by "the general tenor" of Scripture. The analogy to which it refers is "the close and intimate connexion between the chief heads" of the faith. In "The End of Christ's Coming," he says that the essence of the Christian religion "runs through the Bible from the beginning to the end, in one connected chain. And the agreement of every part of it with every other is properly the *analogy* of *faith*."[60] For him, Scripture is consistent in all its parts and there is a general theme of the text that can be identified.

Second, the wholeness of Scripture is constituted by its doctrinal content. In his note, he describes the analogy of faith as forming a "grand scheme of doctrine."[61] In the Preface to the Old Testament *Notes*, Wesley refers to it as "the connexion and harmony there is between those grand, fundamental doctrines. . . ."[62] Rather than any of the other logical possibilities noted by Kelsey,[63] it is the Bible's system of doctrines that gives it wholeness and unity. In other words, the Bible is a whole because all of it functions to teach a system of doctrines which is coherent and consistent.

Third, the analogy of faith pertains to those doctrines which have to do with the order of salvation. In the note, three doctrines are included: original sin, justification by faith, and present, inward salvation. The Preface to the *Explanatory Notes upon the Old Testament* has original sin, justification by faith, the new birth, and inward and outward holiness.[64] "Causes of the Inefficacy of Christianity" has the natural corruption of man, justification by faith, the new birth, and inward and outward sanctification.[65] In "The End of Christ's Coming," "real religion" is described more generally as the restoration of humanity "not only to the favour, but likewise to the image of God; implying not barely deliverance from sin but the being filled with the fulness of God."[66] All of these are substantially equivalent ways in which Wesley formulates the order of salvation. The restoration to the image of God is a change from original sin through repentance, justification, and the new birth to entire sanctification. His formulations of the order may vary, but all relate to one basic scheme.

For Wesley, the elements of the order of salvation are the "chief heads of that faith 'which was once delivered to the saints.'"[67] Although Wesley makes extensive use of the distinction between essential doctrines and opinions, it is difficult to state exactly which doctrines are essential and which are not. The lists he gives vary from one another in substantive ways, and he will occasionally refer to a doctrine as essential which never shows up in any of his summaries of the essentials.[68] The doctrines that appear most frequently in such summaries are three: original sin, justification by faith, and holiness of heart and life. It is these three that form the basis of his proposed union of evangelical clergymen in 1764.[69] In his *Principles of a Methodist Farther Explained*, he lists those three (described here as repentance, faith, and holiness) and says that these include all other Methodist doctrines, and are the basic doctrines of Christianity.[70]

Fourth, the analogy of faith functions as a norm for theology both as a guide to correct conclusions and as a preventive to incorrect ones. It is mentioned as a guide in the Preface to the Old Testament *Notes*, where he says that Henry's exposition "is also *sound*, agreeable to the tenor of Scripture, and to the analogy of faith."[71] It is mentioned as a limit in *The Principles of a Methodist*: "If there be anything unscriptural in these words, anything wild or extravagant, anything contrary to the analogy of faith, or the experience of adult Christians, let them 'smite me friendly and reprove me'; let them impart to me of the clearer light God has given them."[72] By this Wesley means he is going to be guided by Scripture understood in its entirety. Adult Christians are those who have discovered that the promises of Scripture, read in light of the analogy of faith, are true. Therefore their experience functions as a reinforcement to the testimony of Scripture on those matters.

Fifth, the analogy of faith functions as the rule to be used in interpreting Scripture. In the note to Romans 12:6, he says that "every doubtful scripture [should be] interpreted according to the grand truths which run through the whole." When he cites the Reformation principle of using Scripture to interpret Scripture, he understands that as interpretation according to the analogy of faith.[73] In his "Address to the Clergy," he refers to the analogy of faith as "the clue to guide me through the whole" of Scripture.[74]

Thus, for Wesley, the general tenor of Scripture teaches the analogy of faith: the system of doctrine whose content is the order of salvation and whose function is to serve as a normative guide and limit for theology and as a rule for interpretation. The wholeness of Scripture is constituted by the analogy of faith. The places where Wesley makes reference to the wholeness of Scripture support this interpretation of the analogy of faith. Wesley says the doctrine that human beings were created in the image of God is witnessed "in every page" of the Bible.[75] In his *Thoughts on a Late Publication,* he talks about human sinfulness as being part of the message of the whole tenor of Scripture.[76] The necessity of inward holiness is declared "everywhere" in Scripture.[77] In his sermon "On Divine Providence" he writes, "all the oracles of God, all the Scriptures both of the Old Testament and the New describe so many scenes of divine providence."[78] In *Predestination Calmly Considered* he argues that the doctrine of reprobation is "utterly irreconcilable to the whole scope and tenor both of the Old and New Testament."[79]

These claims about Scripture's witness to sin, holiness, providence, and free grace are all species of the larger claim that the Scripture's general content is the order of salvation. It is in this light, for example, that one understands Wesley's note on Ephesians 5:14 where he says that the general tenor of Scripture is concerned with awakening sleeping sinners.[80] Whereas that "awakening" is not the chief concern of every verse, the general tenor of Scripture is interested in the entire process of awakening sinners, from the first dawn of conviction to the blazing noon of perfection.

The Trinity is the one doctrine mentioned by Wesley as being taught by the entire Bible that is not directly entailed by the doctrines pertaining to salvation. In the *Notes* he writes: "Nothing can separate the Spirit from the Father and the Son. If he were not one with the Father and the Son, the apostle ought to have said, *The Father and the Word*, who are one, *and the Spirit, are two*. But this is contrary to the whole tenor of revelation. It remains that *these three are one*."[81] It is interesting that for Wesley "the whole tenor of revelation" testifies to the unity of the Godhead. In his sermon "On the Trinity," he says that the doctrine of the Trinity "is a truth of the last importance. It enters into the very heart of Christianity; it lies at the root of all vital religion."[82] His point here is that the doctrine of the Trinity, while not explicitly a soteriological doctrine, is nevertheless a necessary presupposition of any Christian soteriology. Thus, while not directly a part of the analogy of faith, the analogy of faith presupposes it and thus it is part of the whole message of Scripture.

Two questions can be raised about Wesley's position on this matter. The first is why Wesley appeals to the analogy of faith at all, given that some prominent theologians had criticized the concept as a subjective construct imposed upon Scripture. How would Wesley respond to Locke's rejection of the analogy of faith because it is interpretation "according to the system of his particular sect?"[83] Is Wesley subject to Locke's critique? Locke argues that a simple reading of the text, without commentaries or other traditional interpretations, will yield a better understanding of the true meaning of Scripture. His ultimate goal is to have a simplified version of Christianity which could overcome the destructive divisions among Christians. *The Reasonableness of Christianity* describes his view of that simplified scheme of doctrine. Wesley, too, appeals to Scripture in its plainest form.[84] The methodological difference between Wesley and Locke is that Wesley explicitly appeals to Christian antiquity and the Church of England for help in Scripture's interpretation. Chapter 3 of this study will detail the ways in which Wesley argues that these traditional authorities ought to be utilized. Locke, however, sees the accretion of human commentary as obscuring the simple message of the text. While he does in fact rely on contemporary commentators for help, he does not mention them often and attempts to minimize the influence of any portion of Christian tradition in his interpretation. Wesley would argue that traditional sources have a better understanding of the general tenor of Scripture, and that traditional understandings are in fact useful in eliciting the true, simple meaning of the text.

However, the analogy of faith is not for Wesley simply a traditional construct external to Scripture. He believes that it arises out of the text itself and represents the best construal of its general tenor. The second question to be raised is why Wesley sees this particular scheme of doctrine as the content of Scripture's general tenor. Other views of how the wholeness of Scripture should be construed were available from the primitive church and Protestant theology. An answer must consider how Wesley's understanding of the general tenor of Scripture changed in 1738 and must begin with references to four places where he appeals to the whole message of Scripture. In the 1726 sermon "On Guardian Angels," it is clear that the analogy of faith functions as a norm for Christian understanding. He is willing to speculate about the reasons why God sends the angels to help human beings "provided we proceed with due reverence and humility, and do not contradict the analogy of our faith."[85] Taken in conjunction with his mother's letter of 1725 quoted earlier, it is clear that Wesley is using this means of interpreting Scripture. Further, the content of that sermon shows Wesley is prepared to speculate about the angels along the lines of their holiness and happiness, even when he has no scriptural warrants for his conclusions. The "analogy of our faith" is clearly God's design for all his creatures, angels and human beings, to be both holy and happy.

Two other references indicate the content of the "general tenor of Scripture" in Wesley's view. The 1733 sermon "The Love of God" has Mark 12:30—"Thou shalt love the Lord thy God with all thy heart, and with all thy soul, and with all thy mind, and with all thy strength"—as its text. In §I he argues that the plain sense of the commandment is to "love God alone for his own sake, and all things else only so far as they tend to him." Wesley then seeks to show that this is the true interpretation, arguing that "from every part of the Holy Scriptures it appears that love is the proper worship of a reasonable nature."[86] There follow references to Mark,

Psalms, Micah, Deuteronomy, Matthew, Romans, 1 John, James, and 1 Corinthians. For Wesley, the whole Scripture teaches that every reasonable creature should love God. He understands the entire Scripture to teach the importance of holiness understood as the unbounded love of God.

In a 1734 letter to Richard Morgan, Senior, Wesley argues that "a good Christian" must avoid sins of omission as well as sins of commission:

> Whether divines and bishops will agree to this I know not. But this I know: it is the plain Word of God. God everywhere declares: (1), that without doing good as well as avoiding evil, shall no flesh living be justified. (2). That as good prayers without good works attending them are no better than a solemn mockery of God, so are good works themselves without those tempers of heart, from their subserviency to which they derive their whole value. (3). That those tempers which alone are acceptable to God, and to procure acceptance for which our Redeemer lived and died, are, (i), Faith, without which it is still impossible either to please him or to overcome the world; (ii), Hope, without which we are alienated from the life of God, and strangers to the covenant of promise, and (iii), Love of God, and our neighbour for his sake, without which, though we should give all our goods to feed the poor, yea, and our bodies to be burned, if we will believe God, "it profiteth us nothing."[87]

The key phrase "God everywhere declares" signals that the whole Scripture teaches the three doctrines he lists. Justification depends on doing good and avoiding evil. Prayers require good works and a proper temper of the heart to be efficacious. The three "tempers," faith, hope, and love are necessary to gain acceptance by God.

These three references provide evidence that during the years from 1725 through 1738, Wesley understands that the whole Scripture teaches God's demand for holiness. The understanding of faith as a "temper" is typical of his theology prior to 1738. He defines faith as "an assent to what God has revealed, because he has revealed it."[88] Assent is a disposition of the mind, just as hope and love are dispositions of the heart and soul.[89] Holiness is the final goal and purpose of religion. Many of Wesley's early sermons center on this theme; his 1733 sermon "The Circumcision of the Heart" is an early example, and Wesley says forty-five years later that he cannot improve upon it.[90] Timothy Smith is basically correct when he argues that holiness is a constant emphasis in Wesley's hermeneutics from 1725 to the end of his life.[91]

If holiness of heart and life is the dominant emphasis of Wesley's hermeneutics in his early ministry, it occupies a different place after 1738. The theological transition Wesley made during that year altered his understanding of faith and its relationship to holiness. From that time on, he insisted that faith alone was necessary for salvation, though he continued to emphasize that good works were both the fruit of faith and a necessary condition for its continuance.[92]

This theological transition is apparent in his understanding of the general tenor of Scripture. Wesley's fifth argument against predestination in the 1739 sermon "Free Grace" is that it "directly tends to overthrow the whole Christian revelation," partly by making the Bible contradict itself. The idea that God would save some and not others is contrary to "the whole scope and tenor of Scripture" as well as particular passages like "God is love."[93] Other specific passages are quoted, but the significant point is that the entirety of Scripture is used to rule out a specific interpretation of certain passages. He goes so far as to assert that "better it were to say it had no sense at all than to say it had such a sense as this. It cannot mean, whatever it mean besides, that the God of truth is a liar. . . . No Scripture can mean that God is not love, or that his mercy is not over all his works."[94]

Wesley's understanding of the wholeness of Scripture changes after 1738. Until that time, the general tenor of Scripture is the commandment to be holy, understood as the love of God and the love of humankind. In 1739, the general tenor of Scripture concerns the whole order of salvation. In the 1742 *Principles of a Methodist,* Wesley uses "the analogy of faith" as the standard by which his doctrine of perfection is to be judged.[95] In this work he defends his teaching of justification by faith alone and Christian perfection. Thus 1738 marks a distinct change in his understanding of the general tenor of Scripture, and no further changes in his view can be found after that time.

The Relation of the Old Testament and the New Testament

Wesley's views on the relation of the Old Testament and the New Testament reflect a type of dispensational understanding that allows for both continuity and change in God's relationship with humankind. This understanding leads to an ambivalence about the authority of the Old Testament. On the one hand, Wesley emphasizes that the Old Testament is sacred Scripture and therefore binding on all human beings. On the other hand, he emphasizes that there are aspects of the gospel available only in the New Testament which supersede portions of the Old. We will consider each side of the ambivalence in turn.

In some places, Wesley praises the Old Testament and its importance for Christians. In the sermon "The Law Established through Faith, I," he is concerned to show the proper role and function of the law for Christians. To those who make a distinction between preaching the law and preaching Christ he says this: "Consider this well: that to 'preach Christ' is to preach all things that Christ hath spoken: all his promises; all his threatenings and commands; all that is written in his Book. And then you will know how to preach Christ without making void the law."[96]

What is significant here is that one can "preach Christ" from an Old Testament text. John Deschner argues that there are three ways Christ is related to Old Testament prophecy. First, for Wesley, "Christ, Himself, is simply present and speaking in the Old Testament," for example in the burning bush. Second, Christ is the one who sent the prophets and gives them their message. Third, the Old Testament contains many "types" of Christ, which Deschner defines as "facts, persons, ceremonies, things which, in a measure, embody Christ's significance, and in a sense speak for Christ in the Old Testament, yet remain signs which press for 'an answer' in Jesus Christ Himself."[97] Deschner concludes that the continuity of both testaments is "a presupposition of considerable importance for Wesley."[98]

There are several places where Wesley simply asserts that a particular doctrine is taught by both testaments. Concerning the doctrine of conditional election, for which Wesley argued against the Calvinists, he says, "To this agrees the whole scope of the Christian revelation, as well as the parts thereof. To this Moses and all the prophets bear witness, and our blessed Lord and all his apostles."[99]

There are many other instances where both Old and New Testaments are cited in support of a particular point.[100] The Old Testament is said to have "the most strict connexion" with the gospel.[101] In his sermon "On Divine Providence" he describes the connection:

And this he hath done in his written Word: all the oracles of God, all the Scriptures both of the Old Testament and the New describe so many scenes of divine providence. It is the beautiful remark of a fine writer: "Those who object to the Old Testament, in particular, that it is not a connected history of nations, but only a congeries of broken unconnected events, do not observe the nature and design of these writings. They do not see that Scripture is *the history of God*." Those who bear this upon their minds will easily perceive that the inspired writers never lose sight of it, but preserve one unbroken, connected chain, from the beginning to the end. All over that wonderful book, as "life and immortality" (immortal life) is gradually "brought to light," so is "Immanuel, God with us," and his kingdom ruling over all.[102]

And in "The Means of Grace" he mentions 2 Timothy 3:15-17 in support of the inspiration of Scripture:

It should be observed that this is spoken primarily and directly of the Scriptures which Timothy had "known from a child"; which must have been those of the Old Testament, for the New was not then wrote. How far then was St. Paul (though he was "not a whit behind the very chief of the apostles," nor therefore, I presume, behind any man now upon earth) from making light of the Old Testament! Behold this, lest ye one day "wonder and perish," ye who make so small account of one half of the oracles of God! Yea, and that half of which the Holy Ghost expressly declares that it is "profitable," as a means ordained of God for this very thing, "for doctrine, for reproof, for correction, for instruction in righteousness": to the end [that] "the man of God may be perfect, throughly furnished unto all good works."[103]

The point here is to emphasize that the Old Testament is part of the Bible and as such deserves the respect that is due to all of God's Word. However, Wesley also pointed out the differences between the two testaments, for example in his sermon "Christian Perfection":

It is of great importance to observe, and that more carefully than is commonly done, the wide difference there is between the Jewish and the Christian dispensation, and that ground of it which the same Apostle assigns in the seventh chapter of his Gospel, verse thirty-eight, etc.[104]

It should be noted that Wesley uses this point to rule out arguments from the Old Testament that would provide a different interpretation of Paul. His method of differentiating between the levels
of authority of the two testaments is to assign them to different
dispensations. He describes these dispensations as having different
characteristics in his *Advice to the People Called Methodists with Regard
to Dress* (1780): "The Jews and we are under different dispensations.
The glory of the whole Mosaic dispensation was chiefly visible and
external; whereas the glory of the Christian dispensation is of an
invisible and spiritual nature."[105] He goes so far as to describe the
New Testament, in a rhetorical question, as "a far more perfect
dispensation than that which He delivered in Hebrew."[106] At several
points in his *Notes*, Wesley has occasion to comment on the relation
between the testaments. On 1 John 2:8 he writes, "For there is no
comparison between the state of the Old Testament believers, and
that which ye now enjoy: the *darkness* of that dispensation *is passed
away; and* Christ *the true light now shineth* in your hearts."[107] Similar
comments are made at 2 Corinthians 3:6 and 2 Peter 1:19. Deschner
describes this superiority of the New Testament by saying, "The
light of Old Testament prophecy, taken in its entirety, is as lamplight
before the daylight of the New."[108]

Basic to the distinction between the testaments is Wesley's view
that the Mosaic law had three parts, two of which had been nullified
by Christ. In *Farther Thoughts Upon Christian Perfection*, Wesley responds to a question about Christ being the end of the law, as in
Romans 10:4, saying:

> In order to understand this, you must understand what law is here
> spoken of; and this, I apprehend, is . . . the Mosaic law, the whole
> Mosaic dispensation; which St. Paul continually speaks of as one,
> though containing three parts, the political, moral, and ceremonial.[109]

In his 1787 sermon "The Duty of Reproving Our Neighbour," he
makes clear his view that the ceremonial law had been abolished:

> A great part of the book of Exodus, and almost the whole of the book
> of Leviticus, relate to the ritual or ceremonial law of Moses, which was
> peculiarly given to the children of Israel; but was such "a yoke," says
> the apostle Peter, "as neither our fathers nor we were able to bear."
> We are therefore delivered from it: and this is one branch of "the

liberty wherewith Christ hath made us free." Yet it is easy to observe that many excellent moral precepts are interspersed among these ceremonial laws.[110]

Further, Wesley's note on Ephesians 2:14 suggests a similarity between the "middle wall of partition," which was broken down, and "the ceremonial law, which Christ had now taken away." In commenting on Galatians 2:4, Wesley construes Christian liberty to mean "from the ceremonial law." The note on Galatians 3:19 is even more extensive:

> Probably, the yoke of the ceremonial law was inflicted as a punishment for the national sin of idolatry, Exod. xxxii. 1, at least the more grievous parts of it; and the whole of it was a prophetic type of Christ. The moral law was added to the promise to discover and restrain transgressions, to convince men of their guilt, and need of the promise, and give some check to sin. And this law passeth not away; but the ceremonial law was only introduced *till* Christ, *the seed to* or through *whom the promise was made, should come.*[111]

A similar note is given at Romans 3:20, where Wesley refers to "the moral part of [the law] . . . which alone is not abolished."[112]

The ceremonial law, though abolished, is useful because it points to Christ. In the note to Galatians 3:19 just quoted, the ceremonial law was understood to be a type of Christ. The note to 1 Timothy 1:8 makes this explicit: "*We* grant *the* whole Mosaic *law is good,* answers excellent purposes, *if a man use it* in a proper manner. Even the ceremonial is good, as it points to Christ."[113]

The ambivalence with which Wesley approaches the Old Testament's relation to the New is both coherent and in keeping with traditional Christian interpretation of the Hebrew Scriptures. The coherence of his view rests on the division of salvation history into dispensations. It is the same God working in two different time periods toward the same end. Because of the coming of Christ, new possibilities are open to humankind that did not exist before. In a 1758 letter to Elizabeth Hardy he expresses it clearly:

> I do by no means exclude the Old Testament from bearing witness to any truths of God. Nothing less. But I say the experience of the Jews is not the standard of Christian experience; and that therefore, were it true "The Jews did not love God with all their heart and soul," it

would not follow "Therefore no Christian can," because he may attain what they did not.[114]

The Old Testament does give a valid witness to the truths about God. At the same time, Christians recognize that the new covenant in Christ Jesus has fulfilled and superseded the old. In one place Wesley argues that the covenant of grace existed under the Jewish dispensation.[115] In another place, he refers to Christianity as a doctrine that describes a certain character:

> It describes this character in all its parts, and that in the most lively and affecting manner. The main lines of this picture are beautifully drawn in many passages of the Old Testament. These are filled up in the New, retouched and finished with all the art of God.[116]

Here Wesley talks about the outlines being present in the Old Testament, but the entire picture being finished in the New. He does not negate what is present in the Old, but takes the position that it points to what comes in the New.

Wesley's dispensational view is in keeping with traditional Reformed interpretation of the Old Testament as exemplified in chapter seven of the Westminster Confession. There the Puritan divines distinguish between two covenants, a covenant of works which applied before the Fall and one of grace which applied after Adam's sin. The second covenant is "differently administered in the time of the law and in the time of the gospel." The former is characterized by, among other things, promises and prophecies. The latter exhibits the substance of Christ instead of promises. It has fewer ordinances, but in them is "more fullness, evidence, and spiritual efficacy," which is offered to the whole world. The chapter concludes, "There are not, therefore, two covenants of grace differing in substance, but one and the same under various dispensations."[117]

Although there are significant difficulties about the precision of his language, with "covenant" and "dispensation" often used interchangeably, it seems fairly clear that Wesley subscribed to the basic scheme of two covenants and two dispensations within the second covenant.[118] By adopting this Reformed understanding of how the two testaments are related, Wesley stands well within the tradition of Protestant interpretation of the Old Testament.

The Canonicity of Scripture

Wesley defends a traditional Protestant view of the canonicity of Scripture. Article V in the Articles of Religion sent to the American Methodist Church retains the listing of Old Testament books named in the Thirty-nine Articles. Wesley removes the paragraph which said that the Apocrypha is to be read "for example of life and instruction of manners" but not "to establish any doctrine."[119] In *Popery Calmly Considered* he specifically attacks the Church of Rome for accepting noncanonical books of the Old Testament:

> The Church of Rome not only adds tradition to Scripture, but several entire books; namely, Tobit and Judith, the Book of Wisdom, Ecclesiasticus, Baruch, the two books of Maccabees, and a new part of Esther and of Daniel; "which whole books," says the Church of Rome, "whoever rejects, let him be accursed."
>
> We answer, We cannot but reject them. We dare not receive them as part of the Holy Scriptures. For none of these books were received as such by the Jewish Church, "to whom were committed the oracles of God" (Rom. 3:2): Neither by the ancient Christian Church, as appears from the 60th Canon of the Council of Laodicea; wherein is a catalogue of the books of Scriptures, without any mention of these.[120]

Wesley's thinking on the canon is not well developed, because the "Canons of the Council of Laodicea" do not include the book of Revelation.[121] He does, however, take very seriously the sin of adding to or taking away from what is written in the book, with the warning in Revelation 22:18-19 as a foundation. His note to that passage applies the warning to those who tamper not only with the book of Revelation, but also with the whole New Testament. Further, he understands that God himself closed the canon of the Old Testament.[122] A letter of 1731 to Mary Pendarves shows that he took those sanctions seriously for his own practice as a Christian.[123]

Wesley clearly stands with the larger Protestant tradition in rejecting the Apocrypha as part of the Bible. All of his references to it reject its inclusion in Scripture. If his editorial work on the Articles of Religion is given any weight at all, he appears to oppose even the limited use of the Apocrypha for example and instruction. However, this is one of the places where the distinction between Wesley's conception of Scripture and his use of it is illuminating. Wesley is far more willing to use the Apocrypha than his conception would indicate, as will be shown in chapter 6.

Conclusion

With one exception, Wesley's view of the characteristics of Scripture stands in the mainstream of Protestant theology. Scripture is seen to be sufficient for all matters of faith and practice, but not to conflict with new scientific discoveries. It is clear in its main points, but does need explanation of its more obscure parts. Wesley views the Old Testament with an ambivalence that is characteristic of much of Christian teaching, and resolves the tension between the testaments by using a dispensational scheme taken from the teachings of the Church of England. He defends the Protestant view of the Old Testament canon, apparently rejecting any use of the Apocrypha, even "for instruction in life and manners."

The one exception where Wesley stands out is his view of the wholeness of Scripture. Even here he uses the concept of the analogy of faith to argue for a particular version of the general tenor of Scripture. However, Wesley's view (after 1738) that the analogy of faith is constituted by the order of salvation distinguishes him from others. Earlier writers are more general: Bucanus defines it in terms of the Creeds, the Lord's Prayer, and the Ten Commandments, and Whitby uses the general term "fundamentals of faith" without specificity. In contrast, Wesley offers a specific proposal that it is constituted by the doctrines of original sin, justification by faith alone, and sanctification.

Historically, Wesley's changed understanding of the content of Scripture's general tenor is correlated with his theological transition in 1738 (whether or not one concludes that he was personally converted to Christianity at that time or before).[124] Kelsey's claims about the wholeness of Scripture and the content of a theologian's writings are borne out in Wesley's case. Theologically, however, we are no closer to discovering why and how Wesley came to see soteriology as comprising the general tenor of Scripture.

Wesley assumes that the whole point of religion is salvation, an assumption widely shared by other theologians of his time, such as Locke.[125] Wesley reads the Scripture with that concern uppermost in his mind. The claim that salvation is the general subject matter of Scripture was not controversial in the eighteenth century. What *was* controversial was Wesley's particular formulation of it. He speaks of it having three parts: original sin, justification by faith alone, and sanctification. Wesley's formulation focuses on salvation as an experience of an individual and plays down the role of the church as a formal community.

Kelsey's *Use of Scripture* demonstrates that the wholeness of Scripture has been characterized in a number of different ways, and that "there is an irreducible variety of kinds of wholeness that may be ascribed to the texts."[126] While the variety may be irreducible, it is possible that some method of arguing for one view over another might be devised. Whether such an argument is possible or not, Wesley's view that the wholeness of Scripture is constituted by this understanding of salvation should receive consideration along with others. However, Locke's objection that the analogy of faith is the result of a particular sect's system must be addressed. Locke's own interpretation, as well as all other claims to a correct understanding of the general tenor of Scripture, must demonstrate that Scripture itself authorizes that view. Wesley has not yet provided any such argument to warrant selecting his view of the analogy of faith over other possibilities. In the remaining portions of this study, we will seek further clues to his position and draw whatever conclusions are possible in the concluding chapter.

CHAPTER 3

The Authority of Scripture in Tension with Other Authorities

Wesley's commitment to the authority of Scripture alone did not exclude other authorities. It was noted earlier that Wesley, while proclaiming himself *homo unius libri*, was manifestly a man of many books with a wide range of learning who used these other books as both sources and authorities. Wesley was committed to the authority of Scripture, but his professed allegiance to *sola Scriptura* was more complicated than it first appears.

The analysis which follows will discuss the relation between five different authorities Wesley recognizes. The identification of five authorities stands in explicit disagreement with a number of Wesley scholars who argue that Wesley has a fourfold doctrine of religious authority. Ted Campbell has traced the history of the term "the Wesleyan quadrilateral" and noted that it has become commonplace among Wesleyans to refer to four authorities at work in Wesley's theological writings: Scripture, reason, tradition, and experience.[1] Colin Williams, in *John Wesley's Theology Today*, summarizes each of these, noting that while Scripture is primary, the other three have roles to play as well.[2] Albert Outler was the first to use the term "quadrilateral" to describe the fourfold authority in Wesley's thought. Although he later regretted the term, he defended it as an accurate description of Wesley's method.[3] More recently, Donald Thorson's *Wesleyan Quadrilateral* argues for this fourfold structure as the essence of Wesley's theological method.[4]

After tracing the origin of the term "quadrilateral," Campbell argues that this fourfold view of authority cannot be directly attributed to John Wesley, and that the understanding of tradition commonly presumed in modern formulations of the quadrilateral is anachronistic.[5] In my view, Campbell is correct. When they employ the category of tradition, Williams, Outler, and Thorson are using a term that does not appear explicitly in Wesley's writings as an authority for faith and practice. The term "tradition" has instead only negative connotations for Wesley. The best he can say about the Christian tradition as a whole is that "God never left himself without witness. In every age and in every nation there were a few that truly feared God and wrought righteousness."[6]

Tradition in fact comes in for heavy criticism in Wesley's writings against Roman Catholicism, such as his 1779 tract *Popery Calmly Considered*:

> Yet the Papists add tradition to Scripture, and require it to be received with equal veneration. By traditions, they mean, "such points of faith and practice as have been delivered down in the Church from hand to hand without writing." And for many of these, they have no more Scripture to show, than the Pharisees had for their traditions.[7]

Wesley has in mind here the teaching of the Roman Catholic Church as expressed in the canons of the Council of Trent. Trent's "Decree Concerning the Canonical Scriptures" refers to the truth of the gospel being contained "in libris scriptis et sine scripto traditionibus," that is, "in the written books and the unwritten traditions" which were passed on "from hand to hand . . . preserved in the Catholic Church by a continuous succession."[8] This argument for an unbroken parallel transmission of Christian truth was the primary content of the term "tradition" as used by both Catholics and Protestants in the eighteenth century. Wesley was in complete accord with fellow Protestants of his time when he condemns Roman Catholics on this point.

Thus, for Wesley, "tradition" has a negative connotation and could never be invested with authority in religious matters. He regards the bulk of Christian history as a period of decline for Christianity, with only a few spots where true religion was strong enough to be clearly seen. In the sermon "The Mystery of Iniquity," Wesley notes the purity of the church at Pentecost. With Ananias and Sapphira, iniquity began to work covertly, and then overtly in Corinth and other places discussed in the New Testament itself.[9] The second century exhibited further decline, but he writes, "It is true that during this whole period, during the first three centuries, there were intermixed longer or shorter seasons wherein true Christianity revived." But the greatest blow [that genuine Christianity] ever received, the grand blow which was struck at the very root of that humble, gentle, patient love, which is the fulfilling of the Christian law, the whole essence of true religion, was struck in the fourth century by Constantine the Great, when he called himself a Christian, and poured in a flood of riches, honours, and power upon the Christians, more especially upon the clergy.[10]

Instead of seeing this as a triumph of Christianity, Wesley calls it "the coming of Satan and all his legions from the bottomless pit." He concludes, "Such has been the deplorable state of the Christian church from the time of Constantine till the Reformation."[11] Campbell concludes that Wesley's thought has "a clear sense of the decline in the purity of the ancient church throughout the first four centuries, with a particularly precipitous decline in the age of Constantine, but with some pockets of pure faith remaining even in the fourth century and beyond."[12] Thus, to talk about the whole Christian tradition as being authoritative for him is grossly to misrepresent Wesley's position. Campbell is correct when he argues that it is anachronistic to apply a nineteenth-century understanding of tradition to Wesley.[13] Such anachronism obscures the way in which Wesley sees two distinct periods of the larger Christian tradition as authoritative: antiquity and the then-current doctrines of the Church of England.

Whereas Williams, Outler, and Thorson refer to four authorities, Wesley is more accurately understood as conceiving religious authority to have five components: Scripture, reason, Christian antiquity, experience, and the Church of England. The relation between these elements has been discussed in various ways. No one who reads Wesley carefully could possibly miss the primacy of Scripture over the others. However, the introduction of geometric metaphors is a mistake from the start. For Wesley the elements are defined in such a way that they constitute one locus of authority with five aspects. Christian faith and practice are governed by Scripture, which is reasonable in its claims, exemplified in antiquity, vivified in personal experience, and most fully institutionalized in the Church of England.[14] Potential conflicts between any of the five are reduced, and often ruled out by formulations that distinguish between the true authority and some impure corruption of it, for example, between reason and "idle reasonings" or between scriptural, rational experience and enthusiasm. Indeed, each of the elements is defined in such a way as to make it interdependent with the others.

Part of the complexity in sorting out Wesley's thinking on these matters arises from the fact that he was very careful to consider the type of evidence required to answer a particular question or to respond to a particular adversary, as in a letter of 1762 to Dr. Horne: "Our Church, adopting the words of St. Chrysostom, expressly affirms in the passage above cited he was justified by faith alone. And her authority ought to weigh more than even that of Bishop Bull, or of any single man whatever. Authority, be pleased to observe, I plead against authority, reason against reason."[15] In this case, Wesley matches the authority chosen by his critic, and argues that the authority of the whole Church of England outweighs that of any single individual. In other cases, Wesley suits the type of evidence to the subject matter. If it is a matter of fact that is to be proved, he argues this is done "by the testimony of competent witnesses." Doctrines are to be proved by "Scripture and reason."[16] Thus, in interpreting Wesley, one must be careful to note what sort of question is being discussed and the type of authority that Wesley understands to be appropriate to that question.

Scripture and Reason

Our discussion of Scripture and reason will be divided into three sections: the definition of reason, reason's competence and limits, and Scripture and reason as joint authorities.

Definition of Reason

Wesley's most comprehensive definition of reason is given in his sermon "The Case of Reason Impartially Considered." He first identifies two definitions: argument and eternal reason. Wesley then proceeds to give a third definition, which he intends to use for reason in the strict sense.

In another acceptation of the word, reason is much the same with *understanding*. It means a faculty of the human soul; that faculty which exerts itself in three ways: by simple apprehension, by judgment, and by discourse. *Simple apprehension* is barely conceiving a thing in the mind, the first and most simple act of understanding. *Judgment* is the determining that the things before conceived either agree with or differ from each other. *Discourse* (strictly speaking) is the motion of

65

progress of the mind from one judgment to another. The faculty of the soul which includes these three operations I here mean by the term *reason*.[17]

The same point is made in other places.[18]

Rex Matthews correctly summarizes Wesley's understanding of reason as a faculty:

> So, for Wesley, in this primary sense, reason (noun) is a faculty of the human soul, the mind or the understanding, which has a three-fold operation: simple apprehension, judgment, and discourse. To reason (verb) is to employ the mind or understanding in this three-fold way (though he does on occasion use "inferring" or "reasoning" as equivalent to the highest of these three operations, discourse, by way of synecdoche). Something is "reasonable" (adjective) if it is governed by or in accordance with the three-fold operation of reason, and the adverbial use corresponds. Reasoning (noun) is the use of this faculty of the soul, and by extension refers also to the evidence or arguments used in reasoning. And the use of the term "reason" as synonymous with motive, argument, or explanation is dependent upon and derivative from this more fundamental meaning of the term.[19]

By extension, also, the term "reason" is sometimes used for the conclusions of the reasoning process as constituting a body of knowledge which ought to be self-evident. It is in this sense that reason is used by Wesley as a shorthand name for an entire approach to life that is presumed to be available to all human beings as rational creatures. Endowed by God with the faculty of reason, they are able to use that faculty to reach conclusions about a wide variety of subjects.

It is thus possible to talk about "reason's" position on any number of subjects and expect agreement by all "reasonable" people. Because of this, appeals to "reason" in eighteenth-century England carried weight even if the details of one's reasonings were not given. Thus, Wesley writes to John Valton that the practice of separating men and women during preaching services "is a Methodist rule, not grounded on caprice, but on plain, solid reason."[20] The appeal is made to reason as if reason's conclusions are clear and obvious to all: nowhere does Wesley give an exposition of the reasons for the separation of men and women at preaching services, yet he claims that such separation is according to "plain, solid reason." Reason's conclusions are presumed to be self-evident.

This view of reason approaches the etymological root of "common sense." Something is "reasonable" because a common person with sense would come to the same conclusion. Wesley uses "common sense" in the same way he does "reason" in several cases. He notes that certain behaviors offend religion as well as common sense.[21] He appeals to scripture and common sense.[22] In one place he states that "on Scripture and common sense I build all my principles."[23] Further, in *A Dialogue Between an Antinomian and His Friend*, the Friend (Wesley's persona) uses "common sense" and "reason" as synonymous terms.[24] While this may not be the case in every usage, the two terms are usually equivalent.

Wesley notes three definitions of reason, then, but consistently uses the term to refer to a faculty of the soul that is otherwise known as the understanding. Its functions are apprehension, judgment, and discourse, and its conclusions are presumed to be obvious to all. Wesley lived in the period described by historians as "The Age of Reason"; like his contemporaries, he placed a high degree of confidence in this faculty. He also saw its limits, however, and his methods of preaching often caused him to be attacked as unreasonable.

Reason's Competence and Limits

Wesley was often accused of abandoning reason to be an "enthusiast," and requiring the same of his followers. In the eighteenth century few things were worse in the religious sphere of national life than being an enthusiast. To counter these charges, Wesley's apology *An Earnest Appeal to Men of Reason and Religion* intended to demonstrate the reasonableness of his position. At several points Wesley strives to emphasize that reason is important to him, that it is not important to enthusiasts, and that he is therefore not an enthusiast. He often takes great pains to emphasize the importance of reason to true religion. In such cases, as in a letter of 1768 to Dr. Rutherforth, he gives his most unqualified approbation to reason as an authority in religion without reference to Scripture: "It is a fundamental principle with *us*, that to renounce reason is to renounce religion; that religion and reason go hand in hand, and that all irrational religion is false religion."[25] In a similar vein, he writes in a 1760 letter to the editor of *Lloyd's Evening Post*, "True religion is the highest reason. It is indeed wisdom, virtue, and happiness in one."[26]

Clearly, Wesley sees only harmony, not conflict, between religion and reason, at least when both are truly what they are supposed to be. Reason as a faculty leads to judgments about God and the world which produce virtue and true human happiness. When reason is correctly employed, its conclusions point to the same truths that are taught by religion. This harmony between reason and religion is a key presupposition of Wesley's theological method. Whereas some facets of his theology underwent development and change during his lifetime, his commitment to a reasonable religion was unwavering during his whole life. In 1733 he wrote in the sermon "The Love of God" that "reason, as well as the Holy Scriptures, requires that we should so love God with all our heart as to love nothing else but for his sake, and in subordination to the love of him."[27] He writes in 1784, "We all aim at one point . . . to spread true religion through London, Dublin, Edinburgh, and, as we are able, through the three kingdoms; that truly rational religion which is taught and prescribed in the Old and New Testament."[28]

Frequently, Wesley uses the disjunction Scripture or reason and says that he will abide by the conclusions of either. In the published *Letter to the Author of "The Enthusiasm of Methodists and Papists Compared,"* he writes, "I am not above either reason or Scripture. To either of these I am ready to submit."[29] He even goes so far as to say that if given sufficiently weighty arguments, he will give up Christianity.[30] The importance of reason is thus clear in Wesley's thought; the critical question then becomes determining reason's competence. On the positive side, Wesley sees reason as being extremely useful in both daily life and religious matters. Consider four places where he outlines what reason can do.

In the sermon "The Case of Reason Impartially Considered," Wesley says that reason is of great use in "the affairs of common life." It can direct "servants how to discharge their duty," the "mariner to steer his course," and "those who study the art of healing to cure most of the maladies to which we are exposed." Further, "reason can assist us in going through the whole circle of arts and sciences." In the area of religion, reason can do very much.

Now of what excellent use is reason if we would either understand ourselves, or explain to others, those living oracles! And how is it possible without it to understand the essential truths contained therein? . . . Is it not reason (assisted by the Holy Ghost) which enables us to understand what the Holy Scriptures declare concerning the being and attributes of God? . . . It is by reason that God enables us in some measure to comprehend his method of dealing with the children of men; the nature of his various dispensations, of the Old and New Covenant, of the law and the gospel.[31]

He continues by saying that "many cases of conscience are not to be solved without the utmost exercise of our reason."[32]

Because of the use of reason in interpreting Scripture and resolving difficulties in life, a good minister must be able to reason well. In *An Address to the Clergy,* he writes, "Ought not a Minister to have, First, a good understanding, a clear apprehension, a sound judgment, and a capacity of reasoning with some closeness?"[33] In some references to reason, Wesley praises it while noting its limitations. In the sermon "Original Sin" he says reason, apart from revelation, teaches us about God. However, it does not tell us all we need to know.

We had by nature no knowledge of God, no acquaintance with him. It is true, as soon as we came to the use of reason we learned "the invisible things of God, even his eternal power and godhead," from "the things that are made." From the things that are seen we inferred the existence of an eternal, powerful being that is not seen. But still, although we acknowledged his being, we had no acquaintance with him.[34]

Further, reason does teach one general truth about God's nature and activity, as Wesley writes in "The Reward of Righteousness":

Reason alone will convince every fair inquirer that God "is a rewarder of them that diligently seek him." This alone teaches him to say, "Doubtless there is a reward for the righteous; there is a God that judgeth the earth." But how little information do we receive from unassisted reason touching the particulars contained in this general truth! As eye hath not seen, or ear heard, so neither could it naturally enter into our heart to conceive, the circumstances of that awful day wherein God will judge the world. No information of this kind could be given but from the great Judge himself.[35]

Four points ought to be noted about the positive view of reason given in these examples. First, there is an instrumental role that reason plays. It is necessary to understanding and communicating the Bible and the doctrines of Christianity. Without the ability of reason to understand the Scriptures, there would be no communication of God's revelation. Good ministers will have the ability to reason well. Second, there is a substantive role that reason plays in daily life. The routines of different occupations depend on it as well as the whole of the arts and sciences. Reason by itself reaches conclusions in practical arts like medicine as well as bodies of knowledge like logic, mathematics, and metaphysics. Third, reason plays a substantive role in the area of religious knowledge. Wesley has here accepted some of the basic tenets of natural religion as proposed by the Deists. Unassisted reason teaches the existence of God and that God rewards people for their lives on earth. These are two of the five basic truths of natural religion as expounded by Lord Herbert of Cherbury, a seventeenth-century philosopher whom some account the originator of Deism.[36] Fourth, in each of these cases, Wesley places some sort of limit on the powers of unassisted reason. Five pages after saying a minister ought to reason well, Wesley says this ability is inconsequential compared with the minister's being animated by the grace of God.[37] In the third example, he says we learn of God's existence, but we lack "acquaintance with him." We know God rewards people, but we actually have very little information about that process. And the reason that enables us to understand the Scriptures is said to be "assisted by the Holy Ghost." Wesley continues in the sermon "The Case of Reason Impartially Considered" to say that reason by itself cannot produce faith, hope, or love, and thus cannot make us happy.[38]

Wesley's understanding of reason as a faculty of the human being is inevitably tied up with his anthropology of fallen humanity. For him, there is no doubt that Adam was a perfect creature, and he speculates that Adam may not have reasoned before the Fall.[39] However, a present understanding of the human being's capacity to reason must take into account the effects of the Fall, namely that all of Adam and Eve's children inherit impaired faculties because of the first parents' sin:

> Hence, at present, no child of man can at all times apprehend clearly, or judge truly. And where either the judgment or apprehension is wrong, it is impossible to reason justly. Therefore, it is as natural for

a man to mistake as to breathe; and he can no more live without the one than without the other.[40]

Thus, in *The Doctrine of Original Sin*, Wesley refers to human beings as if their capacity to reason is largely gone:

And surely all our declamations on the strength of human reason, and the eminence of our virtues, are no more than the cant and jargon of pride and ignorance, so long as there is such a thing as war in the world. Men in general can never be allowed to be reasonable creatures, till they know not war any more.[41]

But later in the same treatise, he interprets Romans 2:14 this way: "May not men have some reason left, which in some measure discerns good from evil, and yet be deeply fallen, even as to their understanding as well as their will and affections?"[42]

Wesley is generally skeptical about reason's ability to know much about God. In the comment on the Romans passage, Wesley notes that such knowledge of God's existence does not provide acquaintance with God. Further, the quotation from "The Reward of Righteousness" notes that reason can give no particulars of God's rewards, and it is the particulars that are most important. Concerning the doctrine of God in general, he writes, "But in the tracing of this we can neither depend upon reason nor experiment. Whatsoever men know or can know concerning them, must be drawn from the oracles of God."[43] It seems, then, that reason can discover certain general truths about God, but that for significant and particular understandings Wesley claims neither it nor experience can provide any new knowledge. We must rely on Scripture. He departs from the natural theology of the Anglican rationalists at an early point. Human beings know enough of God to recognize his existence, but not enough for a significant relationship with him.

Seen in this light, it is not surprising that Wesley frequently advises people to refrain from dependence upon reason. Matthews takes note of this phenomenon, but fails to see its breadth in terms of the number of years Wesley held this view and the numbers and types of persons to whom he expressed it.[44] Forty places have been identified where Wesley specifically advises against reasoning or makes explicit reference to the devil reasoning.[45] Between 1763 and 1789 he mentions the subject thirty-one times in correspondence

71

with eighteen different men and women. Twenty-six of these usages are in letters written to women, and it is this that Matthews has correctly highlighted. In a typical letter, Wesley writes to Miss March in 1764,

> But the most frequent cause of this second darkness or distress, I believe, is evil reasoning: by this, three in four of those who cast away their confidence are gradually induced so to do. And if this be the cause, is there any way to regain that deliverance but by resuming your confidence? And can you receive it unless you receive it freely, not of works, but by mere grace? This is the way: walk thou in it. Dare to believe! Look up and see thy Saviour near! When? to-morrow, or to-day? Nay, to-day hear His voice! At this time; at this place! Lord, speak; Thy servant heareth![46]

Three significant points in this letter must be noted. First, the wilderness state of doubt comes after justification. Of the forty references being analyzed, twenty-six can clearly be identified as referring to doubts that come after the experience of justification and while the believer is striving for full salvation. In some of these cases, as Wesley notes in the letter to March, the crisis comes even after the believer has attained entire sanctification or "deliverance from sin." These doubts often take the form of raising questions about the state of one's soul and then seeking "rational" answers to them. In one case, Wesley urged guarding against "reasoning in that dangerous manner."[47]

The second point is that Wesley sees the cause of this wilderness state as being "evil reasoning." The wilderness state is a significant problem among a large number of Methodist people. The majority of persons are "induced" into this state by evil reasoning. Although he does not refer to the devil in this letter, it is clear from other references that it is Satan who does the inducing. Wesley refers to him as the "subtle adversary," the "old sophister," and the "old deceiver."[48] In fact, the whole question of the role of reason in this situation is not internal to the mind of the believer, but has the character of an external struggle. Three times he makes reference to the "reasoning devil."[49] Thirteen of the thirty-one usages mention the devil in some way whether it be a reference to the "reasoning devil" or to "reasoning with him [Satan]."[50] Indeed, Wesley's *Journal* entry in 1739 includes a mention of Satan. Thus, a connection of the devil with this abuse of reason is a frequent and long-lasting theme in Wesley's writings.

The third point is the prescription that Wesley gives for dealing with the problem: he characterizes it as a problem of confidence, and the remedy is faith. "Dare to believe! Look up and see thy Saviour near! . . . to-day hear His voice!" Wesley frequently recommends belief to people who have trouble with evil reasoning, idle reasoning, or Satan's inducements to reason.

The question which is raised by all these negative references to reason is how Wesley, who has such good things to say about reason as an authority in religion, can warn off his readers from reasoning about important questions in their faith. The beginning of an answer comes in his *Letter to the Right Reverend the Lord Bishop of Gloucester*, where he distinguishes between reason itself and idle reasonings: "But *reason* is good, though *idle reasonings* are evil. Nor does it follow that I am an enemy to the one because I condemn the other."[51] When Wesley says "to renounce reason is to renounce religion,"[52] he has in mind reason that is rightly employed. Thus, idle reason might be understood as reason that has a flaw in it somewhere. Matthews is correct in his conclusion:

> Reason, in its three-fold functioning, depends at the outset on accurate perception or apprehension. If these people are not correctly apprehending their actual spiritual condition, then their judgments will be faulty, and consequently (and unsurprisingly) their reasoning can lead to nothing but trouble, since it rests on an inaccurate or inadequate foundation. Hence, simplicity, humility, and trust are the remedies which Wesley repeatedly stresses for these "wandering thoughts" and temptations.[53]

Wesley, then, has a balanced view of reason's competence and limits. On the one side, he acknowledges the importance of reason as a tool in everyday life and human knowledge generally. It is even necessary in religious matters, and he sees true religion and reason correctly employed as a unity. Wesley is always seeking a rational explanation of the world. On the other side, Wesley sets clear limits to what reason can accomplish on its own. It cannot produce the most important virtues—faith, hope, and love—and thus cannot lead an individual to salvation. It cannot give more than a superficial knowledge of God. For all these things, an acquaintance with the Bible is necessary. Reason thus becomes a tool that is subordinate to Scripture. Further, like all human capacities, reason has been disfigured since the Fall. Not all human reasoning is done correctly, and the capacity to reason improperly leads many people to false conclusions which are spiritually dangerous. Thus, reason as a faculty is susceptible to abuse, but reason properly employed is part of God's creation of humanity in God's own image.

Scripture and Reason as Joint Authorities

Wesley's understanding that Scripture and reason, when properly employed, warrant the same conclusions is manifested in a number of places where Wesley appeals to both as joint warrants for his views. In *A Farther Appeal* he writes,

> Miracles therefore are quite needless in such a case. Nor are they so conclusive a proof as you imagine. If a man could and did work them in defence of any doctrine, yet this would not *supersede other proof.* For there may be τέρατα ψεύδους, "lying wonders," miracles wrought in support of falsehood. Still therefore his doctrine would remain to be proved from the proper topics of Scripture and reason. And those even without miracles are sufficient. But miracles without these are not. Accordingly our Saviour and all his apostles, in the midst of their greatest miracles, never failed to prove every doctrine they taught by clear Scripture and cogent reason.[54]

In at least three other places he states that the Methodists prove all their doctrines from Scripture and reason. As he puts it in a letter to the editor of the *London Magazine,* the Methodists "follow no *ignis fatuus,* but 'search the Scriptures freely and impartially.' And hence their 'doctrines are not the dogmas of particular men,' but are all warranted by Scripture and reason."[55] This same formula is found slightly altered in two other places, and in both he notes that antiquity also is used "if needed." In *A Farther Appeal, Part III,* he says that "we prove the doctrines we preach by Scripture and reason; and, if need be, by antiquity."[56] And in the published *Letter to the Author of The Enthusiasm of Methodists and Papists Compared* (i.e., Bishop Lavington), he once again rebuts the charge of "enthusiasm":

> "Here we have," say you, "the true spirit and very essence of enthusiasm, . . . which sets men above carnal reasoning, and all conviction of plain Scripture." It may, or may not; that is nothing to me. I am not

above either reason or Scripture. To either of these I am ready to submit. But I cannot receive scurrilous invective instead of Scripture; nor pay the same regard to low buffoonery as to clear and cogent reasons.[57]

The combination of the adjectives "scriptural" and "rational" used in approbation of a position or person shows the way in which these two criteria functioned together in Wesley's thought.[58] In the sermon "The Danger of Increasing Riches," he asks, "And if you have not children, upon what scriptural or rational principle can you leave a groat behind you more than will bury you?"[59] Although this was written in 1790, the same use appears in a 1769 letter to Mary Bishop: "We have but one point in view—to be *altogether Christians*, scriptural, rational Christians."[60]

The question is what to make of these intertwined references to Scripture and reason. In the various citations given here, four points deserve mention. First, Wesley speaks of Scripture and reason without specifying the precise relation between the two; he does not qualify the phrase at all, but urges them as joint authorities whose conclusions are the same. It is obvious here that Wesley does not sense any divergence between the claims of reason and those of Scripture. He has dismissed the Deistic critique of prophecy fulfillment; he has ignored Hume's criticism of miracles; and he does not yet understand that scientific conclusions bring the biblical world picture into serious question. Wesley fails to meet these critical questions with sustained argument.

One of the key biblical texts in this regard is Joshua 10:12, interpreted in light of the astronomical conclusions commonly accepted in his day. Because of the work of Isaac Newton, and one hundred and sixty years of research and theorizing by Copernicus, Kepler, and Galileo which it crowned, the heliocentric conception of the solar system was now fully accepted by educated persons in England. Joshua 10:12, where God makes the sun stand still for the Hebrews' battle, appears to be a direct contradiction of the new science. Wesley's exegesis of this passage raises no questions about the heliocentric theory. His concern is to assert that the miracle truly did take place as "a deviation from the general laws of nature."[61] In the sermon "Spiritual Worship," Wesley accepts the new cosmology and acknowledges that the proper view is that the earth and other planets move around the sun.[62] In the sermon "On the Trinity," he points out the conflicts between the various cosmological theories and argues that we do not really know why the planets behave the way they do.[63] The significance lies in the fact that for Wesley, scientific truth about the heavens is not dependent on scriptural authority. Further, in the places where Scripture makes claims about the world that science has disproved, it is Scripture that is to be reinterpreted in a nonliteral manner.

The second point to be made about the selection from *A Farther Appeal, Part III*, is that Wesley suggests that even Christ and the apostles always used Scripture and reason to prove their doctrines.[64] This claim comes in the midst of an argument that Scripture and reason are the appropriate authorities for doctrine, and not miracles. Nevertheless, it is surprising that Wesley would claim that Christ himself always used the Old Testament and reason. In his first sermon "Upon Our Lord's Sermon on the Mount," Wesley extols the personal authority with which Christ speaks. Christ is described there as "ὁ ὤν, the being of beings, Jehovah, the self-existent, the supreme, the God who is over all, blessed for ever!"[65] His claim that Christ always used Scripture and reason must be seen as a measure of how strongly he viewed the importance of these two authorities in formulating Christian doctrine.

Third, the two occasions[66] where Wesley mentions antiquity along with Scripture and reason as warrants for doctrine point to a more complex understanding of authority than the simple formula "Scripture and reason." It is true that he qualifies the appeal to antiquity by saying it is to be used only if needed, but clearly it has a role to play as well. This will be discussed later in this chapter.

Fourth, Wesley occasionally uses the formulation "Scripture or reason." In his response to Bishop Lavington he notes that "to either of these I am ready to submit."[67] In the letter to Freeborn Garrettson, he seeks to follow "plain Scripture or plain reason."[68] Most of the time Wesley cites "Scripture and reason" as if they held some sort of joint authority. In the letter to Mary Bishop, he joins the adjectives "scriptural" and "rational" to describe the same thing—genuine Christianity.[69] When the disjunctive "or" is used, it appears that either one alone is sufficient.

Are Scripture and reason mutually dependent or mutually independent authorities? The best answer is that for Wesley, Scripture and reason form a type of joint authority and are thus mutually dependent. Scripture rightly interpreted is eminently reasonable. The doctrine it teaches is in accordance with the dictates of reason so far as it goes. Reason is limited, and is dependent on revelation for much of its data. But the data it gets there does not violate what it already knows. Thus, reason and Scripture are two parts of one locus of authority, yet the precise relation of these parts needs to be described.

There are two ways in which reason relates to Scripture that have not been covered in our analysis so far: the role of reason as a supplement to Scripture, and as interpreter of Scripture. The role of reason as supplement to Scripture arises because there are places where Scripture does not give sufficiently detailed commandments and reason must be employed. In his *Plain Account of the People Called Methodists*, he defends the structure of societies and classes against objections that had been raised:

> Another objection was, "There is no scripture for this, for classes and I know not what." I answer, (1.) There is no scripture against it. You cannot show one text that forbids them. (2.) There is much scripture for it, even all those texts which enjoin the substance of those various duties whereof this is only an indifferent circumstance, to be determined by reason and experience. (3.) You seem not to have observed, that the Scripture, in most points, gives only general rules; and leaves the particular circumstances to be adjusted by the common sense of mankind.[70]

In these cases, reason supplements Scripture by applying its general principles to particular situations it has not foreseen. In the sermon "The Nature of Enthusiasm," Wesley asks the hypothetical question whether marriage is, for a particular man, in accord with the will of God. The scriptural principle is "The will of God is our sanctification," found in 1 Thessalonians 4:3. Wesley then suggests that the person ascertain whether marriage will further his sanctification or not. That is a matter of judgment that is best left to reason to decide.[71] Thus, where Scripture is not specific in giving guidance, reason and experience are permitted to find the right way to implement the general guidance that Scripture does give. The supplementation of Scripture by reason does not call into question the former's sufficiency. Scripture's sufficiency in matters of faith and practice is demonstrated by its stated principles. It need not, and could not, give

77

specific guidelines for every situation. It is the role of reason to bridge the gap between the general rule and the particular situation.

Reason helps us interpret Scripture in two ways. First, reason is necessary simply to make contact with the message the Bible is trying to convey, to gain any understanding of what the Scripture says. We reason about ideas and interpret what other people say:

> Now of what excellent use is reason if we would either understand ourselves, or explain to others, those living oracles! . . . Is it not reason (assisted by the Holy Ghost) which enables us to understand what the Holy Scriptures declare concerning the being and attributes of God? Concerning his eternity and immensity, his power, wisdom, and holiness? It is by reason that God enables us in some measure to comprehend his method of dealing with the children of men; the nature of his various dispensations, of the Old and New Covenant, of the law and the gospel. It is by this we understand (his Spirit opening and enlightening the eyes of our understanding) what that repentance is, not to be repented of; what is that faith whereby we are saved; what is the nature and the condition of justification; what are the immediate and what the subsequent fruits of it. By reason we learn what is that new birth, without which we cannot enter into the kingdom of heaven, and what that holiness is, without which no man shall see the Lord. By the due use of reason we come to know what are the tempers implied in inward holiness, and what it is to be outwardly holy, holy in all manner of conversation—in other words, what is the mind that was in Christ, and what it is to walk as Christ walked.[72]

Here Wesley is making the basic point frequently made in the history of biblical interpretation, that reasoning ability is necessary even to understand what Scripture is teaching. The Protestant scholastics distinguished between this form of reason, which they called *"organic or instrumental"* and the *"normal* use of philosophical principles, when they are regarded as principles by which supernatural doctrines are to be tested. *The former* we admit, *the latter* we repudiate."[73] As they affirmed the former, so does Wesley, arguing that it is a gift from God of which we are to make use. In fact, this is an acknowledgment that in doing theology—or preaching or even talking about Christian faith—a process of reasoning is involved.

Also significant in this passage is the role of the Holy Spirit in guiding and directing human reason. The role of the Holy Spirit in

Wesley's thought is hard to describe precisely. One of the Spirit's functions to which he refers several times is to guide the believer. This extends to a relationship with reason as well. His version of what a Christian character looks like includes the following relations within the person: "This implies not only a power over anger, but over all violent and turbulent passions. It implies the having all our passions in due proportion; none of them either too strong or too weak, but all duly balanced with each other, all subordinate to reason; and reason directed by the Spirit of God."[74] This implies that the Spirit and reason are cooperating hierarchically, with the Spirit's influence being determinative.

Another aspect of the Holy Spirit's work with reason is to enlighten it. In a letter to Miss March in 1768, Wesley writes, "We are reasonable creatures, and undoubtedly reason is the candle of the Lord. By enlightening our reason to see the meaning of the Scriptures, the Holy Spirit makes our way plain before us."[75] All of this leads to the general statements which place reason and the Holy Spirit together in guiding the life and faith of believers. The idea is underscored in Wesley's letter to "John Smith": "I entirely agree with you, that the children of light walk by the joint light of reason, Scripture, and the Holy Ghost."[76]

The second function of reason in the interpretation of Scripture is to determine when there is an absurdity in Scripture. In "The Love of God," an early sermon, Wesley writes, "'Tis true, if the literal sense of these Scriptures were absurd, and apparently contrary to reason, then we should be obliged not to interpret them according to the letter, but to look out for a looser meaning."[77] This principle of interpretation was one Wesley held during all of his ministry. His 1785 sermon "Of the Church" says plainly, "It is a stated rule in interpreting Scripture never to depart from the plain, literal sense, unless it implies an absurdity."[78] The implications of this rule for Wesley's hermeneutics will be discussed in chapter 4. Here we need to ask, What constitutes an absurdity, and how is that judgment made? We have already seen that Wesley regards the Ptolemaic cosmology of the world as an absurdity. Biblical verses that imply such a cosmology must be reinterpreted in a nonliteral way because of that. It is reason based on experience that must decide whether something is absurd or not. This gives reason a role in interpreting

Scripture. Conceivably, Wesley is prepared to adjust many things in the Scripture to modern scientific discoveries.

To apply this principle Wesley utilizes the concept of things "contrary to reason," which can be found in other eighteenth-century discussions of scriptural authority. John Locke suggests three categories for adjudicating the claims of faith: above, contrary to, and according to reason.[79] The crucial point about the relation between revelation and reason is that no direct revelation can be contrary to reason. Traditional revelation, or the relating in words of the original experience, carries even less weight when it contradicts our reason.[80] Locke summarizes his position by saying, "*Reason* must be our last judge and guide in every thing."[81] Anthony Collins surpasses Locke when he argues that reason requires not only the credibility of the person giving the testimony, but that the content be credible as well.[82] Collins builds on this argument to reject Locke's category of propositions above reason. Because there is no category of revelation whose content is beyond human judgment, all ideas must either agree or disagree. Thus, "All Propositions consider'd as Objects of Assent or Dissent, are adequately divided into Propositions agreeable or contrary to Reason; and there remains no third Idea under which to rank them."[83]

Collins continues by arguing that the category of "above reason" is used by divines to hide doctrines that are really contrary to reason.[84] It should be noted, however, that Wesley nowhere uses a concept of things "above reason." Every question Locke would put in that category Wesley sees as "according to reason." Reason is not competent to adjudicate matters of faith, and the only reasonable course is to submit to Scripture's authority in those matters. Whereas Locke judges the resurrection of the dead to be a matter "above reason," Wesley sees it as the only reasonable belief in light of scriptural testimony.[85]

The ability of reason to discover an absurdity in Scripture, then, is limited to two specific areas. First, matters of fact to which experience and natural science testify can supersede the literal sense of Scripture. Second, where the Scripture appears to contradict itself, reason sees the conflict and determines that it must be resolved. Outside of these two areas, reason is not allowed to contradict the Bible.

Scripture and Christian Antiquity

For Wesley, Christian antiquity ranked third in importance among the five sources of authority. He would sometimes say that doctrines should be proved by Scripture and reason, and by antiquity if need be. This is not the same as an appeal to the whole of Christian tradition. Wesley learned from the Nonjurors that there had been a pristine age of Christianity where the faith and practice of Christians had not yet been corrupted. Reference to that age as a model would guide him at many points throughout his life.

Ted Campbell has noted that "Wesley appears to have used the term [Christian antiquity] as a straightforward designation of Christianity in the ancient world, inclusive of the scriptural age, although it often denoted the post-canonical age alone." His terminology varied, sometimes using "primitive" in phrases such as "primitive church," "primitive Christianity," or "primitive Fathers."[86] "Primitive" carried connotations of simplicity and purity. Wesley believed that there had been a period when Christianity was pure and simple. George Boas defines "primitivism" in its chronological form as the cluster of ideas which

> maintains that the earliest stage of human history was the best, that the earliest period of national, religious, artistic, or in fact any strand of history was better than the periods that have followed, that childhood is better than maturity. In short, it argues that to discover the best stage of any historical series one must return to its origin.[87]

On this definition, Wesley joins the many other Christians who saw Christianity at its best in its first centuries.

Theodore Bozeman argues that biblicist "primitivism" was also characteristic of the Puritans. It was one of three interlinked agendas defining the content of Puritan dissent.[88] However, Bozeman notes that Puritan thought from the 1580s onward tended to minimize patristic jurisdiction. He argues that the primitivist appeal was agreed upon by both Puritans and Anglicans, though they differed in the scope of the ideal period to which appeal could justifiably be made.[89] Baxter exemplifies this. Against a Catholic position that the unanimous testimony of the Fathers is authoritative, Baxter argues that they "never unanimously consented in any exposition of the greatest part of the Scriptures at all." "The chief use of the Fathers is

81

to know Historically what Doctrine was then taught."[90] Quotations from the Fathers frequently appear in the margins of his works, but he says that he uses them "both for the sweetness of the matter [of their writings] as also to free my self from the charge of singularity."[91]

On this issue, Wesley clearly sided with the Anglicans more than with the Puritans, though the duration of that period was a question about which Wesley changed his mind during his career. Wesley's development on this issue can be traced. During the years 1732–35 he was influenced strongly by the Nonjuror movement through his friendship with John Clayton. The Nonjurors had a very high regard for the primitive church, and their influence is seen in the memo he wrote to himself on January 25, 1738:

> But it was not long before Providence brought me to those who showed me a sure rule for interpreting Scripture, viz., *consensus veterum*—"quod ab omnibus, quod ubique, quod semper creditum." At the same time they sufficiently insisted upon a due regard to the One Church at all times and in all places.[92]

However, the high view that he held in 1735 was modified while he was in Georgia. Indeed, part of his trouble with the colonists there can be traced to his enthusiasm for applying in his ministry among them the Apostolic Canons, of which they had never before heard.[93] His failure there as well as his reading persuaded him to alter his perspective. In his *Journal* for September 13, 1736, he writes,

> I began reading, with Mr. Delamotte, Bishop Beveridge's *Pandectae canonum conciliorum*. Nothing could so effectually have convinced us that both particular and "general councils may err, and have erred"; and that "things ordained by them as necessary to salvation have neither strength nor authority unless they be taken out of Holy Scripture."[94]

The memo to himself of January 25, 1738, continues:

> Nor was it long before I bent the bow too far the other way: (1) by making antiquity a co-ordinate (rather than subordinate) rule with Scripture; (2) by admitting several doubtful writings as undoubted evidences of antiquity; (3) by extending antiquity too far, even to the middle or end of the fourth century; (4) by believing more practices

to have been universal in the ancient Church than ever were so; (5) by not considering that the decrees of one provincial synod could bind only that province, and the decrees of a general synod only those provinces whose representatives met therein; (6) by not considering that most of those decrees were adapted to particular times and occasions, and consequently when those occasions ceased, must cease to bind even those provinces.[95]

Wesley's respect for the ancient church was further battered as he discovered that it was neither as pure nor as unified as he had thought. In his sermon "A Caution Against Bigotry" he writes in 1750:

There was a time when all Christians were of one mind, as well as of one heart. So great grace was upon them all when they were first filled with the Holy Ghost. But how short a space did this blessing continue! How soon was that unanimity lost, and difference of opinion sprang up again, even in the church of Christ! And that not in nominal but in real Christians; nay, in the very chief of them, the apostles themselves! Nor does it appear that the difference which then began was ever entirely removed. We do not find that even those pillars in the temple of God, so long as they remained upon earth, were ever brought to think alike, to be of one mind, particularly with regard to the ceremonial law.[96]

In 1738 Wesley was prepared to acknowledge that the age of the pure church did not extend into the fourth century. By 1750 he acknowledges that problems arose even in the days of the apostles. In his note on 2 Thessalonians 2:3, written in 1755, he suggests that the falling away from the pure faith of the gospel "began even in the apostolic age."[97]

Wesley's conception of the purity of the early church is one of gradual decline. He begins with the New Testament and notes the doctrinal and moral problems already in evidence there. In the 1787 sermon "On Attending the Church Service" he says that the unity of the primitive church exemplified at Pentecost lasted only a short time. "How soon did 'the fine gold become dim!'" And

Thus did "the mystery of iniquity" begin to "work" in the ministers as well as the people, even before the end of the apostolic age. But how much more powerfully did it work as soon as those master-builders, the apostles, were taken out of the way! Both ministers and people were then farther and farther removed from the hope of the gospel. . . . But the corruption which had been creeping in drop by drop during the second and third century, in the beginning of the fourth, when Constantine called himself a Christian, poured in upon the church with a full tide.[98]

Note that here the decline is seen as gradual, with a distinct dividing line at the accession of Constantine. This dividing line explains Wesley's strong preference for the authority of the Ante-Nicene Fathers.[99] But he is not precise in cutting off the age of purity with the rise of Constantine; in his sermon at the opening of the New Chapel on City Road, he includes certain Post-Nicene Fathers:

This is the *religion of the primitive church,* of the whole church in the purest ages. It is clearly expressed even in the small remains of Clemens Romanus, Ignatius, and Polycarp. It is seen more at large in the writings of Tertullian, Origen, Clemens Alexandrinus, and Cyprian. And even in the fourth century it was found in the works of Chrysostom, Basil, Ephrem Syrus, and Macarius.[100]

Wesley's concept of Christian antiquity is fundamentally flawed. There is an essential ambivalence that stems from two convictions which Wesley knew to be mutually contradictory. The first conviction, learned from the Nonjurors, was that the primitive church was pure and ought to serve as a model for later ages. The second conviction, learned through study and further reading, was that the "mystery of iniquity" invaded the church even in apostolic times and gradually grew until very few real Christians were left. Note here that Scripture is necessary for determining what the "primitive age" is. Wesley has no precise definition of a pure age of Christianity and no credible way to reach such a definition. Since Wesley is unwilling to say that everything done in the apostolic age or any other defined period of time is authoritative on its own, Christian antiquity as a source of doctrine and practice is dependent upon Scripture. As one pushes Wesley's view of Christian antiquity, it becomes clear that certain authors in certain time periods are judged to be primitive because they preserve a "scriptural" approach to Christian life and doctrine. It is only the truly scriptural elements of those purer ages that are authoritative.

Nevertheless, Wesley is convinced that primitive Christianity is authoritative. Despite the problem of definition, Wesley is convinced that the early centuries of Christianity were in fact more scriptural and therefore should function as an authority for modern Christianity. He understands antiquity to have three functions as an authority for faith and practice. First, antiquity functions as a warrant for theological arguments. In his Preface to the "Epistles of the Apostolical Fathers"—the volume of the *Christian Library*, published in 1749, that included the writings of Clement, Ignatius, and Polycarp—Wesley goes so far as to call the Fathers "inspired":

> . . . we cannot with any reason doubt of what they deliver to us as the Gospel of Christ; but ought to receive it, though not with equal veneration, yet with only little less regard than we do the sacred writings of those who were their masters and instructors. . . .
>
> The plain inference is, not only that they were not mistaken in their interpretations of the Gospel of Christ; but that in all the necessary parts of it, they were so assisted by the Holy Ghost, as to be scarce capable of mistaking. Consequently, we are to look on their writings, though not of equal authority with the holy Scriptures, (because neither were the authors of them called in so extraordinary a way to the writing them, nor endued with so large a portion of the blessed Spirit,) yet as worthy of a much greater respect than any composures which have been made since; however men have afterwards written with more art, and a greater stock of human learning, than is to be found not only in the following pieces but in the New Testament itself.[101]

In his 1755 letter to Richard Tompson, he refers to "the whole Christian Church in the first centuries."[102] In his sermon "On Laying the Foundation of the New Chapel," he even defines the primitive church as "the whole Church in the purest ages."[103]

The second part of antiquity's authority is with regard to practice. He writes to his Moravian friend James Hutton, "And the primitive church may thus far at least be reverenced, as faithfully delivering down for two or three hundred years the discipline which they received from the apostles, and th[e apostles] from Christ."[104] Wesley believed that the primitive church had "genuine Christians" in it, and he valued it for this reason, as he explains in his 1749 letter to Conyers Middleton:

All this [being mistaken and holding indefensible opinions] may be allowed concerning the primitive Fathers; I mean particularly Clemens Romanus, Ignatius, Polycarp, Justin Martyr, Irenaeus, Origen, Clemens Alexandrinus, Cyprian; to whom I would add Macarius and Ephraim Syrus.

I allow that some of these had not strong natural sense, that few of them had much learning, and none the assistances which our age enjoys in some respects above all that went before.

Hence I doubt not but whoever will be at the pains of reading over their writings for that poor end, will find many mistakes, many weak suppositions, and many ill-drawn conclusions.

And yet I exceedingly reverence them, as well as their writings, and esteem them very highly in love. I reverence them, because they were Christians, such Christians as are above described. And I reverence their writings, because they describe true, genuine Christianity, and direct us to the strongest evidence of the Christian doctrine.[105]

Wesley admits freely that there are shortcomings in the Fathers, but the shortcomings he admits are literary and intellectual, not moral or religious. He argues that one should read them not because they are necessarily good literature, but as those who point the way to genuine Christianity.

Third, antiquity serves as an interpreter of Scripture. Wesley specifies that the Fathers of the primitive church are the best interpreters of Scripture. They serve as hermeneutical guides, helping to prevent us from interpreting Scripture into our own image. In his 1740 letter to Zinzendorf, he charges, ". . . you receive not the ancients but the modern mystics as the best interpreters of Scripture; and in conformity to these you mix much of man's wisdom with the wisdom of God."[106] This fits Wesley's description of his self-understanding while in Georgia: "Our common way of living was this: from four in the morning till five each of us used private prayer. From five to seven we read the Bible together, carefully comparing it (that we might not lean to our own understandings) with the writings of the earliest ages."[107]

In the correspondence with "John Smith," he appeals to "Scripture, as interpreted by the writers of the earliest Christian church."[108] Sometimes, the correct interpretation of Scripture is said to come from both the primitive church and the Church of England. In his *Short History of Methodism*, he writes about the Oxford Methodists:

But they observed neither these [the university statutes] nor anything else any further than they conceived it was bound upon them by their one book, *the Bible,* it being their one desire and design to be down-right *Bible Christians*—taking the Bible, as interpreted by the primitive Church and our own, for their whole and sole rule.[109]

However, it is important to understand the relationship between antiquity and Scripture. Wesley's clear understanding is that the primitive church, like all other parts of tradition and all other authorities, is subordinate to Scripture. As early as 1736 Wesley had affirmed his commitment to Scripture over the primitive church.[110] His 1782 letter to Joseph Benson makes the same clear point: "I regard no authorities but those of the Ante-Nicene Fathers; nor any of them in opposition to Scripture."[111] Even his citations of antiquity as an authority for a position sometimes show its status as lower than Scripture and reason, as in Part III of the *Farther Appeal:*

What is it you would have us *prove* by miracles? That the *doctrines* we preach are true? This is not the way to prove that—as our first Reformers replied to those of the Church of Rome who, you may probably remember, were continually urging them with this very demand. We prove the doctrines we preach by Scripture and reason; and, if need be, by antiquity.[112]

And in his 1749 letter to Conyers Middleton he makes clear that the primitive church is valuable, but still subordinate to Scripture: "The esteeming the writings of the first three centuries, not equally with, but next to, the Scriptures, never carried any man yet into dangerous errors, nor probably ever will."[113]

Where antiquity is unnecessary for the argument, it is superfluous and can be ignored.[114] Arguments from antiquity are not only un-necessary, they are sometimes unreliable. He admits to Middleton that some of the fathers erred, but that does not mean all of them were wrong:

I grant, in three or four opinions, some (though not all) of these [early church Fathers] were mistaken, as well as those two. But this by no means proves that they were all knaves together; or that if Justin Martyr or Irenaeus speaks wrong, I am therefore to give no credit to the evidence of Theophilus or Minutius Felix.[115]

This unreliability means that Christian antiquity cannot be trusted as a whole. In *The Advantage of the Members of the Church of England* (1753), he writes, "As to the Fathers and Councils, we cannot but observe, that in an hundred instances they contradict one another: Consequently, they can no more be a rule of faith to us, than the Papal decrees, which are not grounded on Scripture."[116] By "rule of faith" Wesley is here talking about the absolute standard of Christian teaching. Against the Roman Catholics, he argues that only Scripture can be such a rule, and that the primitive church, however helpful in interpreting Scripture and as a model for how to implement scriptural practices, must remain subservient to the Scripture as a rule for doctrine and practice.

How could Wesley have said what he did about the Fathers' being "inspired" and yet making mistakes, about their being the best interpreters of Scripture, and yet fallible? Does Wesley appeal to a category that has integrity, or is this so internally contradictory as to be useless? It cannot be stressed too much that Wesley saw Christian antiquity as an authority only in subservience to Scripture. His acceptance of antiquity's influence was based on his finding that the writers of the first four centuries embodied "Scriptural Christianity." When he became convinced that the "mystery of iniquity" had begun working very early in the apostolic age, he was forced to differentiate between the pure and impure parts of antiquity. Thus, the authority of antiquity for Wesley does not arise *sui generis*. It is dependent on Scripture and is only authoritative insofar as it genuinely reflects scriptural teaching. But then why should he distinguish between the first four centuries and the rest of Christian tradition?

The key to understanding Wesley on this point is his judgment that *in fact*, the first four centuries were more nearly pure than any other period of tradition. The rise of Constantine was for him the fall of true Christianity, and the brilliant lights of antiquity became fewer and fewer after Christianity received its honors and riches from the Emperor. Wesley grows to have a carefully nuanced view of the early church. While he makes references to it as an entire unit, he really understands that it had diversity and problems like the church in other times. There were, however, certain leading lights who were pure and among themselves united. Thus he can cite certain Fathers as representing pure Christianity when he knows that they were not representative of the church in their time.

Despite the nuances, Wesley's overall judgment continues to be that, on the whole, the primitive church was more scriptural than the Christian church at any other time. In addition, he argues for its authority on the basis of its unity.[117] Thus, the primitive church is not useless as an authority, but it must be used carefully on account of its diversity and always in subordination to Scripture. Scripture is the criterion by which the pure and impure parts of antiquity can be distinguished. Despite the difficulties of isolating the authoritative aspects, antiquity still provides a better insight into true Christianity than any other period of tradition.

Scripture and the Church of England

A fourth authority for theology in the thought of John Wesley is the Church of England, in which he was an ordained priest. On his own understanding, Wesley never left the church.[118] Further, most of the people to whom he preached and with whom he engaged in theological discussion were members of the Church of England. The Methodist Revival was, to a great extent, a movement within the Church of England during Wesley's lifetime. During four decades of discussion with the Methodist people and preachers, he consistently argued against any separation from the church.

In a letter of 1738 to James Hutton, a fellow member of the Fetter Lane Society, he stresses the connection between membership in the Church of England and following its laws and regulations: "I believe you don't think I am (whatever I was) bigoted either to the ancient church or the Church of England. But have a care of bending the bow too much the other way. The national church to which we belong may doubtless claim some, though not an implicit, obedience from us."[119] Four days later he writes to Hutton again, urging that their membership in the Church of England entailed obedience to her laws.[120] And in *A Short History of Methodism*, he describes Methodism as loyal to the Church of England in every respect: "At present those who remain with Mr. Wesley are mostly Church of England men. They love her Articles, her Homilies, her Liturgy, her discipline, and unwillingly vary from it in any instance."[121]

It was the discipline of the Church of England that was most distasteful to the Methodists. They chafed under the normal practices of the church, because they had discovered unusual methods that were effective in reaching people and helping them grow in grace. Their preaching services were irregular, their class meetings were unusual, and their "enthusiastic" work among the lower classes struck fear into the hierarchy. But even for the discipline of the church, Wesley professes a regard next to that he has for Scripture: "As to your next advice, 'to have a greater regard to the rules and orders of the Church,' I *cannot;* for I now regard them next to the Word of God."[122] The key here is that Wesley understood the commandments of Scripture to be more broad and insistent than they were normally interpreted as being. He took the imperative to save souls to be stronger than a bishop's commandment not to preach in his diocese. He further drove a wedge between the Anglican hierarchy and the Articles and Homilies of the church, arguing that by disobeying the bishops he was being more true to their beliefs than they were.

It should also be noted here that Wesley did not believe himself to be in violation of the discipline of the church. He made the argument that his ordination, being a university ordination, gave him the right to preach anywhere. The well-known saying "The world is my parish" thus refers to his right to preach anywhere in England. In his view, the lay preachers derived their right to preach through him, functioning as his assistants. The closest the Methodist movement came to violating English religious law was in holding unauthorized religious meetings that were not registered under the acts to protect Non-conformity. Wesley saw his work as being similar to religious societies which had not had to register under those acts, and he generally did not take that legal step. Other people, however, saw him as creating a different church and argued that he was undermining the Church of England.

In 1773, Wesley told James Creighton, the curate at Swanlinbar in Ireland, that the Methodists "observe more of the Articles, Rubrics, and Canons of the Church than any other people in the three kingdoms."[123] Telford tells us that Creighton was at first resolved to preach against the Methodists, but later became one of them. The tension that existed between the Methodists and people like Creighton became evident in the discussion when the definition of the Church was discussed. Clearly, Wesley was at odds with the Anglican hierarchy and the majority of parish priests. Many like Creighton were determined to oppose this new movement for violating the principles of good order. Doubtlessly remembering the religious character of the civil war a century earlier, they saw Wesley as introducing enthusiasm and fanaticism into the lower classes of the population. Thus, when they charged Wesley with breaches of propriety, it was often with failing to obey Anglican polity.

Wesley's own definition of the Church differed from the hierarchy's emphasis on church order. He consistently defined the essence of the Church as its liturgy, articles, and homilies, and not its order or episcopacy. Further, when attacked by priests or bishops, he frequently referred them back to the essential documents of Anglican theology and confronted them with their own deviation from those standards. Doctrinally and liturgically, the unity of the Church of England was found in the Articles of Religion and the *Book of Common Prayer*. The Articles make reference to the Homilies as containing godly doctrine and deserving to be read in churches by the ministers. Clergy had to subscribe allegiance to the Articles and *Book of Common Prayer* for ordination.[124] These elements of the Elizabethan Settlement provided both clear boundaries and room for flexibility within those boundaries. After the civil war, they were reinstated without change. Wesley was on strong grounds in appealing to these standards over the heads of the existing Anglican authorities.

In his 1745 correspondence with "John Smith," the unknown churchman, Wesley clarifies his position:

> In saying, "I teach the doctrine of the Church of England," I do and always did mean (without concerning myself whether others taught them or no, either this year, or before the Reformation), I teach the doctrines which are comprised in those Articles and Homilies to which all the clergy of the Church of England solemnly profess to assent, and that in their plain, unforced, grammatical meaning.[125]

Later, in a letter to Samuel Walker, he explicitly rejects an alternative answer to the issue:

> My difficulty is very much increased by one of your observations. I know the original doctrines of the Church are sound. I know her worship is (in the main) pure and scriptural. But if "the essence of the Church of England, considered as such, consists in her orders and laws" (many of which I myself can say nothing for), "and not in her

worship and doctrines," those who separate from her have a far stronger plea than I was ever sensible of.[126]

It was during this time that the Methodist preachers and laity were pressing to separate from the Church of England and form an independent church. Wesley was resisting this move, arguing that Methodists had no quarrel with the most important parts of the Church of England. Clearly, if he granted that order and laws were essential, then the irregular Methodist proceedings would require dissolution of the Methodist societies or separation from the church.

For Wesley, however, the authority of the church was clearly limited by its subordination to Scripture. In his *Farther Appeal*, he answers his critics in these terms: "It was not quite clear to me that the Canon he cited was against extempory prayer. But supposing it were, my plain answer would be: 'That Canon I dare not obey; because the law of man binds only so far as it is consistent with the Word of God.'"[127] Here the pronouncements of the church are counted as human words, which cannot contradict Scripture. In a letter to Gilbert Boyce, Wesley makes the point that it is Scripture which is supreme, because the church is judged by it:

> If I were in the Church of Rome I *would* conform to all her doctrines and practices, so far as they were not contrary to plain Scripture. And (according to the best of my judgment) I conform so far only to those of the Church of England . . .
> I am not conscious of embracing any opinion or practice which is not agreeable to the Word of God. And I do believe the doctrines, worship, and discipline (so far as it goes) of the Church of England to be agreeable thereto.[128]

In his correspondence with John Smith he makes the same point.[129] In a letter to Charles Wesley, he once again categorizes the teachings of the church as among the teachings of men and contrasted with Scripture: "All men may err: but the word of the Lord shall stand forever."[130] And he clearly sorts out the relation between Scripture, the primitive church, and the Church of England in his *Farther Thoughts on Separation from the Church*:

> From a child I was taught to love and reverence the Scripture, the oracles of God, and next to these to esteem the primitive Fathers, the writers of the three first centuries. Next after the primitive Church I

esteemed our own, the Church of England, as the most scriptural national church in the world. I therefore not only assented to all the doctrines, but observed all the rubric[s] in the Liturgy, and that with all possible exactness, even at the peril of my life.[131]

Wesley was clear that he regarded the Church of England as an authority, but one that ranked after the primitive church. His departure from being a "regular" clergyman came, on his own understanding, when he was "constrained" to preach in the open air. It was only Scripture that had the authority to constrain him over the rules of his own church. Throughout his life, he saw himself as varying from the church only where faithfulness to the Bible forced him to do so.

We have already noted that the teaching of the church itself points back to the supreme authority of Scripture. Article VI of the Thirty-nine Articles is explicit in saying about Scripture that "whatsoever is not read therein, nor may be proved thereby, is not to be required of any man, that it should be believed as an article of the Faith, or be thought requisite or necessary to salvation."[132] Wesley's revision of the Articles for the American Methodists retained this same language. In a 1756 letter to James Clark, he explicitly claims the authority of Article VI to support the authority of Scripture in matters of doctrine.[133]

The key to understanding how Wesley relates these ecclesiastical authorities to Scripture is to understand that in his view, all of them are in fundamental agreement about the doctrine, faith, and practice of the church. In this case as with all the others so far, Wesley can quote both Scripture and the church in support for his positions. As Wesley saw it, the Scripture and the doctrines and liturgy of the Church of England formed a unity which guided him and which he was willing to defend. At no point does he ever criticize the doctrine or liturgy of the Church of England as contrary to Scripture. In a letter to the editor of *Lloyd's Evening Post*, he writes,

> You say: (1) "You have impiously apostatized from those principles of religion which you undertook to defend." I hope not. I still (as I am able) defend the Bible, with the Liturgy, Articles, and Homilies of our Church; and I do not defend or espouse any other principles, to the best of my knowledge, than those which are plainly contained in the Bible as well as in the Homilies and Book of Common Prayer.[134]

However, the role of the Church of England differs from that of the primitive church in that the mature Wesley never mentions his contemporary church as an interpreter of Scripture. On one occasion, he mentions that the Oxford Methodists believed in the Bible as interpreted by the primitive church and the Church of England; that is simply another way of saying that the Church of England is scriptural and that he agrees with the church's interpretation. To be sure, he notes in 1733 that the Church of England urges everyone to look to the Fathers and the primitive church for guidance in interpretation.[135] For Wesley, the relation between Scripture and the church is entirely one-sided, with the latter being subject to what the former teaches. Nevertheless, it is Wesley's judgment that the Church of England is the "most scriptural national church in the world,"[136] and is therefore deserving of his allegiance.

The two authorities, Christian antiquity and the Church of England, together constitute the only aspects of the history of Christianity that Wesley acknowledges as authoritative. His opposition to Christian tradition in general stems from the judgment that Christianity entered into severe decline and corruption, which was alleviated only during the Reformation. Wesley's comments on the state of Christianity in England during his own time reveal his view that the Church of England's practice does not match the purity of her doctrine.

Scripture and Experience

During the seventeenth and eighteenth centuries, experience was attaining significant authority as a source of knowledge. John Locke's *Essay on Human Understanding* revived the ancient idea that all our ideas are based on experience. Locke's statement of this epistemology had achieved wide influence by Wesley's day. As a man of the eighteenth century, Wesley adopted this strong emphasis on experience. Sometimes Wesley uses "experience" to refer to the common body of knowledge available to everyone. When he does so, it is often with adjectives like "all" or "universal." In his sermon "On Riches" he writes, "Nearly related to anger, if not rather a species of it, are *fretfulness* and *peevishness*. But are the rich more assaulted by these than the poor? All experience shows that they are."[137] He can also appeal to "universal experience" to make logical distinctions between types of love[138] and to contradict Horace on the joys of the country life.[139]

Wesley's primary reference, however, was not to common experience but to religious experience. He revived the Puritan and Pietist emphasis on the individual's experience of God, and turned it into an authority for Christian theology. Religious experience was, for Wesley, as objective a reality as sensory experience was for Locke. Thus, he also referred to it in universal terms. He talks about the experience of "all real Christians" in "The Witness of the Spirit, I": "But I contend not; seeing so many other texts, with the experience of all real Christians, sufficiently evince that there is in every believer both the testimony of God's Spirit, and the testimony of his own, that he is a child of God."[140] In the sermon "On Working Out Our Own Salvation," he writes, "All experience, as well as Scripture, shows this salvation to be both instantaneous and gradual."[141] A few pages later he adds,

> We know indeed that word of his to be absolutely true, "Without me ye can do nothing." But on the other hand we know, every believer can say, "I can do all things through Christ that strengtheneth me."
>
> Meantime let us remember that God has joined these together in the experience of every believer. And therefore we must take care not to imagine they are ever to be put asunder.[142]

He can also refer to this experience of God's children as being "constant."[143] The experience to which Wesley is appealing is one that all Christians share. In a 1766 letter to Mrs. Bennis, he adds, "In the *Thoughts on Christian Perfection* and in the *Farther Thoughts* you have the genuine experience of the adult children of God. Oppose that authority to the authority of any that contradict (if reason and Scripture are disregarded), and look daily for a deeper and fuller communion with God."[144]

The experience he is speaking of is something that is objectively real and available to all believers. Whereas he refers to it as constant and universal, what he really means is that it is constant and universal for all who believe. Those who do not yet have that experience testify to it by either wanting it or ignoring it, showing thereby their unbelief.[145] This is an experience that is described in Scripture and is available to those who seek the Lord. So far, he does not show any understanding that there are varieties of "sound" experience. All who truly believe share the experience that Scripture describes, and that Wesley himself describes at various places in his sermons and letters. The experience has a specific content, so Wesley can tell his hearers what they should expect to experience when it comes. It is important to note, however, that Wesley's appeals to universal human experience and to specifically religious experience have a subtle but significant difference. His appeal to the former implies that any unbiased observer would reach the same conclusion. His appeal to the latter, however, requires that the observer share the specific experience that is being described. Words such as "believer" and "genuine experience" are capable of being construed in such a way that anyone who disagrees has not experienced the reality being discussed and so is incapable of rendering a true judgment. The claim "all true believers know this" is an analytic judgment, since anyone who disagrees must, by that very fact, not be a true believer.

This second usage of "experience" construes it as first and foremost a goal. He preaches in order to lead people to faith in Christ, and to experience all that goes along with faith. Properly understood, the whole point of religion is the re-creation of the human being to become what God had originally intended them to be.[146] Once the individual has begun the re-creative process and has thus experienced justification, new birth, adoption, and at least partial sanctification, his or her experience then validates the theology of the preaching. It is to that role of experience as authority to which we now turn.

George Croft Cell argues that Wesley's doctrine was a "theocentric doctrine of Christian experience."[147] He suggests that Wesley's theology rested on the twin pillars of Scripture and experience, taken as "cognate and congenial principles."[148] There is evidence to support such a view, for on many occasions Wesley states his understanding of experiential authority in very high terms. The earliest reference comes in a letter to his father, Samuel Wesley, written December 10, 1734, in which John discusses his reasons for staying at Oxford, and how being more holy would make him a better instrument of God's for healing the souls of others:

> But for the proof of every one of these weighty truths experience is worth [a] thousand reasons. I see, I feel them every day. Sometimes I cannot do good to others because I am unwilling to do it; shame or pain is in my way, and I do not desire to serve God at so dear a rate . . .

From all this I conclude that where I was most holy myself, there I could most promote holiness in others; and consequently that I could more promote it here than in any place under heaven.[149]

In his manuscript journal for May 25, 1737, he refers to "the strongest of all proofs, experience,"[150] but only with reference to reclaiming souls. On January 8 of the following year, in midst of the spiritual crisis that started with his return voyage to England, he writes,

In the fullness of my heart I wrote the following words:
By the most infallible of proofs, inward feeling, I am convinced.
1. Of unbelief, having no such faith in Christ as will prevent my heart from being troubled; which it could not be if I believed in God, and rightly believed also in him [i.e., Christ].
2. Of pride, throughout my life past, inasmuch as I thought I had what I find I have not.
3. Of gross irrecollection, inasmuch as in a storm I cry to God every moment, in a calm, not.
4. Of levity and luxuriancy of spirit, recurring whenever the pressure is taken off, and appearing by my speaking words not tending to edify; but most, by my manner of speaking of my enemies.[151]

And in his sermon "The Witness of the Spirit, I," he refers to an individual's evaluation of whether he loves God or not, and says, "And of his thus loving God he has an inward proof, which is nothing short of self-evidence."[152]

Perhaps the strongest statement of the authority of experience comes in a letter to the Reverend Dr. Conyers Middleton, written in 1749, in which Wesley evaluates the relative merits of experience and "traditional evidence" in these terms:

So Christianity tells me; and so I find it, may every real Christian say. I now am assured that these things are so: I experience them in my own breast. What Christianity (considered as a doctrine) promised, is accomplished in my soul. And Christianity, considered as an inward principle, is the completion of all those promises. It is holiness and happiness, the image of God impressed on a created spirit; a fountain of peace and love springing up into everlasting life.

And this I conceive to be the strongest evidence of the truth of Christianity. I do not undervalue traditional evidence . . .

Traditional evidence is of an extremely complicated nature, necessarily including so many and so various considerations, that only men of a strong and clear understanding can be sensible of its full force. On the contrary, how plain and simple is this; and how level to the lowest capacity! Is not this the sum: "One thing I know; I was blind, but now I see?" An argument so plain, that a peasant, a woman, a child, may feel all its force. . . .

If, then, it were possible (which I conceive it is not) to shake the traditional evidence of Christianity, still he that has the internal evidence (and every true believer hath the witness or evidence in himself) would stand firm and unshaken. Still he could say to those who were striking at the external evidence, "Beat on the sack of Anaxagoras." But you can no more hurt my evidence of Christianity, than the tyrant could hurt the spirit of that wise man.[153]

While these appeals to experience give some weight to Cell's thesis, they must be considered in the context of the whole of Wesley's thought. John Wesley was frequently given to making extreme statements because of the audience he was addressing and the polemical character of the discussion. He exaggerated points in order to communicate them under hostile circumstances, and he overstated his position in order to guard against a misunderstanding. Thus, it is very misleading to take Wesley's own words without looking for evidence that would more carefully nuance his position. In this case, Wesley provides a clue to the proper understanding of these passages. He was attacked because of the 1737 *Journal* entry just quoted,[154] and offered this explanation in his *Second Letter to the Author of "The Enthusiasm of Methodists etc."*:

To support this weighty charge you bring one single scrap, about a line and a quarter from one of my *Journals*. The words are these: "By the most *infallible of proofs, inward feeling*, I am convinced." Convinced of what? It immediately follows: "Of unbelief, having no such faith as will prevent my heart from being troubled."

I here assert that *inward feeling*, or consciousness, is the *most infallible of proofs* of unbelief, of the want of such a faith as will prevent the heart's being troubled. But do I here "advance impressions, impulses, feelings, etc., into 'certain rules' of conduct"? Or anywhere else? You may just as well say I advance them into certain proofs of transubstantiation.

Neither in writing, in preaching, nor in private conversation, have I ever "taught any of my followers to depend upon them as sure guides or infallible proofs" of anything.[155]

Wesley cannot escape the charge that his teaching has occasionally misled both his followers and his opponents, but his point is clear enough. Different types of evidence are appropriate to different questions. The question of an individual's own spiritual state is best answered by evidence of that person's feelings. There is an immediate consciousness of whether one loves God or not that is readily apparent to the individual.

Wesley talks about the experience of salvation, with its related experiences of love and faith, and so forth, as very important. But that understanding of a certain type of experience as the *goal* of the Christian life must not be confused with experience as a principle by which theological and doctrinal decisions are made. In his discussion with Conyers Middleton quoted earlier,[156] Wesley distinguishes between "Christianity considered as doctrine" and "Christianity considered as an inward principle." What the former promises is completed in the latter. Christianity promises holiness and happiness, and those promises are fulfilled in the lives of believers. It is the fact that Christianity actually works these miracles that provides evidence for the truth of Christianity. Wesley does not claim here that such experience becomes a criterion for the promises, only that when the promises are fulfilled, the whole system is then validated, and validated in such a way as to be irrefutable. Scripture teaches what should be expected, and experience teaches Wesley that the promises were actually fulfilled in the lives of real human beings.

Given this understanding of experience, it is possible to consider the relationship between Scripture and experience as authorities for Christian teaching. The key text for understanding the mutual roles of Scripture and experience comes in "The Witness of the Spirit, II." In this sermon Wesley is careful to make his method of arguing explicit. His opening sentence claims that the doctrine of the Spirit's witness is taught by Scripture: "a truth revealed therein not once only, not obscurely, not incidentally, but frequently, and that in express terms."[157] After defining μαρτυρία by its biblical usage, he proceeds in §III to argue for the doctrine. After a long exegetical argument, he says, "And here properly comes in, to confirm this doctrine, the experience of the children of God—the experience not of two or three, not of a few, but of a great multitude which no man can number."[158] Wesley then deals with a number of objections in proving the doctrine:

> It is objected, first, "Experience is not sufficient to prove a doctrine which is not founded on Scripture." This is undoubtedly true, and it is an important truth. But it does not affect the present question, for it has been shown that this doctrine is founded on Scripture. Therefore experience is properly alleged to confirm it.[159]

If we take the distinction we have mentioned between Christianity considered as a doctrine and considered as an inward principle, Wesley allows no use of experience in determining what Christian doctrine is. It is used to confirm what Christianity teaches, by giving evidence of those doctrines being accomplished in the souls of believers.

Thus, in those places where Wesley sees that Scripture and experience diverge, he characterizes Scripture as trustworthy and experience as untrustworthy. While the emphasis of his preaching in the Revival was on the experience of salvation, he also cautioned the Methodists against relying on that experience rather than Scripture. They were "to be tried by a farther rule, to be brought to the only certain test, 'the law and the testimony.'"[160] A key passage for understanding this comes in the *Journal* for September 6, 1742:

> I then heard each of them relate her experience at large. I afterwards examined them severally touching the circumstances which I did not understand; on which I then talked with several others also. And thus far I approved of their experience (because agreeable to the written Word) as to their *feeling* the working of the Spirit of God, in peace and joy and love. But as to what some of them said farther concerning feeling the blood of Christ running upon their arms, or going down their throat, or poured like warm water upon their breast or heart, I plainly told them, the utmost I could allow, without renouncing both Scripture and reason, was that *some* of these circumstances might be from God (though I could not affirm they were), working in an unusual manner, no way essential either to justification or sanctification; but that all the rest I must believe to be the mere, empty dreams of an heated imagination.[161]

Here it is clear that Wesley subordinates the claims of experience to the teaching of Scripture. Those experiences which are "agreeable to the written word" are judged to be of divine origin, and those that go beyond what Scripture teaches are held to be possibly divine but more probably products of imagination.

But there is also one instance in which Wesley addresses the possibility that experience might not confirm the doctrine of perfection as the Methodists understood it. In his sermon "Christian Perfection," he had called this doctrine the "plain, natural, obvious meaning" of the text.[162] In the 1766 work "A Plain Account of Christian Perfection" he writes,

> Q. But what does it signify, whether any have attained it or no, seeing so many scriptures witness for it?
> A. If I were convinced that none in England had attained what has been so clearly and strongly preached by such a number of Preachers, in so many places, and for so long a time, I should be clearly convinced that we had all mistaken the meaning of those scriptures; and therefore, for the time to come, I too must teach that "sin will remain till death."[163]

For years he had based his preaching on the doctrine of perfection on the clarity of key Scripture passages. Experience functioned to show that his interpretation was correct, because people did actually experience what the Scripture had promised. But here Wesley suggests that if such confirmation had not taken place, his original exegesis might be thrown into question—he might have "mistaken the meaning of those scriptures." This passage gives further evidence that Scripture and experience are interdependent. Although experience is usually shown to be the weakest authority in determining Christian doctrine, yet it too has a place. Because it is possible to make mistakes about interpretation and because a certain type of experience is the goal of the Christian life, repeated failures to make it happen the way the Scripture promises must mean the interpretation has been wrong. Note here that Wesley is talking about a large amount of effort to test the obvious meaning of the text. He is prepared to admit error in interpretation only after the doctrine "has been so clearly and strongly preached by such a number of Preachers, in so many places, and for so long a time." Further, he is talking about a doctrine where he knows confirmation has already been found. But the theoretical possibility of such experiential correction does exist.

Conclusion

It is clear that Wesley's five authorities (Scripture, reason, Christian antiquity, the Church of England, and experience) form a unified witness to the truth of the Christian faith. On one occasion, he stated that position in these terms: "Methodism, so called, is the old religion, the religion of the Bible, the religion of the primitive church, the religion of the Church of England."[164] A few pages later he makes the point that the Methodists at Oxford were good Church of England men because of their zeal for Scripture and the primitive church: "The Methodists at Oxford were all one body, and as it were one soul, zealous for the religion of the Bible, of the primitive church, and in consequence of the Church of England; as they believed it to come nearer the scriptural and primitive plan than any other national church upon earth."[165] Here Wesley ties together Scripture, the primitive church, and the Church of England as all witnessing to the same religion. The words "in consequence" show the strict connection that exists between the first two and the last of these three authorities.

There is a great deal of variation in Wesley's doctrine of the five authorities for faith and practice. It is possible to cite single quotations from Wesley that would appear to prove contradictory positions. However, when one considers all the evidence that has been proposed, Wesley's view is seen to be consistent. This view is that Scripture, reason, Christian antiquity, the Church of England, and experience together form a single but complex locus of authority. A correct understanding of Scripture is dependent on the other four. Reason and antiquity are needed for proper interpretation. The Church of England is the best transmitter of Scripture because it is, in Wesley's view, "the most Scriptural national church" of his time. Experience proves the promises of Scripture to be true and can even correct one's interpretation at times. Conversely, the very definitions of how the other four are properly used involve their fidelity to Scripture. Any position that denies the inspiration and authority of Scripture is irrational. Only those parts of antiquity and the Church of England that conform to Scripture are authoritative. Experience alone cannot prove or generate doctrine; it merely confirms or corrects what Scripture teaches.

These authorities are not really five but one. It is inconceivable for Wesley that there is any real conflict between them when they are properly used. Of course, the definition of "properly used" includes the *a priori* commitment that such conflict must ultimately be seen as illusory. It is true that this unified locus of authority is sometimes not apparent in individual formulations. This is in character with the rest of Wesley's theology. Writing as he did for plain people in the midst of a very hectic schedule, his theological formulations are geared to particular audiences and to the dangers and needs he saw at the time. For example, he can stress the importance of reason to his intellectual audience in the *Appeals,* and then caution his followers against evil reasoning when it threatens their assurance of salvation. The two positions appear incompatible when taken out of context and put side by side. But when one understands that reason has its limitations for Wesley, then a coherent position can be seen to underlie the various formulations.

One key that ties the various formulations together is that for Wesley, each authority is competent in its proper areas. Over and over he argues that Scripture and reason are the only authorities for proving doctrine. Between the two of them, Scripture is supreme, and yet it requires reason for correct interpretation. Experience is the only authority that can supply evidence for the state of one's soul. One's salvation is a question of fact for which experience is the only competent authority. One cannot get this from a book or from reasoning upon abstract concepts. One *feels,* one *knows* that God is at work, or that God has pardoned one's sins. At that level, experience is indisputable. Yet, it must be judged in the light of how Scripture and reason say God will act, in order to know if a particular experience is really the act of God or of some other being. Antiquity and the Church of England are clearly the weakest authorities. They have no exclusive realm of competence, yet they do contribute to the argument. Their authority is derivative in the sense that they are helpful in showing how Scripture is to be interpreted and applied.

Another key to their unity is that they all make the same witness. When properly used, all five have the same content. The "general tenor" of Scripture delivers a reasonable message which was the basic teaching of the primitive church, is also taught by the Church of England, and has been shown to be real by the experience of many individuals. This unity forms a web of interrelated ways of talking about the central truths which they all proclaim. As understood by John Wesley, they all point in the same direction.

CHAPTER 4

Interpretation of Scripture

Purpose

The purpose of biblical interpretation, according to Wesley, is the salvation of souls. In his Preface to *Sermons on Several Occasions*, he writes,

> I want to know one thing, the way to heaven—how to land safe on that happy shore. God himself has condescended to teach the way: for this very end he came from heaven. He hath written it down in a book. O give me that book! At any price give me the Book of God! I have it. Here is knowledge enough for me. Let me be *homo unius libri.* Here then I am, far from the busy ways of men. I sit down alone: only God is here. In his presence I open, I read his Book; for this end, to find the way to heaven.[1]

Although this precedes a description of Wesley's sermons, it applies to all of his interpretation of the Bible. He purposely approaches the Bible not with "curious, critical inquiries" but as one "who desires only the salvation of his soul."[2] He says that he found the doctrine of perfection "in the oracles of God, in the Old and New Testament; when I read them with no other view or desire but to save my own soul."[3]

It is in this sense that Wesley understands searching the Scriptures to be a "means of grace." In the sermon of that title he defines the means of grace as "outward signs, words or actions ordained of God, and appointed for this end—to be the *ordinary* channels whereby he might convey to men preventing, justifying or sanctifying grace." Three such means are discussed there: prayer, receiving the Lord's Supper, and "searching the Scriptures (which implies reading, hearing, and meditating thereon)."[4] He argues that Christ commanded people to "search the Scriptures" in John 5:39.[5] As a means of grace, it is a channel God uses to bring people out of their sin and toward full salvation.

This purpose of interpretation is crucial to understanding what follows. Wesley is interested in historical questions about the background of biblical times only insofar as the answers might help Scripture speak to soteriological issues. In a similar way he does not seek a "minute, philosophical account of the *manner*" in which the Holy Spirit causes the new birth.[6] He is only interested in what Scripture says about its nature and the means to attain it. For the most part, Wesley brings to the text practical questions, centering on "What must persons do to be saved?"

Prerequisites

Three attributes of the reader are discussed as being helpful to correct interpretation of Scripture: inspiration of the Holy Spirit, faith, and knowledge. Strictly speaking, only the first is a prerequisite. In the Preface to his 1765 *Explanatory Notes upon the Old Testament*, Wesley argues that meditating on the Scriptures will make people holy. He gives a number of directions for reading the Scriptures in the most profitable way, one of which is "Serious and earnest prayer should be constantly used before we consult the oracles of God; seeing 'Scripture can only be understood through the same Spirit whereby it was given.' Our reading should likewise be closed with prayer, that what we read may be written on our hearts."[7] Prayer before studying the Bible is thus seen as a means of receiving the inspiration of the Holy Spirit. This inspiration is understood by Wesley as a necessary prerequisite for proper interpretation. In his letter to William Warburton, published in 1763, Wesley defends his doctrine of the inspiration of the Holy Spirit: "I do firmly believe (and what serious man does not)—*omnis scriptura legi debet eo spiritu quo scripta est:* we need the same Spirit to *understand* the Scripture which enabled the holy men of old to *write* it."[8]

As a means of grace, the letter of Scripture is dead unless the Spirit enlivens it.[9] In his 1741 preface to *An Extract of the Life and Death of Mr. Thomas Haliburton*, Wesley suggests this response to an accusation of enthusiasm:

> Ask such a one, (but with meekness and love,) "Are you taught of God? Do you know that he abideth in you? Have you the revelation

105

of the Holy Ghost" (they are the words of our own Church) "inspiring into you the true meaning of Scripture? If you have not, with all your human science and worldly wisdom, you know nothing yet as you ought to know. Whatever you are in other respects, as to the things of God, you are an unlearned and ignorant man. And if you are unstable too, you will wrest these, as you do also the other scriptures, to your own destruction."[10]

By "the words of our own Church," Wesley is referring to the *Homily of Reading the Holy Scriptures,* whose first paragraph Wesley has quoted with his customary imprecision.[11] And Wesley's note on 2 Timothy 3:16 makes a similar point: "*All Scripture is inspired of God*—The Spirit of God not only once inspired those who wrote it, but continually inspires, supernaturally assists, those that read it with earnest prayer. Hence *it is so profitable for doctrine,* for instruction of the ignorant . . ."[12]

Several interpreters of Wesley have concluded that Wesley stands in the Reformed tradition of an internal testimony of the Holy Spirit. Larry Shelton refers to the Westminster Confession as background.[13] Duncan Ferguson refers to Wesley's abridgment of Cranmer's homily, part of which was quoted earlier.[14] George Lyons[15] and Timothy Smith[16] also give it prominence. Colin Williams says, "It is true that, with the Reformers, he insisted on the *testimonium Spiritus Sancti internum*—the need for the Spirit to illumine the heart of the reader so that he may receive the truth of Scripture."[17]

It is clear that Wesley believed in the internal witness of the Holy Spirit, and the Reformed tradition which lay behind the Homilies and the Puritan influences in Wesley's early training are sufficient to account for how he got the idea. He clearly stands in the Reformed tradition in this matter. But what has he done with it? He is not simply citing Calvin or repeating Cranmer. Rather, Wesley understands the role of the Holy Spirit in a different way. He places a significant restriction on the influence of the Holy Spirit because of the danger of enthusiasm. He defines enthusiasm as "a religious madness arising from some falsely imagined influence or inspiration of God; at least from imputing something to God which ought not to be imputed to him, or expecting something from God which ought not to be expected from him."[18] One type of enthusiasm comes to people who expected to be directed of God, either in spiritual things or in common life, in what is justly called an *extraordinary* manner. I mean by visions or dreams, by strong impressions or sudden impulses on the mind. I do not deny that God has of old times manifested his will in this manner, or that he can do so now. Nay, I believe he does, in some very rare instances. But how frequently do men mistake herein![19]

He then describes the assistance that the Spirit gives as one searches out the will of God:

Meantime the assistance of his Spirit is supposed during the whole process of the inquiry. Indeed 'tis not easy to say in how many ways that assistance is conveyed. He may bring many circumstances to our remembrance; may place others in a stronger and clearer light; may insensibly open our mind to receive conviction, and fix that conviction upon our heart.[20]

What is striking here is Wesley's reticence about the role of the Spirit. Here is no guarantee of the Spirit's acting in a certain manner; the assistance of the Spirit is "supposed," and the manner is left vague. The best explanation for this reticence is that Wesley also has in his background the excesses of the Puritans during the seventeenth century. Richard Baxter argues for two ways in which the testimony of the Spirit works. First, the Spirit enabled the Apostles to work miracles "to seal their doctrine." Second, it comes "in the *Sanctifying Illumination* of our *understandings* to see that which is Objectively Revealed. So that this *Testimony* is the *efficient* and not *objective Cause* of our *Belief* in this latter sense."[21] Yet, N. H. Keeble claims that Baxter "warred unceasingly against unreasoning fanaticism and enthusiasm,"[22] which in the seventeenth century often came under the heading of the witness of the Spirit. Keeble quotes Baxter as saying, "It is *true,* that the saving knowledge of Divinity, must be taught by the Spirit of God: But it is false that *labour* and *humane teaching* are not the means which must be used by them, who will have the teaching of the spirit."[23] Baxter denies that the Spirit gives new revelations. It "only reveals what is revealed already in the Word; by illuminating us to understand it."[24]

Thus Baxter carefully qualifies the inspiration of the Spirit. In an age even more devoted to reason than was Baxter's, Wesley talks more about the Spirit enlightening our reason than giving direct messages about the meaning of the Scripture. Indeed, the key to Wesley's understanding of the internal witness of the Spirit is that it acts primarily on our reason. In a 1750 letter to George Stonehouse, he refers to "the Spirit of God not putting out the eyes of my understanding, but enlightening them more and more."[25] We noted earlier that reason has a role to play in interpreting Scripture and guiding our actions. But Wesley comments in a 1786 letter to Elizabeth Ritchie:

> It is doubtless the will of the Lord we should be guided by our reason so far as it can go. But in many cases it gives us very little light and in others none at all. In all cases it cannot guide us right but in subordination to the unction of the Holy One. So that in all our ways we are to acknowledge Him, and He will direct our paths.[26]

He makes the same point in a letter to Miss March in 1768: "We are reasonable creatures, and undoubtedly reason is the candle of the Lord. By enlightening our reason to see the meaning of the Scriptures, the Holy Spirit makes our way plain before us."[27] And in a letter to "John Smith" he says that "I entirely agree with you, that the children of light walk by the joint light of reason, Scripture, and the Holy Ghost."[28]

Wesley thus draws on the Reformed tradition for his understanding that the inspiration of the Holy Ghost is required for proper interpretation of the Bible, but he significantly modifies that tradition by insisting that the Holy Spirit's influence is always on our reasoning powers, and works jointly with reason. This is one more indication of the unity that exists between the various parts of religious authority for Wesley. If the inspiration of the Holy Spirit is an experiential matter, such experience works together with reason to interpret the meaning of Scripture correctly.

The second prerequisite for correct interpretation of Scripture is harder to specify. At several points Wesley seems to suggest that faith is such a prerequisite. He most frequently defines faith in the terms of Hebrews 11:1—"the evidence of things not seen." It is this spiritual realm which is also revealed in Scripture, so that the content of Christian faith is the same as the content of the Scripture. In his 1788 sermon "The Discoveries of Faith," he says, "Faith, on the other hand, is the 'evidence of things not seen,' of the *invisible world*; of all those invisible things which are revealed in the oracles of God. But indeed they reveal nothing, they are a mere 'dead letter,' if they are 'not mixed with faith in those that hear them.'"[29] Yet, in "The Means of Grace" Wesley said of the Scripture, "Nor is this profitable only for the men of God, for those who walk already in the light of his countenance, but also for those who are yet in darkness, seeking him whom they know not."[30] His story of how salvation comes to "a stupid, senseless wretch" includes Scripture as a means of conversion.[31] Is faith as a supernatural gift independent of Scripture's description of "spiritual" reality? Is faith required to understand Scripture?

The answers to these questions are not clear in Wesley's writings. What seems probable is that the work of the Holy Spirit is involved in Wesley's view here. Faith is a gift of the Holy Spirit. The Spirit uses Scripture to give grace to the sinner. As that grace is received, spiritual sight is given and reason is enlightened, so that the recipient can better understand the Scriptures, which will be an even more powerful means of grace than before. Thus, faith is not independent of Scripture, but is the spiritual gift which enables the believer to see the realities it describes. Further, any believer's understanding of Scripture involves the work of the Holy Spirit who is using the text as part of the work of grace in the life of the reader. Faith is not required to understand Scripture, but anyone reading Scripture without the aid of the Holy Spirit, who always produces faith in those who receive him, will not understand it properly. Faith and a correct understanding of Scripture are both produced by the same Spirit. Thus, while faith is not necessary, it is always present in those who read Scripture correctly.

Wesley understands that knowledge of certain areas is expedient, but not necessary, to a correct interpretation of the Scriptures. In his 1756 *Address to the Clergy*, he goes on at some length about the qualifications necessary to be a good clergyman.[32] Of the eight qualifications he discusses there, five are areas of knowledge that relate directly to the minister's ability to interpret the Bible. Second on the list is a knowledge of the whole Bible, because "scripture interprets scripture." Third is knowledge of the original tongues, Greek and Hebrew. Fourth, knowledge of profane history "though not absolutely necessary, yet [is] highly expedient, for him that would throughly understand the Scriptures." Fifth, some knowledge of the sciences is expedient, including natural philosophy and metaphysics. Sixth, knowledge of the Fathers as "the most authentic commentators on Scripture" is important. Wesley is very clear that knowledge is extremely useful in interpreting the Bible, and even necessary to fulfilling the office well. The only area of knowledge that Wesley deems necessary to correct interpretation of Scripture is logic, which is said to be "necessary next, and in order to, the knowledge of the Scripture itself."[33] While this is clearly an area of knowledge, it is also part of the faculty of reasoning and can be counted as another instance of Wesley's use of reason in the interpretation of Scripture.

Wesley's view that knowledge is not necessary for correct interpretation of Scripture is made clear in his defense of the itinerant preachers in the Methodist movement. He argued that, despite their lack of a university education, they were better interpreters than the educated but unfaithful parish clergy.[34] Knowledge of history, the sciences, the Fathers, Greek and Hebrew are less important than a living faith and the inspiration of the Spirit.

Rules of Interpretation

Wesley nowhere provides an exhaustive list of hermeneutical rules. In fact, as with other aspects of his doctrine of Scripture, he casually refers to principles and rules which he presupposes in the discussion. By compiling all of those rules to which he makes reference at various times, it is possible to list his hermeneutical rules. They are as follows:

1. Speak as the oracles of God.
2. Use the literal sense unless it contradicts another Scripture or implies an absurdity.
3. Interpret the text with regard to its literary context.
4. Scripture interprets Scripture, according to the analogy of faith and by parallel passages.
5. Commandments are covered promises.
6. Interpret literary devices appropriately.
7. Seek the most original text and the best translation.

Two cautions about these hermeneutical rules are in order. First, not all of them are explicitly stated in these words as rules of interpretation. While some of them are so stated, notably the rule about using the literal sense, others are appealed to in less obvious fashion. Second, this formulation of these rules is somewhat arbitrary. I have presented them here in a pattern that is meant to provide a comprehensive and clear description of Wesley's conception. For the sake of clarity, I have grouped some rules together that could conceivably have been separated. By making different distinctions, it would be possible to list either more or fewer.[35]

Speak as the Oracles of God

When Wesley advocates speaking "as the oracles of God," he is following the rule even in its formulation, since it is taken from 1 Peter 4:11 in the AV. Wesley is here advocating a minimalist hermeneutic; taken strictly, it implies that the best interpretation is no interpretation at all. The point, made clearly in a 1745 letter to "John Smith," is that using the very words of Scripture is the best way of remaining faithful to it: "But I cannot call those uncommon words which are the constant language of Holy Writ. These I purposely use, desiring always to express Scripture sense in Scripture phrase. And this I apprehend myself to do when I speak of 'salvation' as a *present* thing."[36] Here Wesley argues that the best way to religious truth is to use the same words and definitions that are found in Scripture. Wesley is prepared for the argument that the ancient language is no longer applicable to the modern period:

> For however the propriety of those expressions may vary which occur in the writings of men, I cannot but think those which are found in the Book of God will be equally proper in all ages. But let us look back, as you desire, to the age of the apostles. And if it appear that the state of religion now is (according to your own representation of it) the same in substance as it was then, it will follow that the same expressions are just as proper now as they were in the apostolic age.[37]

Note that he is willing to consider that the times may render the concepts with different meanings, or might invalidate them. But it is not the use of language that invalidates those meanings, but whether the basic human condition has changed. Wesley goes on to argue that the conditions are indeed similar.

This rule gets quoted explicitly in at least eight places outside the New Testament *Notes*. In two of these places, he simply urges the value of speaking "as the oracles of God."[38] In two places, this scriptural admonition applies to the content of the oracles of God: the preacher or Christian is to speak the same message contained therein.[39] But in four places, the text is applied in such a way as to suggest that the Christian is to use the actual words of Scripture as much as possible.[40] In fact, Wesley's comment on 1 Peter 4:11 authorizes both speaking the same message and speaking in the same words as Scripture:

> *If any man speak, let him*—In his whole conversation, public and private. *Speak as the oracles of God*—Let all his words be according to this pattern, both as to matter and manner, more especially in public. By this mark we may always know who are, so far, the true or false prophets. *The oracles of God* teach that men should repent, believe, obey. He that treats of faith and leaves out repentance, or does not enjoin practical holiness to believers, does not speak as the oracles of God: he does not preach Christ, let him think as highly of himself as he will.[41]

While Wesley interprets this rule to apply to both "matter and manner," it is with the latter that we are concerned here. The most extensive application of the rule in this regard occurs in the sermon "On Knowing Christ After the Flesh." There he argues that we must not know Christ after the flesh, but must refer to him in ways that are appropriate to his being God as well. He writes about use of the word "dear":

> Is there any Scripture, any passage either in the Old or New Testament, which justifies this manner of speaking? Does any of the inspired writers make use of it, even in the poetical Scriptures? . . . Therefore I still doubt whether any of the inspired writers ever addresses the word either to the Father or the Son. Hence I cannot but advise all lovers of the Bible, if they use the expression at all, to use it very sparingly, seeing the Scripture affords neither command nor precedent for it. And surely, "if any man speaks," either in preaching or prayer, he "should speak as the oracles of God"![42]

In his *Journal* for July 18, 1765, he makes the same point, referring to 1 John as "the deepest part of the Holy Scripture," "by which, above all other even inspired writings, I advise every young preacher to form his style. Here are sublimity and simplicity together, the strongest sense and the plainest language! How can any one that would 'speak as the oracles of God' use harder words than are found here?"[43]

However, this rule cannot be expanded to claim that Wesley thought all interpretation was unnecessary. Indeed, if interpretation were not necessary, we would not need any hermeneutical rules or even any *Explanatory Notes* to help us understand. In his correspondence with "John Smith," Wesley defends himself against the charge of proof-texting. He first quotes Smith and then responds:

> "Another objection" (you say) "I have to make to your manner of treating your antagonists. You seem to think you sufficiently answer your adversary if you put together a number of naked Scriptures that sound in your favour. But remember, the question between you and them is not whether such words are Scripture, but whether they are to be so interpreted."
> You surprise me. I take your word, else I should never have imagined you had read over the latter *Appeal,* so great a part of which is employed in this very thing, in fighting my ground, inch by inch, in proving, not that such words are Scripture, but that they must be interpreted in the manner there set down.[44]

And in a letter to William Dodd, he agrees that it is "absolutely necessary" sometimes to add words explanatory of the sense of Scripture, so long as they are not subversive of that sense.[45]

Yet, Wesley is aware that interpretation of Scripture is a human activity and therefore subject to human mistakes. He writes in the sermon "Christian Perfection,"

> Nay, with regard to the Holy Scriptures themselves, as careful as they are to avoid it, the best of men are liable to mistake, and do mistake day by day; especially with respect to those parts thereof which less immediately relate to practice. Hence even the children of God are not agreed as to the interpretation of many places in Holy Writ; nor is their difference of opinion any proof that they are not the children of God on either side. But it is a proof that we are no more to expect any living man to be *infallible* than to be *omniscient.*[46]

By this rule Wesley is advocating the minimal amount of interpretation necessary to render the meaning of the text clear. By and large, the words of Scripture are the clearest and most fitting words to use in expressing scriptural truth. When they do require interpretation and explanation, human fallibility requires additional rules for guidance.

Use the Literal Sense Unless It Contradicts Another Scripture or Implies an Absurdity

The second hermeneutical rule, which gives priority to the literal sense of Scripture, receives explicit mention in at least seven places.[47] In each of them, the necessity of using the literal sense is either assumed or asserted, unless an absurdity or contradiction is involved. In his 1785 sermon "Of the Church" he writes, "But it is a stated rule in interpreting Scripture never to depart from the plain, literal sense, unless it implies an absurdity."[48] In his 1738 letter to Lady Cox, it is contradiction which receives mention as a condition requiring another sense:

> To anyone who asketh me concerning myself or these whom I rejoice to call my brethren, what our principles are, I answer clearly, We have no principles but those revealed in the Word of God. In the interpretation whereof we always judge the most literal sense to be the best, unless where the literal sense of one contradicts some other Scripture.[49]

In his 1778 sermon "A Call to Backsliders," he puts both into the mouth of a presumed opponent:

> It is true, some are of opinion, that those words, "it is impossible," are not to be taken literally as denoting an absolute impossibility, but only a very great difficulty. But it does not appear that we have any sufficient reason to depart from the literal meaning, as it neither implies any absurdity, nor contradicts any other Scriptures.[50]

In order to understand what Wesley means by this rule, we need to ask three questions: (1) What does he mean by the "literal sense"? (2) What constitutes a contradiction or absurdity? and (3) What is the proper substitute when the literal sense is rejected? First, Wesley frequently calls the literal sense the "plain, obvious meaning" of the passage.[51] One of the places where these terms are found together is in his *Farther Thoughts on Christian Perfection*, where he says, "Try all things by the written word, and let all bow down before it. You are in danger of enthusiasm every hour, if you depart ever so little from

Scripture; yea, or from the plain, literal meaning of any text, taken in connection with the context."[52]

For Wesley, the literal sense of Scripture is equivalent to its plain, obvious, natural meaning. The background for Wesley's emphasis on the "plain, literal meaning" goes back at least as far as the Reformation. The reformers' insistence on the authority of Scripture included the insistence on its literal sense as opposed to the four senses frequently used in medieval exegesis.[53] The Protestant Scholastics were emphatic on this point. "There is but one proper and true sense of each passage, which the Holy Spirit thereby intends, and which is drawn from the proper signification of the words, and only from this *literal sense* available arguments may be derived."[54] The Puritans were noted for their commitment to both plainness in preaching style and in biblical interpretation during the seventeenth century.[55] In *The Saints' Everlasting Rest*, Richard Baxter writes, "O when will the Lord once perswade his Churches to take his Written Word for the only Canon of their Faith! and that in its own naked Simplicity and Evidence, without the Determinations and Canons of men!"[56] After the Restoration, many Anglicans reaffirmed their commitment to the plain sense of Scripture. Edward Stillingfleet says that scriptural interpretation should be "plain and easie and agreeable to the most received sense."[57] In this matter Stillingfleet represents the other Latitudinarian theologians who emphasized the plain meaning of the text. John Locke sees the Scripture as basically simple. He writes that "all the duties of morality lie there clear and plain, and easy to be understood."[58] Scripture is suited to its audience of common men and women who lived long ago: "'Tis plain that the teaching of Men Philosophy, was no part of the Design of Divine Revelation; but that the Expressions of Scripture are commonly suited in those Matters to the Vulgar Apprehensions and Conceptions of the Place and People where they were delivered."[59] The Latitudinarians, building on the Puritans before them, set the tone with regard to simplicity of interpretation. In mathematics, astronomy, and many other fields, complex problems were being broken down into simple answers. Biblical interpreters were driven by the same desire to eliminate the complexity of the older views and find the plain, simple meaning of the text.

Thus, Wesley is in the mainstream of his time when he emphasizes the plain sense of Scripture. He is prepared to place a great deal of emphasis on that meaning. He is seeking the straightforward, basic, reliable word of God. It is his understanding that the Scriptures deliver this, at least in many places, with "inimitable simplicity"[60] and with "no laboured pomp of words."[61] When Wesley speaks of designing "plain truth for plain people" in his sermons, it is possible because the Scriptures provide that same sort of plain clarity themselves, and are to be interpreted "simply": "I set aside the glosses of men, and simply considered the words of God, comparing them together and endeavouring to illustrate the obscure by the plainer passages."[62] When such plain clarity is achieved in Scripture and interpreted plainly as well, then as little as a single passage can settle an issue. In the sermon "On Faith (Hebrews 11:1)," he asks how it is that disembodied spirits know each other after death: "I answer plainly, I cannot tell. But I am certain that they do. This is as plainly proved from one passage of Scripture as it could be from a thousand. Did not Abraham and Lazarus know each other in Hades, even afar off?"[63]

All of this discussion about the literal sense of Scripture, however, is complicated by several references to the spiritual sense of Scripture. There are also references to the literal sense being of lesser value than the spiritual sense.[64] In his *Address to the Clergy*, Wesley urges a number of necessary skills, one of which is "a knowledge of the Scriptures":

> So that, whether it be true or not, that every good textuary is a good Divine, it is certain none can be a good Divine who is not a good textuary. None else can be mighty in the Scriptures; able both to instruct and to stop the mouths of gainsayers.
>
> In order to do this accurately, ought he not to know the literal meaning of every word, verse, and chapter; without which there can be no firm foundation on which the spiritual meaning can be built?[65]

And in his *Notes* on John 6:63, he writes,

> *It is the Spirit*—The spiritual meaning of these words, by which God giveth life. *The flesh*—The bare, carnal, literal meaning, *profiteth nothing. The words which I have spoken, they are spirit*—Are to be taken in a spiritual sense. *And*—When they are so understood, *they are life*—That is, a means of spiritual life to the hearers.[66]

His note on 2 Corinthians 3:6 identifies the law as the *"letter*, from God's literally writing it on the two tables" and thereby includes the whole "Mosaic dispensation": "Yea, if we adhere to the literal sense even of the moral law, if we regard only the precept and the sanction as they stand in themselves, not as they lead us to Christ, they are doubtless a killing ordinance, and bind us down under the sentence of death."[67] According to this passage, the difference between the spiritual meaning and the literal meaning of a text is whether one understands the literal meaning as "leading to Christ." It is not that the spiritual meaning involves a completely different grammatical understanding of the words. Rather, it involves understanding the literal sense in the context of a larger whole. This larger whole testifies to "Christ," and is also referred to as the general tenor of Scripture or the analogy of faith. Supporting this understanding of Wesley is his use of the term "dead letter" to refer to those who argue away the real meaning and spirit of a text whereby "the Word of God is made of none effect."[68] In his note on Mark 4:2, he says:

> A parable signifies, not only simile or comparison, and sometimes a proverb, but any kind of instructive speech, wherein spiritual things are explained and illustrated by natural. Prov. i. 6. "To understand a proverb, and the interpretation."—The proverb is the literal sense, the interpretation is the spiritual: resting in the literal sense killeth; but the spiritual giveth life.[69]

As noted earlier, Wesley insists on following the literal sense of the text unless it contradicts another Scripture or leads to an absurdity. The second question concerning this hermeneutical rule of Wesley's is, What constitutes a contradiction or absurdity? A contradiction exists when two or more different texts say mutually exclusive things. In a letter to Samuel Furly, Wesley says, "The general rule of interpreting Scripture is this: the literal sense of every text is to be taken, if it be not contrary to some other texts. But in that case, the obscure text is to be interpreted by those which speak more plainly."[70]

In his reply to Furly, Wesley slides from a text that is "contrary to other texts" to those that are "obscure." While a text may be obscure for other reasons, all of those that contradict another part of Scripture are for that very reason obscure. However, some contradictions are only apparent and can be resolved without leaving the literal sense.

In such cases, Wesley treats the "plain, literal sense" as one that resolves the contradiction with the least amount of change made to the texts in question. In his sermon "On Sin in Believers" he is concerned to explain texts such as Galatians 5:17, "The flesh lusteth against the spirit, and the spirit against the flesh: these are contrary the one to the other." He interprets Paul as saying that inward sin still exists in the believer.[71] But he then considers the "chief arguments" of those who disagree with him. The first such argument is based on 2 Corinthians 5:17 (AV, adapted): "If any man be (a believer) in Christ, he is a new creature. Old things are passed away; behold all things are become new." Wesley says,

> But we must not so interpret the Apostle's words as to make him contradict himself. And if we will make him consistent with himself the plain meaning of the words is this: his *old judgment* (concerning justification, holiness, happiness, indeed concerning the things of God in general) is now "passed away"; so are his *old desires, designs, affections, tempers,* and *conversation.* All these are undeniably "become new," greatly changed from what they were. And yet, though they are *new,* they are not *wholly* new.[72]

Wesley claims that the "plain meaning" of the text is one that adds a crucial limitation. While Wesley does not explicitly say that this is the literal sense of the text, its status as "the plain meaning" connotes that it is. Because Paul could not possibly have contradicted himself, the correct understanding is that Paul really meant for the limitation to be applied. As noted earlier, this understanding that a correct interpretation must avoid biblical self-contradiction stems from Wesley's conviction of divine authorship of the text.

Determining what Wesley means by an absurdity is somewhat more difficult. An early unpublished sermon, "The Love of God," states the rule for interpretation: "'Tis true, if the literal sense of these Scriptures were absurd, and apparently contrary to reason, then we should be obliged not to interpret them according to the letter, but to look out for a looser meaning."[73] He appears to use the term as something contrary to reason or to obvious truth.[74]

The third question to be answered with regard to this hermeneutical rule is, What is the proper substitute when the literal sense is rejected? Frequently Wesley states the hermeneutical rule without specifying the alternative. All he says is that when absurdity or biblical contradiction prevent the use of the literal sense, then one is permitted to leave it. The answer to this question is not at all clear; one must weigh the evidence and make the best inferences possible.

The answers are of two types. When a text is contradictory or absurd, it should be "interpreted" by others that are more clear. But what happens in that process of interpretation? Is the original text ignored in favor of others? Is there any sense at all in a text that is absurd? Or does its meaning become so flexible that any meaning is suitable if there are other, clearer texts to support it? Unfortunately, Wesley does not give any indications as to how these questions should be answered.

The second type of answer mentions another sense of the problematic text. In the sermon "The Love of God," just quoted, Wesley refers to "a looser meaning."[75] Perhaps the clearest indication of what he means comes in an earlier, unpublished sermon "On the Sabbath":

> Indeed, so soon as it shall be proved that there is an absurdity in taking this in the plain literal sense, then we shall be forced to take it in a less plain, in a figurative sense, and to say, "Though this is related as done at the creation, it was not done till the giving of manna in the time of Moses, four or five and twenty hundred years after the creation." But till this absurdity be shown we have no pretence for giving up the letter.[76]

The key words here are "figurative sense." What does Wesley mean by this?

An exhaustive search of his writings shows seven places in the *Explanatory Notes upon the New Testament* where the figurative sense is mentioned. Five of these are in Revelation where he is concerned with whether to take the images used there as literally true or only figurative.[77] On Revelation 21:15 he writes,

> In treating of all these things a deep reverence is necessary; and so is a measure of spiritual wisdom; that we may neither understand them too literally and grossly, nor go too far from the natural force of the words. The gold, the pearls, the precious stones, the walls, foundations, gates, are undoubtedly figurative expressions; seeing the city itself is in glory, and the inhabitants of it have spiritual bodies: yet these spiritual bodies are also real bodies, and the city is an abode distinct from its inhabitants, and proportioned to them who take up

a finite and a determinate space. The measures, therefore, above mentioned are real and determinate.[78]

The other two uses of "figurative" shed more light on what Wesley might mean by the term. His comment on Luke 18:34:

They understood none of these things—The literal meaning they could not but understand. But as they could not reconcile this to their pre-conceived opinion of the Messiah, they were utterly at a loss in what parabolical or figurative sense to take what he said concerning his sufferings; having their thoughts still taken up with the temporal kingdom.[79]

Here it seems that "figurative" is to be understood as "parabolical." The comment on Luke 14:7, while not using the term "figurative," does note that a discourse is called a parable because "several parts are not to be understood literally." Wesley's comment on Galatians 4:24 also contains the term "figurative": *"Which things are an allegory*—An allegory is a figurative speech, wherein one thing is expressed, and another intended."[80]

While this is one matter on which Wesley's true position cannot be stated with certainty, it is possible to construct a position that fits the hints he has given. Consider these hints laid out in the following order. When the literal sense of the text must be abandoned, one goes to a "looser" or "figurative" sense. Wesley never defines what these terms mean, but we know that parables and allegories are both types of figurative speech. It is plausible, then, to argue that Wesley means that, when the literal sense is untenable, then allegorical interpretation is acceptable. Indeed, there is some evidence to show that allegorical interpretation, in the proper amount, is acceptable to Wesley. Although his anti-Roman tract *The Advantage of the Members of the Church of England* condemns Roman Catholics for interpreting the Scriptures in "a strained and allegorical sense,"[81] the "Large Minutes" do allow it. Question 37 asks, "Are there any smaller advices relative to preaching, which might be of use to us?" He answers, "Perhaps these: . . . (7.) Be sparing in allegorizing or spiritualizing."[82] If one read only Wesley's anti-Catholic literature, one would believe it was always wrong to allegorize. Here he permits it in small amounts. Later in the same work he seeks to guard against the evils of the Calvinists, urging his preachers, "Do not imitate them in screaming, allegorizing, boasting: Rather mildly expose these things when time serves."[83]

What conclusion can be drawn from this evidence? While it is not possible to say anything with certainty, the most plausible conclusion is that when Wesley finds the literal sense untenable, an allegorical reading is allowed if it is kept under tight control and does not become "strained."

Interpret the Text with Regard to Its Literary Context

The third hermeneutical rule calls attention to the literary context of a passage. Wesley explicitly cites it on four occasions.[84] In *Farther Thoughts Upon Christian Perfection* he speaks about knowing the context as one element of correct interpretation: "Try all things by the written word, and let all bow down before it. You are in danger of enthusiasm every hour, if you depart ever so little from Scripture; yea, or from the plain, literal meaning of any text, taken in connection with the context."[85]

In *Address to the Clergy* he lists a number of ways in which divines should prepare themselves to know the Scriptures. Knowing the Bible means knowing "the context and parallel places" for any passage.[86] Wesley is aware of the many theological arguments that turn on the interpretation of key verses of the Bible. The rule requiring consideration of the context is an assertion that a verse's true meaning is to be found only in its larger setting. Thus, one cannot interpret a single verse from Paul's letters without considering the entire letter. Though Wesley never specifies what he means by the context of a verse, some parts of his meaning are clear. The context clearly includes the verses immediately surrounding the passage under consideration. It also includes any "parallel passages," that is, other places in the Bible which speak of the same subject matter. Further, the context for Wesley ultimately refers to the entire Bible. It is clear from the following rule that Wesley is concerned that each verse be interpreted in a literary context within the Bible that is as wide as possible.

Scripture Interprets Scripture, According to the Analogy of Faith and by Parallel Passages

The fourth hermeneutical rule is a direct result of the Protestant theological principle of *sola Scriptura*. If there is no outside authority to render a definitive interpretation, then the Scripture must be self-interpreting. Here Wesley is following a principle common to Protestant hermeneutics.[87]

There are several places where Wesley explicitly states that Scripture is the best interpreter of Scripture. One of these comes in his early sermon, "On Corrupting the Word of God": "1. If then we have spoken the Word of God, the genuine, unmixed Word of God, and that only; 2, if we have put no unnatural interpretations upon it, but [have] taken the known phrases in their common, obvious sense, and where they were less known explained Scripture by Scripture; . . ."[88]

In his late sermon, "The New Creation," he explicitly refers to "interpreting Scripture by Scripture, according to the analogy of faith."[89] Chapter 2 of this study discussed at length what Wesley means by the wholeness of Scripture and how the analogy of faith functions as the "clue to guide me through the whole."[90] One of the conclusions reached there was that the analogy of faith functions as the rule to be used in interpreting Scripture. For Wesley, the Reformation principle of Scripture interpreting Scripture means looking to the analogy of faith as the doctrinal marrow of the text. One should always interpret unclear places in light of this doctrinal understanding of the "general tenor" of the Bible.

Similarly, the interpreter should consider parallel passages in Scripture. Wesley makes explicit mention of this practice in three places.[91] Again, that crucial section from his *Address to the Clergy* asks rhetorically, "Upon the mention of any text, do I know the context, and the parallel places?"[92] Another indication of Wesley's reliance on this principle comes in the Preface to the 1746 edition of *Sermons on Several Occasions*. After declaring he wants to be *homo unius libri*, he writes, "I then search after and consider parallel passages of Scripture, 'comparing spiritual things with spiritual.' I meditate thereon, with all the attention and earnestness of which my mind is capable."[93]

What Wesley means by "parallel texts" is never fully explained. However, he appears to mean other texts in the Scriptures that address the same subject. One example may suffice. In the sermon "The Witness of the Spirit, II" he devotes much space to a close exegesis of Romans 8:16, "The Spirit itself beareth witness with our spirit, that we are the children of God": "This is farther explained by the parallel text, 'Because ye are sons, God hath sent forth the Spirit of his Son into your hearts, crying Abba, Father.' . . . All these texts, then, in the most obvious meaning, describe a direct testimony of the Spirit."[94] Parallel passages are not restricted to similar accounts of the same event, as in the four Gospels' versions of the crucifixion. Rather, this principle points to the doctrinal wholeness of Scripture. Places where the same subject is addressed are thereby parallel. In trying to understand Scripture, one ought then to use parallel passages to explain each other.

This principle is sometimes formulated as a rule that clearer passages are to be used to explain the more obscure. This formulation is first used in Wesley's manuscript journal as one of several ways the Moravians deal with obscure passages of Scripture.[95] However, when he is debating with Peter Böhler about the relationship between faith and salvation, he writes, "I first consulted the Scripture. But when I set aside the glosses of men, and simply considered the words of God, comparing them together and endeavouring to illustrate the obscure by the plainer passages, I found they all made against me. . . ."[96] Seventeen years later, a letter written to Samuel Furly refers to the same principle: "The general rule of interpreting Scripture is this: the literal sense of every text is to be taken, if it be not contrary to some other texts. But in that case, the obscure text is to be interpreted by those which speak more plainly."[97] The plainer passages help the interpreter understand the more obscure. How to distinguish the plain from the obscure is never explained by Wesley. In the same way that the literal sense is "plain and obvious," obscurity of a text would, in his mind, be clear to all unbiased readers as well.

What does Wesley really mean here? The plain parts of Scripture are those which fit easily into the general tenor of the text. Once the overall pattern of the Scripture's message has been discerned, then the clearest texts are those which are easily understandable within that pattern. Thus, for Wesley, the plain texts are those which speak clearly of the order of salvation—sin, justification, and sanctification—and other essential doctrines of Christianity. Their clarity derives from their relationship to the overall theme of the Bible when taken as a whole. Conversely, the obscure parts are those which are apparently in conflict with that overall message. Such texts present hermeneutical problems to the student of Scripture who seeks to find coherence in the whole Bible.

Commandments Are Covered Promises

The fifth hermeneutical rule is a way of bringing together the two different aspects of Scripture which Wesley describes as law and gospel; it is mentioned in three different places.[98] Perhaps the clearest statement of his principle comes in the sermon "Upon Our Lord's Sermon on the Mount, V." There he is concerned to show the agreement between law and gospel:

> Yea, the very same words, considered in different respects, are parts both of the law and of the gospel. If they are considered as commandments, they are parts of the law: if as promises, of the gospel. Thus, "Thou shalt love the Lord thy God with all thy heart," when considered as a commandment, is a branch of the law; when regarded as a promise, is an essential part of the gospel—the gospel being no other than the commands of the law proposed by way of promises. Accordingly poverty of spirit, purity of heart, and whatever else is enjoined in the holy law of God, are no other, when viewed in a gospel light, than so many great and precious promises. . . .
>
> We may yet farther observe that every command in Holy Writ is only a covered promise.[99]

This rule gives Wesley support for his theological conceptions of that holy living which comes after justification by faith. Wesley's view of the relation of grace and law stipulates that salvation is by grace alone through our faith alone. God's grace imputes righteousness to us, and then imparts it, with our cooperation. Thus, the legalistic commandments must be understood as promises, because when met with faith, God's grace will always enable the believer to fulfill that which has been demanded of him. Conversely, promises are also covered commandments. Even though Wesley nowhere states this reverse of his rule, it is implicit in the concluding sections of "The Witness of the Spirit, II." There he suggests that no one should rest in any fruits of the Spirit without the witness of the Spirit as well, nor should anyone rest in the witness of the Spirit without the fruits.[100] This is typical of Wesley's holistic theology. Those things which are promised—adoption as a child of God and the assurance of salvation—are also expected by God. Each act of God's grace can be viewed as either a promise or a commandment of God.

Interpret Literary Devices Appropriately

The sixth hermeneutical rule points to the use of literary devices embedded in the biblical text. Into this general category should be placed a number of secondary rules which all treat the text as a literary device pointing obliquely to another message. Three approaches are mentioned by Wesley. Two of them are mentioned in the early sermon, "The Love of God":

> It is here enjoined that whatever use we make of any power which God hath given us, whatever act of any faculty we exert, all should tend to the glory, the love, of God. And it is enjoined expressly. We need not argue from a parity of reason—"whether ye eat or drink," therefore, "whether ye rejoice or love." We need not argue from the less to the greater—if every bodily action, which at best profiteth but little, how much more is every movement of our soul to be subordinated to the end of our being! No, we have yet a more sure word of direction; the very terms are, "whatever ye do." This commandment is indeed exceeding broad.[101]

The first is that arguments "by parity of reason" are allowed. A strictly literal interpretation of the given phrase would limit the force of the commandment simply to activities of eating and drinking. But Wesley is prepared to recognize the validity of an argument that would substitute other activities and still hold true. By parity of reason this commandment could be expanded to all other human activities—working, playing, and so forth.

The second approach in this passage is one that moves from the less to the greater. This would have been an argument that if the commandment applies to insignificant bodily functions, how much more should it apply to the whole of our lives. This is not strictly a literal interpretation; rather, it is a way of reading the text and amplifying it by suggesting that the author intended to convey more than was stated.

A third approach that falls under this category of literary devices is Wesley's desire to pay attention to literary style. An author's use of metonymy, transposition, figurative language, and other elements of style affects how the text is read. Thus, Wesley does not take the golden streets in Revelation 21:21 as literally true.[102]

Seek the Most Original Text and the Best Translation

The seventh hermeneutical rule acknowledges the textual uncertainty behind the ancient manuscripts of the Bible as a whole and the derivative nature of any English translation. Wesley is clearly aware of both these factors which affect interpretation of the text. The Preface to his *Explanatory Notes upon the New Testament* addresses the issue:

> In order to assist these in such a measure as I am able, I design, First, to set down the text itself, for the most part, in the common English translation, which is, in general, so far as I can judge, abundantly the best that I have seen. Yet I do not say it is incapable of being brought, in several places, nearer to the original. Neither will I affirm that the Greek copies from which this translation was made are always the most correct: and therefore I shall take the liberty, as occasion may require, to make here and there a small alteration.[103]

Wesley understands in principle the difficulties with textual transmission and seeks the best Greek and Hebrew texts. Further, he is a linguist who understands that some translations are superior to others, and he seeks the best.

Conclusion

The interpretation of Scripture is an eminently practical matter for Wesley. He is concerned to know "the way to heaven," and is convinced that a correct interpretation of Scripture will reveal that. The inspiration of the Spirit and faith are seen as prerequisites to true understanding. While knowledge of both sacred and secular subjects is helpful, it is not required. Those with knowledge will miss the point more often than those who have faith and the Spirit guiding them.

Rules for the interpretation of Scripture are necessary because human beings are fallible and need guidance. We have seen how Wesley uses a number of traditional rules that were widely accepted among Protestants. Other rules, such as "speaking as the oracles of God," are more nearly unique to Wesley. In addition, he was prepared to take advantage of the emerging science of textual criticism and follow its conclusions where they seemed correct to him.

In his approach to hermeneutics, Wesley was clearly in the mainstream of Protestant theology. He is not advocating anything unorthodox. However, his limitation of the Spirit's guidance to the enlightenment of human reason is a significant revision of the Reformed principle of the internal witness of the Spirit. Wesley's insistence on interpretation according to the whole Scripture is somewhat different from his contemporaries, although the difference is largely one of emphasis.

Several problems in Wesley's interpretation have been noted. The most significant of these is the problem of interpretation when the literal sense is contradictory to other texts or absurd. It appears most probable that Wesley intends to suggest an allegorical reading of Scripture as the proper interpretation of such a text. However, the only direction Wesley provides about how allegorical interpretation could properly be used is to be "sparing." When he defines allegory as "one thing expressed and another intended," he opens the door to abuse. Wesley recognizes this potential for abuse in the criticism he aims at Roman Catholics for interpreting Scripture in allegorical ways.

In Wesley's defense, it is probable that he would appeal to two limitations. First, allegory is only to be used where a literal interpretation is impossible. On Wesley's understanding, the number of such texts in Scripture is very low. It is very rare that Wesley admits there is a contradiction or absurdity that requires a different reading. Second, all interpretation is subject to the analogy of faith, and so no "strained and allegorical" interpretation could be permitted in violation of that rule. Wesley's lack of a systematic exposition of hermeneutics leaves much uncertainty regarding his views on interpretation according to the literal sense and the use of allegory. The pieces of a coherent position based on Wesley's views do exist, but it is not clear how Wesley himself would have put them together.

PART TWO

CHAPTER 5

The Function of Scripture as an Authority

Wesley's doctrine of Scripture is the first component of a balanced understanding of his relationship to the Bible. The second component, how he actually uses the Bible, is necessary for a complete view of the matter. What a theologian says about Scripture may or may not be in harmony with what he or she actually does with Scripture. Under this heading, there is a functional analogue to each of the main sections in our treatment of Wesley's doctrine of Scripture. With regard to the authority of Scripture, we will ask about how Scripture actually authorizes his conclusions. For the rules of interpretation, we will ask if Wesley actually interprets Scripture according to those rules, or if there were others that he tacitly employs. It should be noted, however, that in this case our conclusions are based on a representative sample of Wesley's writings (including twenty-five sermons, four books from the *Notes*, and two of his polemical writings), not on the entire corpus of his works.[1]

The Authority of Scripture

Even the casual reader of Wesley's sermons cannot help noticing the abundance of scriptural references intermixed in almost every section. This was evident with the older editions of his works, but the footnotes in the Bicentennial Edition have made it even more obvious. The sheer quantity of scriptural references indicates that the Bible plays an important role in Wesley's thinking and in the presentation of his message. But it is not always clear what Wesley intends by his use of scriptural phrases, which appear in his published works in three different ways.

First, scriptural quotations are sometimes explicit. There is no doubt that Wesley is quoting Scripture and no doubt in the reader's mind that the phrase comes from the Bible. Sometimes, Wesley employs references in his text to indicate where the quotation came from.[2] Such instances are rare, however, and usually come in places where he is seeking to drive home a point in a closely reasoned argument. Much more frequently he introduces a quotation with words such as "thus is the Scripture fulfilled,"[3] "God saith,"[4] "our Lord says,"[5] "St. Peter saith,"[6] or simply with the names of Peter, Paul, John, or "the Apostle."[7] Here he is clearly marking the words as being of scriptural authority by noting their author.

Second, Wesley often sets off the words of scriptural quotations. In the original editions, the quoted words were placed in italics; in subsequent editions they were enclosed in quotation marks. This practice is by far the most frequently used way in which a scriptural quotation is placed in the text. Wesley's quotations are not always exact, but the fact that the words are distinctively marked means that the reader will realize they are special. However, Wesley also highlights in this way some phrases that are not scriptural.[8]

Third, Wesley frequently quotes Scripture without setting off the quoted words in any way. Consider the following selection from "The Means of Grace":[9]

> Without controversy, the help that is done upon earth, he doth it himself.[a] It is he alone who, by his own almighty power, worketh in us what is pleasing in his sight.[b] And all outward things, unless he work in them and by them, are mere weak and beggarly elements.[c] Whosoever therefore imagines there is any intrinsic *power* in any means whatsoever does greatly err, not knowing the Scriptures, neither the power of God.[d]

The Bicentennial Edition identifies the citations included in this passage as being from Psalms, 1 John, Galatians, and Matthew. In the immediately following passage there are five additional quotations from Scripture also not set off in any way. In such cases is Wesley consciously quoting Scripture? Would his quotations be recognized as such by his readers? If spoken, would any of his nonexplicit quotations of Scripture be heard as Scripture? Two considerations suggest that Wesley was consciously using Scripture and that his audience was aware that he was doing so, at least part of the time.

First, a theory of cultural literacy presupposes that in any given culture, the people of that culture will share certain words, phrases, and ideas as cultural landmarks.[10] There is no doubt that parts of the Bible were so well known by people in the eighteenth century that they would recognize them as biblical when they heard them. However, establishing a list of which parts of the Bible a majority of the people in eighteenth-century England would recognize is an extremely difficult, if not impossible, task. If parallels from nineteenth- and twentieth-century Americans are applicable, verses like the Ten Commandments and "Love your neighbor as yourself" would be included in any such list. It is much more doubtful that "weak and beggarly elements," used without identification in "The Means of Grace" just quoted, would be readily identified as biblical, let alone as from Galatians. As Wesley's audiences varied, their ability to recognize different verses would also vary, but any literate person in the eighteenth century would have had a significant acquaintance with the Bible. The Bible was used as a basic text in teaching people to read in the charity schools.[11] In a more traditional society, the traditional source of authority would be at least more familiar than it is today. Thus, the level of familiarity Wesley would expect from his audience would be high enough to enable his listeners and readers to appreciate a large number of his biblical references.

Second, Wesley's personal familiarity with Scripture and his commitment to holiness explain why he might have used such language even if his hearers did not understand all of it. His acquaintance with the Bible began as a young child. His mother said that the Wesley children were taught the Lord's Prayer "as soon as they could speak" and "some portions of Scripture, as their memories could bear."[12] After the Epworth rectory burned in 1709, the family began the daily custom of having the children read to each other the Psalms appointed for the day, a chapter of the New Testament and a chapter of the Old Testament.[13] Wesley was taught the Scriptures from childhood until the time he left home at age eleven. In 1725 he resolved to lead a more holy life. The Holy Club at Oxford focused on common Bible study as one of their activities.

Wesley's attempt to speak as Scripture speaks must have been deliberate. Whereas many modern readers of the paragraph just quoted would not recognize the scriptural phrases embedded in the text, one of Wesley's hearers or readers would have had a better chance at doing so. The most plausible explanation for the frequency of scriptural quotation in Wesley's writings is that he was following his own rule to "speak as the oracles of God." One of the most interesting uses for Scripture in Wesley's writings is a rapid repetition of scriptural phrases all making the same general point. Such concatenations of Scripture are found frequently in his sermons and apologetic writings. Usually, they come at the end of a sermon or a section that is trying to make a point. Consider the closing section of "Christian Perfection" (§II.30):[14]

"Having therefore these promises, dearly beloved," both in the law and in the prophets, and having the prophetic word confirmed unto us in the gospel by our blessed Lord and his apostles, "let us cleanse ourselves from all filthiness of flesh and spirit, perfecting holiness in the fear of God."[a] "Let us fear lest" so many promises "being made us of entering into his rest" (which he that hath entered into "is ceased from his own works") "any of us should come short of it."[b] "This one thing let us do: forgetting those things which are behind, and reaching forth unto those things which are before, let us press toward the mark for the prize of the high calling of God in Christ Jesus;"[c] crying unto him day and night till we also are "delivered from the bondage of corruption into the glorious liberty of the sons of God."[d]

Of 149 words in this paragraph, 104 are in scriptural phrases. A similar concatenation appears in §63 of *An Earnest Appeal*:[15]

And why should it seem a thing incredible to you who have known "the power of God unto salvation"[a]—whether he wrought thus in your soul or no (for "there are diversities of operations, but the same spirit")[b]—that "the dead should hear the voice of the Son of God,"[c] and in that moment live? Thus he useth to act, to show that when he willeth, to do is present with him. "Let there be light (said God), and there was light."[d] "He spake the word, and it was done."[e] "Thus the heavens and the earth were created, and all the hosts of them."[f] And this manner of acting in the present case highly suits both his power and love. There is therefore no hindrance on God's part, since "as his majesty is, so is his mercy."[g] And whatever hindrance there is on the part of man, when God speaketh it is not. Only ask then, O sinner, "and it shall be given thee,"[h] even the faith that brings salvation; and that without any merit or good work of thine, for it is "not of works, lest any man should boast."[i] No; it is of *grace*, of grace alone. For "unto him that worketh not, but believeth on him that justifieth the ungodly, his faith is counted to him for righteousness."[j]

Two points must be made to help us understand the large number of scriptural quotations here. First, eighteenth-century people read and heard the Bible differently from most moderns. Hans Frei, in his *Eclipse of Biblical Narrative*, has suggested that before the Enlightenment, people regarded the Bible's narrative world as normative and viewed the world of empirical experience through scriptural lenses.[16] The seeds of a new perspective had been sown in Wesley's day and the tensions that produced a modern worldview are present in his own thought. Nevertheless, for him and the majority of his hearers, short phrases could evoke a biblical worldview that does not exist for most of us. Second, these concatenations were usually used in exhortations. They were surely effective in driving home the message of the text. When such phrases were used, the authority of the Bible was evoked, and its familiarity gave them great persuasive power. Wesley may simply have found that this technique was effective and could be used to great advantage.

Given the frequency with which scriptural phrases appear in Wesley's writings, it is important to ask what they actually do there. How do they function in the content of his writing? I wish to propose five different categories into which all of his uses can be placed. These are textual, explanatory, definitional, narrative, and semantic.

First, and perhaps most obviously, Scripture often functions as the text of a sermon, or the subject of his "explanatory" notes. In other words, Scripture is the subject of the inquiry. It is the datum to be explained or understood. Each of Wesley's 151 sermons has a Scripture text at the beginning. Those texts function in different ways in the various sermons. Clearly, there are some sermons in which the text is only a stylistic convenience, required by the form of the writing but not playing a determinative role in the content.[17] The sermon "Original Sin" is not primarily an exposition of Genesis 6:5;[18] rather, it uses the text as a starting point and moves from there. But for many of the sermons, the text actually does act as the subject of the inquiry. Consider "The Witness of the Spirit, II," which begins with Romans 8:16—"The Spirit itself beareth witness with our spirit, that we are the children of God." Wesley asks, "But what is 'the witness of the Spirit'?" He then analyzes $\mu\alpha\rho\tau\nu\rho\iota\alpha$ and the meaning of the verse to understand it. Later, he argues that the text implies two witnesses, because it mentions two spirits.[19] The point here is not to understand Wesley's doctrine, but to note that, when Scripture is quoted in such a case, it functions as the subject of explanation. Much of the *Explanatory Notes upon the New Testament* really seeks to explain the text. His comments on Matthew 3:1-2, for example, seek to explain the meaning of the terms "wilderness," "Kingdom of God," and "Kingdom of heaven" and what it means for the latter to be "at hand." Even more focused is the sermon "Dives and Lazarus," where the whole sermon is an explanation of the various facets of the text. It amounts to an extended explanation of the "history" of these two biblical figures.[20] Of the seventy-three Scripture references in the sermon, forty-eight refer to the text.

Second, Scripture sometimes functions as the vehicle for explaining something else, either another passage of Scripture, or a subject that has been raised from another place. Most often this means that it serves as a warrant for a conclusion about the explicandum. A formal argument is made that something must be the case, and the reason given is a passage of Scripture. In his letter to Bishop Lavington, Wesley quotes the bishop as suggesting that Wesley defines conversion as to "start up perfect men at once." Wesley counters: "A man is usually converted long before he is a perfect man. 'Tis probable most of those Ephesians to whom St. Paul directed his epistle were converted. Yet they were not 'come (few, if any) to a perfect man; to the measure of the stature of the fullness of Christ.'"[21] Here the reference to Scripture bolsters Wesley's position that conversion and perfection are different stages in the Christian life. The quoted text functions as a warrant for the conclusion he wants to draw.

Third, Scripture serves as a sort of authoritative dictionary. Important terms in theological discussion are defined by reference to the way in which Scripture uses the term. Sometimes Scripture's use of the term suffices to settle the issue of definition. One of the most crucial definitions Wesley draws from Scripture is his definition of faith. He quotes Hebrews 11:1 for this purpose at least twelve times.[22] Typical is this passage from "The Scripture Way of Salvation": "Faith in general is defined by the Apostle, ἔλεγχος πραγμάτων οὐ βλεπομένων —'an evidence,' a divine 'evidence and conviction' (the word means both), 'of things not seen'—not visible, not perceivable either by sight or by any other of the external senses."[23] Here, as elsewhere, Wesley turns to Scripture to define his terms. Once a clear scriptural definition can be found, that often settles how the concept should be understood. Wesley was not simplistic in this usage, for he could use several scriptural texts to define the same term. For example, he could expand on the definition from Hebrews to include other concepts of faith as well:

> Faith, in general, is a divine, supernatural ἔλεγχος of things not seen, not discoverable by our bodily senses, as being either past, future or spiritual. Justifying faith implies, not only a divine ἔλεγχος that "God was in Christ, reconciling the world unto himself," but a sure trust and confidence that Christ died for *my* sins, that he "loved *me* and gave himself for *me*."[24]

The conviction of the unseen world includes the trust and confidence that Scripture elsewhere describes as faith.

Fourth, Scripture serves as a narrative storehouse, from which stories, characters, and events can be used as illustrations or allusions in his work. In *An Earnest Appeal* he writes, "And not being suffered to preach it in the usual places, we declare it wherever a door is opened, either on a mountain or plain or by a river side (for all which we conceive we have sufficient precedent), or in a prison, or as it were in the house of Justus or the school of one Tyrannus."[25] Here Wesley mentions the stories of Paul being opposed by the Jews and thus going to preach to the Gentiles in the house of Justus in Corinth, or the school of Tyrannus in Ephesus. The stories are not recounted, but merely alluded to as providing precedent for his own activity of field preaching. It should be noted that these stories were presumed to be familiar to Wesley's learned audience, and that the allusion would suffice to press his point.

Fifth, Scripture can provide the words and phrases to make a point that could easily have been made in other words without a change in meaning. This I call a semantic use of Scripture, because it is a substitution of words to take advantage of the authority associated with their source. In this case the use of scriptural words gives an added dimension that is often unstated. This is by far the most common of the functions that Scripture plays in Wesley's preaching and writing. In the sample analyzed for this study, there were a total of 2,181 scriptural references; of these, 1,664 (76 percent) were of this type. Consider Wesley's discussion of sanctification in "The Scripture Way of Salvation":[26]

> From the time of our being "born again"[a] the gradual work of sanctification takes place. We are enabled "by the Spirit" to "mortify the deeds of the body,"[b] of our evil nature. And as we are more and more dead to sin, we are more and more alive to God. We go on from grace to grace, while we are careful to "abstain from all appearance of evil,"[c] and are "zealous of good works,"[d] "as we have opportunity doing good to all men";[e] while we walk in all his ordinances blameless,[f] therein worshipping him in spirit and in truth;[g] while we take up our cross and deny ourselves[h] every pleasure that does not lead us to God.

In this example, Wesley has made a semantic use of eight different passages of Scripture. Five of these are set off with quotation marks, but three are not. None of them is introduced by a phrase that identifies the passage as Scripture. Rather, it is assumed that these are known to be such. In semantic use, Wesley employs scriptural words and phrases to make his point. The same content could be delivered in other words, but the unspoken message of scriptural authority would be missing.

This semantic use of Scripture is Wesley's single most distinctive pattern. It is neither a form of argument nor a form of narration; rather, it provides Wesley with a kind of language that evokes respect because what is being spoken consists of phrases from the Bible. It may be that we are here dealing with a kind of sanctified language for those who are in the process of sanctification.[27] While there is no direct evidence for this in Wesley's writings, it would be interesting to analyze the writings of Wesleyan converts to determine whether this use of Scripture was more characteristic of their language after their experience of justification than before that experience.

These five uses of Scripture all amount to appeals to the authority of Scripture. Each use calls on Scripture to authorize Wesley's points in different ways. The textual use is a corollary to his decision to write theological treatises in sermonic form. Scripture forms Wesley's literary starting point in each case. At times it also forms his starting point in content, as many of his sermons seek to take a particular text with utter seriousness and understand how that can be true. The explanatory use of Scripture calls on its authority to explain other Scriptures or justify conclusions. Here Wesley claims, in effect, that the Word of God is the source of our doctrine, and what it teaches is to be accepted. The definitional use of Scripture plays another role in theological argument. Terms are often used with different understandings in mind. By appealing to Scripture as the source for correct definitions, Wesley can influence the outcome of the discussion, as seen with his definition of faith. There are a number of reasons why Wesley prefers a definition of faith as a type of sense.[28] But Wesley's argument is strengthened by the fact that he can quote Hebrews 11:1 and say that it is the authoritative definition. Wesley's narrative use of Scripture, infrequent though it is, still is authoritative because he is constantly looking for scriptural and early church precedents for his actions. If the apostles had done it, then it must be permissible for the Methodists to do it as well. The authoritative aspect of the semantic use of Scripture is harder to ascertain; precisely because it is without introduction, what it seeks to do is unclear. On the assumption argued earlier that Wesley's audience would recognize these as scriptural phrases, it would seem to lend authority to what he said because these were words from the Bible.

Wesley is inviting his listeners into a different worldview. Hans Frei's point about the shift away from seeing the world through the Bible's perspective means that more men and women began to look at the Bible from a different worldview and find it strange. This use of Scripture is Wesley's resistance to this cultural trend. Albert Outler argued persuasively in his *Theology in the Wesleyan Spirit* that Wesley had one foot in secular culture, but that he "*lived* in the Scripture, and his mind ranged over the Bible's length and breadth and depth like a radar, tuned into the pertinent data on every point he cared to make."[29] Outler lifts up Wesley as an example of a Christian who was well grounded in Scripture and the Christian past, and yet was deeply engaged in the secular culture as well. Our point here is the first half of that tension, the fact that Wesley was deeply grounded in Scripture so that it is not an exaggeration to say that he lived in it. Wesley never finds the world of the Bible strange. He is so familiar with it, its words are a second language that can be woven together in concatenations that flow with powerful rhetoric. Scripture is a source of definitions, pointing toward the true meaning of words and the true nature of reality. Scripture is the defining story of all creation, and especially humankind's interaction with the creator. Frei's argument is that the modern period is a time when that quality of living in the Scripture is lost. Wesley is a bridging figure who is able to retain the ability to see the world from Scripture's point of view while remaining deeply engaged in the various secular parts of his culture that had, in many cases, already left the biblical worldview behind.

In comparison with his doctrine of Scripture, Wesley's use is consistent. He argues that Scripture should be the source and the norm for Christian teaching and practice, and we find that to be the case. Wesley quotes Scripture frequently, and uses it in five different ways to authorize his conclusions. Many times, Wesley takes extreme positions based on his understanding of "the plain sense of the text." Scripture is understood both to permit and to compel such conclusions.

The Inspiration of Scripture

There are two ways to test Wesley's doctrine of inspiration. The first is to examine instances in which he explicitly appeals to the inspired nature of the text. The second is to ask about his use of other, noninspired literary material.

The appeal to the inspiration of Scripture acts to establish or to reinforce its authority. In a letter to William Law, Wesley writes: "In matters of religion I regard no writings but the inspired. Tauler, Behmen, and an whole army of Mystic authors are with me nothing to St. Paul. In every point I appeal 'to the law and the testimony,' and value no authority but this."[30] As Wesley opposes Law's shift to a more philosophical and mystical religion, he insists that the inspired character of Scripture makes it more authoritative than any human beings. In the heat of controversy, he uses hyperbole, declaring that inspired authors are the only authorities he values.

However, two other references illustrate that Wesley sees a human side to Scripture. In the sermon "What Is Man?" Wesley says that the inspired writer of Psalm 8 left certain vital themes out of the account. He says we may cure a fear that arises while reading the psalm

> by considering what David does not appear to have taken at all into his account, namely, that the body is not the man; that man is not only a house of clay, but an immortal spirit; a spirit made in the image of God, an incorruptible picture of the God of glory; a spirit that is of infinitely more value than the whole earth; of more value than the sun, moon, and stars put together; yea, than the whole material creation.[31]

The inspired author of the psalm is understood not to have told the whole story, to have left out an important matter which could lead to misunderstanding. Wesley's note on Acts 21:20 considers the discussion about the application of the law to Gentile Christians at the Jerusalem Conference. For Wesley, it is clear that the ceremonial part of the law was abolished by the ministry of Christ. Wesley expresses astonishment that the apostles could even discuss such an obvious matter. He cannot believe that all of them, with the single exception of Paul, did not know that the Mosaic dispensation had been abolished.[32]

Taken together, these three instances illustrate Wesley's use of inspired texts. On the one hand, Wesley is adamant that the text is inspired and therefore without error. It is trustworthy and its authority derives from its inspiration. On the other hand, Wesley occasionally sees the human side of the text and acknowledges that the human channels of inspiration have some effect on it. However, it should be noted that in neither of the two latter cases does Wesley admit error in the Bible. In the first example Wesley is not saying that the psalmist was wrong, only that there are other arguments which can answer the question better. In the second example, he is astonished at the facts but does not argue with them. While the apostles may have been inspired in the writing of Scripture, they were not necessarily inspired to be correct at every stage of their doctrinal deliberations. Indeed, Wesley's picture of the purity of the early church eventually included an understanding that the mystery of evil had crept in during apostolic times. There is no error here, only some characteristics that result from the human instruments God chose to use.

How, then, does Wesley use noninspired texts? Does he quote them at all? If so does he use them in ways that are similar to his use of Scripture? Are there any differences in the ways that such material is used? In the sample on which this study of Wesley's use of Scripture is based, there are two kinds of material, in addition to Scripture, that Wesley quotes as being authoritative: the Apocrypha and secular literature.[33]

Wesley's Use of the Apocrypha

The Apocrypha consists of those books regarded as canonical Old Testament material by the Roman Catholic Church but not included in the biblical canon by Protestants or Jews. Orthodox Christians call them "Deutero-Canonical," including them as part of the Bible but placing them "on a lower footing than the rest of the Old Testament."[34] Wesley's attitude toward the Apocrypha is not easy to ascertain. The relevant evidence consists of two types: his use of Apocryphal texts, and the teachings of the Church of England, which he often defended in general. Wesley's use of the Apocrypha can be understood by reference to eleven instances that occur within the sample of works analyzed for this study.[35] In all of his sermons, there are only fifty-two such uses. Of these, thirty-five refer to the Book of Wisdom, with Wisdom 9:15 being Wesley's favorite verse in the Apocrypha. He quotes it eleven times.[36] The significance of these uses lies not in their number, but in the way in which Wesley quotes from this material.

Wesley's use of Apocryphal texts is very similar to his use of canonical texts in three respects. First, he uses Apocryphal texts in a semantic way side by side with canonical texts. Frequently there is no formal distinction to indicate they are from different types of sources. Consider §51 of *An Earnest Appeal*:[37] "Bear with me yet a little longer: my soul is distressed for you. 'The god of this world hath blinded your eyes,'[a] and you are 'seeking death in the error of your life.'"[b] Here one quotation from 2 Corinthians is used semantically and placed in quotation marks. In the same sentence the quotation from Wisdom is used in the same way and also placed in quotation marks. The uses of the two texts are identical. In another place, two texts are paired without identifying marks. In "On the Wedding Garment"[38] he writes,

From the very time that the Son of God delivered this weighty truth to the children of men, that all who had not the wedding garment would be cast into outward darkness, where are weeping and gnashing of teeth,[a] the enemy of souls has been labouring to obscure it, that they might still seek death in the error of their life,[b] and many ways has he tried to disguise the holiness without which we cannot be saved.

Here the same conclusion about identical usage must be drawn. In other instances, a passage from Ecclesiasticus is used with passages from 1 Corinthians and Ecclesiastes; Wisdom 1:12 is used with Isaiah 5:20.[39]

Second, there is one place where Wesley explicitly cites a passage from an Apocryphal text in his sermon. Of all his sermons, this one has the most references provided by Wesley himself—fifty-nine. One of these is a translation of the Greek word ἔλεγχος given in the text. All the rest refer to scriptural texts, with the exception of Wisdom 2:13-16:

The world in general were offended, "because they testified of it that the works thereof were evil" [John 7:7]. The men of pleasure were offended, not only because these men were "made," as it were, "to reprove their thoughts" ("He professeth," said they, "to have the knowledge of God; he calleth himself the child of the Lord;" "his life is not like other men's; his ways are of another fashion; he abstaineth from our ways, as from filthiness; he maketh his boast that God is his Father") [Wisdom 2:13-16]; but much more because so many of their companions were taken away and would no more "run with them to the same excess of riot" [1 Peter 4:4].[40]

Here Wesley cites an Apocryphal book in exactly the same manner as his canonical references. This raises the question whether Wesley recognized a distinction in status between canonical and apocryphal books. Albert Outler correctly remarks, "Note how casually Wesley resorts to an Apocryphal text; the line between canonical and apocryphal Scripture is by no means absolute."[41]

More light can be shed on the nature of that dividing line by considering the doctrine of the Church of England. As in many other matters of worship and doctrine, the church takes a middle position between Protestant and Catholic views of the Apocryphal books. Article VI of the Thirty-nine Articles says that "the other Books (as

Hierome saith) the Church doth read for example of life and instruction of manners; but yet doth it not apply them to establish any doctrine." In accordance with this, the "Proper Lessons to be Read at Morning and Evening Prayer on the Sundays and other Holy-days throughout the Year" includes readings from Wisdom and Ecclesiasticus. However, they are not assigned for ordinary Sundays, but only for special "Holy-days." For example, the Old Testament readings for the feast day of the Conversion of Saint Paul are Wisdom 5 and 6. In addition to these two books, "The Kalendar" includes readings from Tobit, Judith, and Baruch.[42] The Authorized Version includes the Apocrypha as an appendix, following a precedent set by the Coverdale and Geneva versions. In 1615 Archbishop Abbot "forbade any to issue the Bible without the Apocrypha, on pain of one year's imprisonment."[43] While the Puritans opposed reading the Apocrypha at all,[44] the Restoration ensured that it would be included in the printing of Bibles in England.

Thus, while they are not Scripture, Apocryphal books are used as lessons by the Church of England in the same way as scriptural books. The Apocryphal lessons appear in the list for "holy-day" readings as well as in the daily table of readings. According to Article VI, those texts are read not for doctrinal instruction but for moral example. However, it would be difficult to distinguish those different purposes when the texts are treated exactly alike in the liturgy. This may be a distinction in doctrine without any difference in practice.

Two of Wesley's editorial works will shed light on his use of the Apocrypha. While not included in the sample analyzed for Part 2 of this study, Wesley's practice in these two cases is significant. The "Sunday Service," his revision of *The Book of Common Prayer* for the American Methodists, reproduces Article VI with the omission of the section on the Apocrypha. Further, Wesley omits the list of "Holy-days" and "The Kalendar" from the American lectionary and thus excludes all of the readings from the Apocrypha. This editorial work does not provide sufficient grounds for firm conclusions about Wesley's view of the Apocrypha. He could have eliminated these tables for any number of reasons, only one of which would have been a rejection of the Apocrypha even for "example of life and instruction of manners."

The second such work is Wesley's 1746 *Lessons for Children*. In this book, Wesley has abridged many parts of the Old Testament and divided them into short lessons. In the Preface he says,

> I have endeavoured in the following Lessons to select the Plainest and the most Useful Portions of Scripture; such as Children may the most easily understand, and such as it most concerns them to know. These are set down in the same Order, and (generally) the same Words, wherein they are delivered by the Spirit of God.[45]

His *Journal* for December 8, 1746, refers to this work as "consisting of the most practical Scriptures."[46] In Part IV, lessons 52-61 are taken from Wisdom and lessons 61-82 from Ecclesiasticus. In no other place in the Wesley corpus does Wesley specifically label a body of quotations from Apocryphal books as Scripture. Here he clearly does. The Preface refers to all of the lessons, including those from the two Apocryphal books, as Scripture delivered by the Spirit of God. They are called "Words of Eternal Life." There are no formal marks to distinguish these lessons from those taken from canonical books. In short, this book is a clear statement that Wesley viewed the Apocrypha as part of Scripture.

In subscribing and frequently appealing to the Thirty-nine Articles and *Book of Common Prayer*, Wesley presumably supported the secondary status for the Apocrypha. All eleven of the Apocryphal texts cited by Wesley appear in the table of "Proper Lessons" or "Kalendar." It would appear that in his treatment of Apocryphal texts, Wesley was following the teaching and practice of the Church of England. There was no formal difference in his treatment of scriptural and Apocryphal texts, and yet Wesley could argue that the latter were used not for doctrinal purposes but "for example of life and instruction of manners."

Wesley might argue that these lessons, professedly written for use with children, are a prime example of using the Apocrypha in that way. However, in all of his other writings, Wesley's use of the Apocrypha is also indistinguishable from his use of Scripture. Outler's assessment that Wesley "casually" resorts to an Apocryphal text is an understatement. Wesley occasionally treats the Apocrypha as Scripture.

Wesley's Use of Secular Literature

Wesley also uses quotations from secular literature in a semantic manner. In the sample of material we are considering, there are fifty quotations from such sources; thirty of these are from seventeenth- and eighteenth-century English sources such as John Milton and Alexander Pope, and twenty are from classical sources such as Virgil, Horace, and Plato.[47] These should be considered in three categories.

First, there are those uses of literary sources that are semantic in the same way that his use of Scripture is semantic. These quotations are without specific attribution and easily fit in the flow of the text. It would be possible to say the same thing in different words without having used the quotation at all. For example, in "The Great Assize" Wesley quotes Milton in this way: "And, indeed, if the whole lives of all the children of men were not manifestly discovered, the whole amazing contexture of divine providence could not be manifested; nor should we yet be able in a thousand instances to 'justify the ways of God to man.'"[48] In another example, Wesley makes the same use of literary sources, but instead of setting them off with quotation marks he indents them in the text. Wesley is even capable of giving the quotation in Latin or Greek, sometimes without translation.

> While not the fabled Rhadamanthus, but the Lord God Almighty, who knoweth all things in heaven and earth,
>> *Castigatque, auditque dolos; subigitque fateri*
>> *Quae quis apud superos, furto laetatus inani,*
>> *Distulit in seram commissa piacula mortem.*[49]

Both of these quotations fit the semantic type of usage. They flow naturally into the sentence Wesley is writing and are used without attribution. In "The Great Assize," he quotes Milton in a way that is formally indistinguishable from his scriptural quotations. For some, the familiarity of Milton and the religious content of *Paradise Lost* would make it hard to tell if the passage is scriptural or not.

Second, Wesley sometimes quotes literary material with attribution. In *An Earnest Appeal*, he quotes Suetonius: "If a day passes without doing good, may one not well say with Titus: 'Amici, diem perdidi?'"[50] Here Wesley is using a literary text of which he approves to make a point. In a similar way, he uses two lines he attributes to

Hesiod to show that even a pagan can sometimes see the truth. In "The Case of Reason Impartially Considered," he writes,

> Hence many hundred years before our Lord was born, the Greek poet uttered that great truth,
>> Millions of spiritual creatures walk the earth
>> Unseen, whether we wake, or if we sleep.[51]

Here Wesley has offered a literary quotation as evidence in his argument that while reason can produce "a shadowy persuasion of a spiritual world," yet it is far from the clear knowledge given by the Scriptures. The same text from Milton (who is quoting Hesiod) is used in *An Earnest Appeal* where Wesley uses it as evidence to support a different claim, that even a heathen like Hesiod can know that there is a spiritual world, and yet suggest that Wesley's audience does not know much about it.[52] In both places this text is used as a warrant in an argument not that there is a spiritual world, but that others believe it to be the case.

Third, Wesley sometimes uses literary material in a negative manner, attributing a quotation to someone only to deny its truth. Several times he quotes someone as giving a position held by his opponents, and either by association or by argument tears it down. In his sermon "Original Sin," he talks about "the pride of life" as a sin and says that men love honor. He continues:[53]

> Yea, eminent Christians, so called, make no difficulty of adopting the saying of the old, vain heathen, *Animi dissoluti est et nequam negligere quid de se homines sentiant:*[a] "Not to regard what men think of us is the mark of a wicked and abandoned mind." So that to go calm and unmoved "through honour and dishonour, through evil report and good report,"[b] is with them a sign of one that is indeed "not fit to live; away with such a fellow from the earth."[c] But would one imagine that these men had ever heard of Jesus Christ or his apostles?

In this passage Wesley introduces the quotation from Cicero and opposes it in three ways. First, it is attributed to the "vain heathen" in the middle of a discussion about the sin of pride. This already suggests that what follows is not exemplary. Second, it is immediately countered with a Scripture passage which suggests that one should do the opposite. The third method is sarcasm wherein Wesley suggests complete ignorance of the gospel.

One similarity and two differences can be noted between Wesley's use of Scripture and his use of literary material. The similarity is that Wesley uses literary material semantically and without attribution, just as he does Scripture. Although one might be tempted to describe his use of Scripture as "authoritative" and his use of literary texts "illustrative," there are no formal grounds for doing so. This distinction might require us to say that when Wesley is using Scripture semantically, he is doing no more than illustrating his text with familiar and moving words.

However, the source of the words is an important factor that adds to whatever formal characteristics can be noted. Milton's *Paradise Lost* is quoted approvingly many times, and never used in a negative way. Wesley's intent with regard to the text must be separated from its perception by his audience. Whereas an educated audience might recognize the difference between a quotation from Milton and one from Romans, many of his hearers presumably would not.

There is a significant difference in the quantity of material used. Scripture quotations permeate Wesley's writings so that few pages lack at least one citation. On the other hand, there are entire sermons where literary material is absent. Another difference is that Wesley quotes literary material in a negative light with Scripture in order to oppose it. In such cases, the interpretation of Scripture need not be argued against the literary material, but simply be stated to contradict it. In contrast, when scriptural passages are used in counterpoint to each other, the conflict raises a problem and the interpretation needs to be argued.

Wesley's Use of Inspired Writings

What does this consideration of Wesley's use of Apocryphal and literary texts say about Wesley's doctrine of inspiration? The most important conclusion is that Wesley's use of authoritative texts is significantly more flexible than his doctrine. His willingness to quote from Apocryphal and literary sources in a manner parallel to his use of Scripture suggests that these books are to be highly valued and used. Wesley found religious truth in many places—not only in Christian literature like that of Milton but also in that of enlightened pagans such as Virgil. His frequent use of this illustrative material is an attempt to communicate his message by using whatever helps are available.

Another conclusion tempers the importance of these nonscriptural sources. The position of the Church of England's Article VI on the use of the Apocrypha helps explain Wesley's practice here. He never uses noncanonical material in a formal argument. Rather, all his references are semantic; they fit the description in Article VI of "example of life and instruction of manners." While his use of Wisdom and Ecclesiasticus in *Lessons for Children* crosses the boundary and labels these books Scripture, Wesley could still argue that he is only following Article VI. However, his practice has blurred the line that his conception drew quite clearly.

The Infallibility of Scripture

The test of a doctrine of infallibility lies in whether any errors in Scripture are admitted to exist, and, if not, how the many "problem" texts are handled. Such texts have been obvious to every serious commentator on Scripture, and have received a variety of solutions down through the centuries. Wesley rarely admits that there even are such problem texts in Scripture. There are only two places within our sample where he recognizes problems and comes close to admitting the presence of error. In his comment on Matthew 1:1, Wesley mentions the problem of differences in the genealogies given in Matthew and Luke:

> If there were any difficulties in this genealogy, or that given by St. Luke, which could not easily be removed, they would rather affect the Jewish Tables, than the credit of the Evangelists: for they act only as historians, setting down these genealogies, as they stood in those public and allowed records. Therefore they were to take them as they found them. Nor was it needful they should correct the mistakes, if there were any. For these accounts sufficiently answer the end for which they are recited. They unquestionably prove the grand point in view, that Jesus was of the family from which the promised Seed was to come. And they had more weight with the Jews for this purpose, than if alterations had been made by inspiration itself. For such alterations would have occasioned endless disputes between them and the disciples of our Lord.[54]

Three points are significant about this comment. First, Wesley never admits there is error in the text. He says, "If there were any difficulties" and "if there were any" mistakes. Never does Wesley admit that those difficulties actually exist. Second, he goes on to explain why such mistakes could still exist in an inspired text. Inspiration could have corrected these mistakes, but such correction was unnecessary. The purposes for which the Gospels were written were better served by simply transmitting the records, even with their flaws, so that needless disputes with the Jews could be avoided. The writers of the Gospels did not make the mistake; rather, they were forced to repeat commonly believed mistakes in order to persuade their audience. Thus, an incorrect statement is not necessarily an error, which would indicate a lack of divine inspiration. Third, Wesley as usual has in mind "the grand point" and does not want to be bothered with trivial details. He is concerned that Jesus really was from the family mentioned in the prophecies, and as long as the texts succeed in establishing that point, "trivial" inconsistencies are to be left alone.

The other place where Wesley finds a significant problem with Scripture comes in the sermon "Free Grace." In this sermon Wesley is at some pains to counter those Calvinist evangelicals who preached predestination, notably George Whitefield. The sermon is sharply polemical in tone and seeks to counter his opponents first by eliminating the possibility of any middle ground, what Wesley refers to as "the election of grace."[55] He then makes seven arguments against the doctrine of double predestination. While four of these are based on experience, for example, the tendencies of the doctrine to destroy holiness, two of them clearly refer to the interpretation of Scripture. One argument says that the doctrine makes Scripture contradict itself. In this part Wesley lists numerous biblical texts presumed to favor his opponents, and then gives his own text with the statement that this represents the whole message of the Bible:[56]

For instance: the asserters of this doctrine interpret that text of Scripture, "Jacob have I loved, but Esau have I hated,"[a] as implying that God in a literal sense hated Esau and all the reprobated from eternity. Now what can possibly be a more flat contradiction than this, not only to the whole scope and tenor of Scripture, but also to all those particular texts which expressly declare, "God is love"?[b]

Wesley repeats this pattern several times, arguing that the doctrine is blasphemous because it destroys the attributes of God. Then he makes a crucial point about the interpretation of Scripture:[57]

> You represent God as worse than the devil—more false, more cruel, more unjust. But you say you will "prove it by Scripture." Hold! What will you prove by Scripture? That God is worse than the devil? It cannot be. Whatever that Scripture proves, it never can prove this. Whatever its true meaning be, this cannot be its true meaning. Do you ask, "What is its true meaning, then?" If I say, "I know not," you have gained nothing. For there are many Scriptures the true sense whereof neither you nor I shall know till death is swallowed up in victory.[a] But this I know, better it were to say it had no sense at all than to say it had such a sense as this. It cannot mean, whatever it mean besides, that the God of truth is a liar. Let it mean what it will, it cannot mean that the Judge of all the world is unjust. No Scripture can mean that God is not love, or that his mercy is not over all his works.[b] That is, whatever it prove beside, no Scripture can prove predestination.

Wesley clearly prefers admitting that a particular text has an unknown meaning to accepting its literal sense, if that sense implies predestination. But note that there is no discussion of error here. He does not say that the text from Malachi quoted in Romans is wrong, that God really did love Esau and the prophet somehow got it wrong. Rather, he suggests that we simply don't know what the prophet meant and will not know until the end of time.

The conclusion to be drawn from all this is that Wesley will not admit error in the text under any circumstances. He prefers meaninglessness to a meaning that acknowledges a contradiction within the Bible. In actuality, however, Wesley never claims a text is meaningless. In cases where the literal sense causes a contradiction, a different interpretation is to be sought within the framework of the whole Scripture. Wesley's point with regard to predestination is that the whole Bible's view of God's grace must determine the meaning of any particular verse.

The Sufficiency of Scripture

With regard to Scripture's sufficiency, two patterns indicate that Wesley's use is in accordance with his doctrine. The first is that Wesley frequently bases a doctrinal position on the "plain word" of

Scripture without regard to other factors at all. His controversial doctrine of the witness of the Spirit has as its chief argument "the plain, natural meaning of the text, 'The Spirit itself beareth witness with our spirit, that we are the children of God.'"[58] The rest of "The Witness of the Spirit, II" is an attempt by Wesley to rebut all who would explain away the clear implication that God's Spirit gives us the assurance we are children of God. The same is true for his doctrine of Christian perfection. Here Wesley seeks to take seriously texts like 1 John 3:9: "Whosoever is born of God doth not commit sin."[59] In each case other arguments are made, and reason, experience, Christian antiquity, and the Church of England are brought in to support the position. But when Scripture is clear, he will often rely on only its authority.

Wesley's conception was seen to assume that the sufficiency of Scripture applies only to matters of faith and practice. He is not prepared to quote Scripture to contradict the conclusions of science. He regards that as reason's sphere and reinterprets Scripture under the category of accommodation. Nowhere in the sample of material analyzed does Wesley use Scripture outside the subjects of faith and practice. Further, if a doctrine is understood to be speculative rather than practical, Scripture might be sufficient only for what human beings need to know for salvation, not in all details. Wesley's hesitation to specify an ontological doctrine of the Trinity is characteristic of this.

The Clarity of Scripture

With regard to the clarity of Scripture, Wesley's use demonstrates harmony with his conception. For the most part, Wesley interprets the Scriptures as though they are clear in their essential points. At points, the Bible is so clear that one passage suffices to establish a doctrine. This is a corollary to his belief in the "plain, natural meaning of the text" which he finds so often. In "The Means of Grace" he notes that God's commands are "express." Wesley argues that the channels of God's grace are expressed in the "plainest manner"[60] and that the only problem lies in following them.[61] He uses adjectives like "clear," "plain," "peremptory," "explicit," and "evident" throughout this sermon.

For Wesley, the clarity of Scripture is related to the literal sense of the text. For him, interpreting the literal sense is a matter of *simply* reading it and understanding what it says. Scripture is perspicuous, the literal sense renders its meaning, and one only need read it to find its true meaning. This point will be examined in greater detail in chapter 7 when considering Wesley's interpretation according to the literal sense of the text. However, Wesley acknowledges places where the Bible is not clear on important points. The verses mentioned in the foregoing discussion based on "Free Grace" are places where the literal sense of an individual verse was contradictory to the whole tenor of Scripture. But Wesley's conviction is that though each text of Scripture is not always clear, the general tenor of Scripture is.

The Wholeness of Scripture

We have seen that Wesley's conception calls for the unclear parts of Scripture to be interpreted with reference to the whole Bible. Indeed, every verse is to be interpreted according to the "analogy of faith." This conception should be tested against his use of Scripture and whether or not he actually does what he says.

In several places Wesley appeals to parts of the Bible as compendia of the whole that clearly reflect Scripture's general tenor. He speaks of three different passages in this way: the Sermon on the Mount, 1 John, and 1 Corinthians 13. In the *Journal* for October 17, 1771, he writes, "About ten, I preached at Oxford, in a room well filled with deeply attentive hearers, on part of the Sermon on the Mount, the noblest compendium of religion which is to be found even in the oracles of God."[62] A year later, on November 9, 1772, he writes, "I began to expound (chiefly in the mornings, as I did some years ago) that compendium of all the Holy Scriptures, the first Epistle of St. John."[63] Twice he refers to the thirteenth chapter of 1 Corinthians as summarizing the whole Bible.[64] Again, in his 1749 letter to Conyers Middleton, he refers to Christianity as a type of character, which is given "in miniature more than once; particularly in the thirteenth chapter of the former Epistles to the Corinthians, and in that discourse which St. Matthew records as delivered by our Lord at his entrance upon his public ministry."[65]

In each of these instances, Wesley appeals to a part of the Bible as containing the essence of the whole. The Sermon on the Mount was interpreted by Wesley as "teaching us the true way to life everlasting, the royal way which leads to the kingdom."[66] First John has its aim "to confirm the happy and holy communion of the faithful with God and Christ, by describing the marks of that blessed state."[67] Wesley describes 1 Corinthians 13 as talking about the necessity, nature, properties, and duration of love. These three portions of Scripture have in common a focus on soteriology, as Wesley's conception of Scripture would indicate. But it is a particular part of salvation—"inward and outward holiness"—on which each of them focuses. This raises the question of whether Wesley's use of Scripture indicates a functional canon within the canon that guides his hermeneutics. Granted that Wesley's conception of Scripture sees its wholeness as constituted by the entire analogy of faith, it is important to ask whether one or more aspects of that doctrinal pattern are really the most important touchstone for what Scripture is all about. We will return to that question after considering other aspects of how the wholeness of Scripture functions for Wesley.

A second usage of Scripture relevant to the concept of the wholeness of Scripture is Wesley's interpretation to avoid contradiction. In the sermon "Christian Perfection" he takes great care in exegeting 1 John 3:8-9 and 5:18, which both refer to those born of God not sinning.[68] He later raises the specific question:

> "But does not St. James directly contradict this? His words are, 'In many things we offend all.' [chap. 3, v. 2] And is not *offending* the same as *committing sin?*" In this place I allow it is. I allow *the persons here spoken of* did commit sin; yea, that they *all* committed *many* sins. But who are "the persons here spoken of"? Why, those "many masters" or "teachers" whom God had not sent (probably the same "vain men" who taught that "faith without works" which is so sharply reproved in the preceding chapter); not the Apostle himself, nor any real Christian.[69]

Thus, Wesley makes a great effort to demonstrate that the Scripture is consistent on this important point. In response to arguments that John contradicts himself, he then undertakes to "reconcile St. John with himself" and finally concludes, "St. John therefore is well consistent with himself, as well as with the other holy writers; . . . In conformity therefore both to the doctrine of St. John, and to the whole tenor of the New Testament, we fix this conclusion: 'A Christian is so far perfect as not to commit sin.'"[70] Wesley is familiar with the many arguments about the possibility of perfection. He knows that others have interpreted different parts of Scripture as being contradictory on this point. But he does not allow the apparent contradictions to stand. Rather, he takes great pains to show that they are not really contradictions.

Another way to explore Wesley's use of Scripture with regard to its wholeness is by reviewing his wide-ranging use of texts from all parts of the Bible. The most significant evidence on this score comes in two different patterns of quotation in which he mixes different books and testaments. The first pattern is evident in concatenations of scriptural quotations which draw on a variety of different books to make the same point. One of the most extended of these comes in the sermon "Catholic Spirit." In §§I.12-18, Wesley is answering the question, "What is properly implied" by "Is thine heart right, as my heart is with thy heart?" In less than three pages of text he quotes Scripture thirty-eight times, from the following places:

Hebrews 1:3	Mark 12:30	Psalms 2:11
2 Corinthians 5:7	Luke 1:46-47	Psalms 2:11
2 Corinthians 4:18	1 Thessalonians 5:18	Isaiah 3:8
Romans 9:5	Psalms 147:1	Psalms 119:104
Galatians 1:16	Matthew 6:20	Acts 24:16
1 Corinthians 2:2	Philippians 3:8	Leviticus 19:18
John 6:56	Galatians 6:14	Luke 6:32
Galatians 4:19	Colossians 3:3	Matthew 5:44
Romans 10:3	John 6:38	Romans 9:3
Romans 3:22	Matthew 7:21	Matthew 5:44
Philippians 3:9	Matthew 6:22	Galatians 6:10
1 Timothy 6:12	Hebrews 12:2	2 Kings 10:15
Galatians 5:6	Colossians 3:17	

Within seven paragraphs, then, there are thirty-eight different quotations from seventeen different books of the Bible. Seven are from the Old Testament, eighteen from Pauline books, eleven from the Gospels and Acts, and two from Hebrews. They all serve to describe a heart that is right with God.[71] While nowhere else in the Wesley corpus can such a long string of quotations be found, there are many occasions where texts from different books and both testaments are put together to make the same point. Wesley is able to do this only because he understands Scripture to be whole.

The second pattern is evident in Wesley's ability to use a text from one part of the Bible to explain or interpret a text from another part. He feels fully justified in amplifying and thus interpreting 1 John 2:12 with Pauline material in his sermon "Christian Perfection":

> And accordingly St. John, in his first Epistle [chap. 2, v. 12, etc.], applies himself severally to those he terms little children, those he styles young men, and those whom he entitles fathers. "I write unto you, little children," saith the Apostle, "because your sins are forgiven you;" because thus far ye have attained, being "justified freely,"[a] you "have peace with God, through Jesus Christ."[b] . . . "I write unto you, fathers, because ye have known him that is from the beginning." Ye have known both the Father and the Son and the Spirit of Christ in your inmost soul. Ye are "perfect men, being grown up to the measure of the stature of the fullness of Christ."[c][72]

And yet the wholeness of Scripture is modified by his understanding of dispensations within Scripture. The Scripture is not one simple story. It is complex, composed of distinct sections to which different levels of authority belong.

His refusal to allow objections to his doctrine of Christian perfection from Old Testament examples is significant. In the sermon "Christian Perfection," Wesley acknowledges that Abraham, David, and others favored by God committed sins. However, he quotes Matthew 11:11, which says, "Among them that are born of women there hath not risen a greater than John the Baptist: notwithstanding he that is least in the kingdom of heaven is greater than he." Wesley goes on to argue that "kingdom of heaven" refers to true believers on earth, and that any one of these is greater than any of the prophets who have gone before, that is,

> greater in the grace of God and the knowledge of our Lord Jesus Christ. Therefore we cannot measure the privileges of real Christians by those formerly given to the Jews. "Their ministration" (or dispensation) we allow "was glorious"; but ours "exceeds in glory."[a] So that whosoever would bring down the Christian dispensation to the Jewish standard, whosoever gleans up the examples of weakness recorded in the law and the prophets, and thence infers that they who have "put on Christ"[b] are endued with no greater strength, doth "greatly err, neither knowing the Scriptures nor the power of God."[c][73]

Here there is evidence of a modification of the simple wholeness to which he sometimes appeals. While Wesley often affirms that various doctrines conform to the "whole tenor of Scripture," it is clear that perfection is something that belongs only to the Christian dispensation. "That this great salvation from sin was not given till Jesus was glorified St. Peter also plainly testifies." Wesley then concludes, "If therefore you would prove that the Apostle's words, 'He that is born of God sinneth not,'[a] are not to be understood according to their plain, natural, obvious meaning, it is from the New Testament you are to bring your proofs."[74]

This ambivalence about the Old Testament in relation to the New directly reflects Wesley's conception of this matter. Wesley wants to stress that the New Testament is a fulfillment of the Old, without being tied to the restrictions perceived to go along with the Jewish Scriptures. This ambivalence is also supported by a statistical analysis of the index to Wesley's Sermons.[75] According to this index, Wesley quotes from every book of the Bible except Ruth, Obadiah, and 3 John. Matthew is his favorite book, quoted 947 times.[76] It is closely followed by Romans with 907, and then Psalms with 750.[77] In total, Wesley cites the New Testament 7,635 and the Old Testament 2,455 times. Of the twenty books quoted most frequently, only three, Psalms, Isaiah, and Genesis, are from the Old Testament. Wesley's nine most quoted verses, as given in his own translation, are as follows:

1. *Philippians 2:5*—52 times:
"Let this mind be in you, which was also in Christ Jesus."
2. *Romans 5:5*—49 times:
"The love of God is shed abroad in our hearts by the Holy Ghost which is given unto us."
3. *Romans 8:16*—45 times:
"The same Spirit beareth witness with our spirits, that we are the children of God."
4. *1 John 2:16*—44 times:
"For all that is in the world, the desire of the flesh, and the desire of the eye, and the pride of life, is not of the Father, but is of the world."
5. *Galatians 2:20*—41 times:
"I am crucified with Christ: and I live no longer, but Christ liveth

in me: and the life that I now live in the flesh I live by faith in the Son of God, who loved me and delivered up himself for me."

6. *Galatians 6:10*—33 times:

"Therefore, as we have opportunity, let us do good unto all men; but especially to them who are of the household of faith."

7. *Romans 14:17*—32 times:

"For the kingdom of God is not meat and drink; but righteousness, and peace, and joy in the Holy Ghost."

8. *Hebrews 12:14*—30 times:

"Follow peace with all men, and holiness, without which no man shall see the Lord."

9. *Hebrews 12:1*—29 times:

"Wherefore let us also, being encompassed with so great a cloud of witnesses, lay aside every weight, and the sin which easily besetteth *us;* and run with patience the race that is set before us."

Three conclusions can be drawn from these statistics. First, Wesley truly does believe in the wholeness of the Bible. The fact that he quotes from 63 of the 66 books is highly significant. Few theologians can claim such a constant use of Scripture and one that is as widespread as that of Wesley. He is using the *whole* of Scripture.[78] Second, within that whole there is a marked preference for New Testament texts over Old Testament ones. In the bulk, his quotations of the New Testament are better than three times the number of his Old Testament quotations. None of his favorite passages is from the Old Testament. Psalm 145:9 (God's mercy is over all his works) and Genesis 1:27 (the image of God) are his two favorite texts from the Old Testament, but they are used only eighteen and seventeen times respectively. Third, Wesley's favorite passages of Scripture are those related to different aspects of his doctrine of salvation. When Wesley claims that the wholeness of Scripture consists in the "grand scheme of doctrine" concerning salvation, he then proceeds to concentrate his use of Scripture on passages most directly related to that doctrine. Of the nine most quoted passages just listed, all fit easily under the categories of sin, justification, assurance, new birth, and sanctification. More specifically, seven of the nine passages (nos. 1, 2, 4, 6, 7, 8, and 9) are directly related to the doctrine of sanctification rather than sin or justification.

Wesley's conception of Scripture constantly insists upon the wholeness and unity of the Bible. The analogy of faith is the starting and ending point of one's interpretation of Scripture, because it is in the light of that "grand scheme of doctrine" that the real message of the whole text is made clear. Whereas Wesley's conception of Scripture would argue that all three parts of the analogy of faith are an inseparable unity, his use of Scripture points a different direction. Soteriology is the main guide to interpretation, but it is the passages relating to Christian perfection and holiness that serve as Wesley's canon within the canon.[79]

That Wesley had a functional canon within the canon is the inescapable conclusion of this analysis of how the wholeness of Scripture actually operates in his works. Three points already outlined in this chapter require this conclusion. First, all the passages which summarize the Scriptures are passages describing God's commandments for holiness. The Sermon on the Mount, 1 John, and 1 Corinthians 13 all describe the character of humanity as God expects it to be. These are not passages which tell the story of God's activity in the world. Nor do they relate directly to sin, repentance, and forgiveness. They do not even describe faith and the internal gift of trust or confidence in God. Broadly speaking, they do describe Christian character and behavior, which Wesley often summarized as "inward and outward holiness." Second, the sharpest distinctions between the Old and New Testaments are seen in the doctrine of perfection. One of the primary functions of Wesley's dispensational understanding of the two testaments is to preclude Old Testament arguments against the possibility of perfection in this life. Even the view that only the ceremonial law has been abolished is an important part of how the doctrine of perfection is construed. Third, the statistical analysis of Wesley's pattern of quotations reveals a strong reliance on passages related to holiness. Of the nine most quoted verses listed here, all but two describe or command the perfection that is love. The witness of the Spirit in Romans 8:16 and Christ living in us in Galatians 2:20 are the only two of the nine that do not precisely fit this pattern.

There is no way one or more texts as a group can exhaustively serve as Wesley's "canon within the canon." His doctrine of the wholeness of Scripture precludes any one verse or verses serving that function in an explicit way. Indeed, if asked if he had such a list of verses at the determinative center he would answer in the negative. However, our analysis of his actual use of Scripture shows that verses most directly related to holiness are the most important ones for him. In addition, any such list of key texts would have to be a selection of verses he quotes frequently, sorted according to subject matter. Differentiation according to subject matter is inevitably blurred because of the nature of the scriptural material. Certain verses, such as Philippians 2:5—"Let this mind be in you, which was also in Christ Jesus"—are obviously related to holiness, when others such as Galatians 2:20—"I am crucified with Christ: and I live no longer, but Christ liveth in me: and the life that I now live in the flesh I live by faith in the Son of God, who loved me and delivered up himself for me"—could be construed in the same way only with some careful interpretative decisions. When Wesley uses Galatians 2:20, it is obviously a text enforcing the goal of holiness. In other theologians' writings, it may function in a different way. It is clear that Wesley's use of Scripture treats the human love of God and love of neighbor as the central theme to which all other interpretation must refer.

This is not inconsistent with his doctrine of salvation, because even there it is holiness that takes center place. Real religion is described in terms of the doctrine of holiness. Salvation is by God's grace and comes through human faith, but the whole point of God's activity is the healing of the human soul and the restoration of humanity as nearly as possible to God's original creation. For Wesley, real religion is "a restoration of man, by him that bruises the serpent's head, to all that the old serpent deprived him of; a restoration not only to the favour, but likewise to the image of God; implying not barely deliverance from sin but the being filled with the fullness of God."[80] When he talks about the religion of the Bible, he repeatedly says it is "no other than love: the love of God and of all mankind."[81]

Conclusion

This analysis of Wesley's use of Scripture as an authority has shown it to be largely congruent with his conception. Wesley does indeed treat Scripture as the authority behind his teachings. He frequently appeals to it in formal arguments and in semantic uses that appear to be primarily illustrative. His frequent citation of

Scripture shows he is immersed in a world that is defined by scriptural phrases and terminology. Hans Frei's observation about persons viewing the world through the framework of biblical narrative is true for Wesley. His intent to "speak as the oracles of God" is correlated with a sanctified speech that uses biblical language to an extraordinary degree. This is the most distinctive aspect of Wesley's use of Scripture.

However, Wesley's use of Scripture is not as rigid as his conception would lead one to expect. While he insists on the inspiration of Scripture as the ground of its authority, we see him treating Apocryphal books in a way similar to his use of Scriptural ones. While he insists that there are no errors in the text of the Bible, we see him acknowledging the possibility that some of the apostles might have been mistaken on a key point of doctrine, and that the evangelists might have written down a mistaken genealogy for Jesus. Such human participation in the transmission of Scripture is not covered by Wesley's most forceful statements about the inspiration and infallibility of Scripture.

Further, we have discovered that the real heart of Scripture, as seen in his use of it, is the doctrine of perfection. While his conception of Scripture makes reference to the whole doctrine of salvation, it is those texts which describe what human beings ought to be like that function as the center of the text. When Wesley speaks about interpreting obscure texts in light of plain ones, the plain ones are those which talk about love and other aspects of "the mind which was also in Christ Jesus."

CHAPTER 6

The Function of Other Authorities in Relation to Scripture

In Wesley's writings, the uses of Scripture vastly outnumber uses of all other authorities put together. Specifically, in the sample we are using, excluding the *Explanatory Notes upon the New Testament*, Wesley uses Scripture 2,181 times. Even the most liberal count of combined uses of reason, Christian antiquity, experience, and the Church of England would show no more than one hundred such instances. In addition, some of these uses of other authorities are in reality negative uses, that is, they refer to the authority only to refute it.

Reason

Wesley's own understanding of reason described it as a threefold faculty whereby the mind apprehends, makes judgments, and discourses from one judgment to another.[1] However, in analyzing Wesley's use of reason in contrast with his use of Scripture, a different set of distinctions will be employed. This is necessary because anyone who seeks to interpret Scripture, use it, and talk about what it means for daily life must use reason to do so. The orthodox Lutheran theologians of the seventeenth century referred to this as the instrumental use of reason.[2] This is different from the use of reason alone to answer questions, whether they be theological, philosophical, or what we would now call "scientific." Thus, we will examine Wesley's use of reason, first as an instrument of interpretation of Scripture, and second, as an independent source of knowledge. Third, we will examine Wesley's negative references to reason. Last, we will consider reason's independent testimony to Scripture's authority.

Reason as an Instrument of Interpretation

Wesley's use of reason to interpret Scripture falls into two broad types. First, there is the basic use of reason to define terms and make distinctions that will help him present what he believes Scripture is trying to say. Second, Wesley often uses reason to examine the implications of Scripture.

Wesley often makes use of very precise definitions and distinctions, which were frequently overlooked by his controversial opponents and ignored by his followers. For example, on the issue of salvation by faith or works, he uses two different understandings of "necessity." Wesley makes the controversial point that "faith is the condition, and the only condition, of justification."[3] He then quotes Matthew 3:8 and Isaiah 1:16-17 to say that repentance and good works are necessary for justification. Wesley must somehow resolve the apparent conflict between these two passages and the text for the sermon, Ephesians 2:8, "Ye are saved through faith." In a crucial move for his soteriology, Wesley distinguishes two senses and two degrees of necessity. Repentance and its fruits

> are not necessary in the *same sense* with faith, nor in the *same degree*. Not in the *same degree;* for those fruits are only necessary *conditionally,* if there be time and opportunity for them. Otherwise a man may be justified without them, as was the "thief" upon the cross. . . . Not in the *same sense:* for repentance and its fruits are only *remotely* necessary, necessary in order to faith; whereas faith is *immediately* and *directly* necessary to justification. It remains that faith is the only condition which is *immediately* and *proximately* necessary to justification.[4]

This is clearly a use of reason to establish the text and to interpret Scripture. By introducing "necessity" and then qualifying it in two different ways, Wesley has provided a logical framework for his interpretation. He can refer the Ephesians passage to immediate and unconditional necessity, and the passages from Isaiah and Matthew to remote and conditional necessity.

This clarifying of terms extends to theological discussion where interpretation of a particular passage is not immediately at issue. The sermon "The Means of Grace" was written to counter the influence of quietist Moravians and defend the active use of the Lord's Supper, prayer, and Bible study for receiving God's grace. Toward the end of the sermon, Wesley responds to objections:

It has been vehemently objected, thirdly, that Christ is the only means of grace. I answer, this is mere playing upon words. Explain your term, and the objection vanishes away. When we say "Prayer is a means of grace," we understand a channel through which the grace of God is conveyed. When you say, "Christ is the means of grace," you understand the sole price and purchaser of it; or, that "no man cometh unto the Father, but through him." And who denies it? But this is utterly wide of the question.[5]

Here the issue is a theological statement, but Wesley's use of reason clarifies the discussion and shows that the argument is only semantic.

Such theological distinctions are not usually of Wesley's own making. He is the inheritor of the whole Christian tradition, which has devised logical distinctions in order to understand and to preach the Christian faith. Wesley's use of reason is often the willingness to make use of such distinctions to clarify his points. In his comment on Romans 3:20, he makes use of the distinction made between the moral and ceremonial aspects of the Old Testament law. He writes,

No flesh shall be justified—None shall be forgiven and accepted of God. *By the works of the law*—On this ground, that he hath kept the law. St. Paul means chiefly the moral part of it, verses 9, 19, ii. 21, etc., 26, which alone is not abolished, verse 31. And it is not without reason, that he so often mentions the works of the law, whether ceremonial or moral; for it was on these only the Jews relied, being wholly ignorant of those that spring from faith.[6]

Within the Old Testament there is no concept of a distinction within the law between ceremonial and moral parts of the law. Even the New Testament does not make an explicit distinction between different sections of the law. Acts 15 does acknowledge the binding character of some Old Testament laws while denying that Christians are required to follow others. But Wesley's interpretation of the Old Testament requires a distinction between the parts of the law that are no longer binding on Christians and the parts that are. So he relies on a logical distinction between two types. A similar distinction is the one between imputed and imparted righteousness, which Wesley uses to distinguish the ways in which Christ makes us holy before God.[7]

In a second use of reason for interpretation, Wesley is often prepared to use reason to determine the implications of Scripture. Going beyond simple definition or distinction, Wesley can argue that a particular interpretation must be true. For example, the "royal law of heaven and earth" is "Thou shalt love the Lord thy God with all thy heart, and with all thy soul, and with all thy mind, and with all thy strength." He then reasons,

> Not that this forbids us to love anything besides God: it implies that we "love our brother also." Nor yet does it forbid us (as some have strangely imagined) to take pleasure in anything but God. To suppose this is to suppose the fountain of holiness is directly the author of sin, since he has inseparably annexed pleasure to the use of those creatures which are necessary to sustain the life he has given us. This therefore can never be the meaning of his command.[8]

Here Wesley uses a *reductio ad absurdam* argument whose conclusion is that an interpretation which prohibits loving other things makes God the author of sin. Such a conclusion is impossible, so the original premise must be wrong.

In another example, Wesley reasons that certain forms of baptism were used by John the Baptist. He makes the point in his comment on Matthew 3:6.

> Such prodigious numbers could hardly be baptized by immerging their whole bodies under water: nor can we think they were provided with change of raiment for it, which was scarce practicable for such vast multitudes. And yet they could not be immerged naked with modesty, nor in their wearing apparel with safety. It seems, therefore, that they stood in ranks on the edge of the river; and that John, passing along before them, cast water on their heads or faces; by which means he might baptize many thousands in a day.[9]

In the notoriously complex arguments about whether Scripture mandates immersion as the correct form of baptism, Wesley here employs an argument based on the single phrase, "Then went out to him Jerusalem, and all Judea, and all the region round about Jordan, and were baptized of him in Jordan, confessing their sins." He draws logical inferences from the verse and its historical context, and arrives at a conclusion.

In the opposite direction, Wesley sometimes resolves conflicts between Scriptures by easing the implications of a particular text. In "Christian Perfection" he writes,

> Well; suppose both Peter and Paul did then commit sin. What is it you would infer from hence? That *all the other apostles* committed sin sometimes? There is no shadow of proof in this. Or would you thence infer that *all the other Christians* of the apostolic age committed sin? Worse and worse. This is such an inference as one would imagine a man in his senses could never have thought of. Or will you argue thus?—"If two of the apostles did once commit sin, then *all other Christians, in all ages,* do, and will commit sin as long as they live." Alas, my brother! a child of common understanding would be ashamed of such reasoning as this.[10]

Wesley here wants to restrict the drawing of broad conclusions from the examples of Peter and Paul. His reading of Scripture has led him to conclude that perfection was God's command to all Christians, and so one or two individual examples would not suffice to negate the commandment. He is, in effect, asking for a strict chain of reasoning to prove that all the early Christians committed sin, knowing that there is no evidence for that in the New Testament.

Reason as Independent Source of Knowledge

Wesley's use of reason as an independent source of knowledge is quite limited. In the sample analyzed, seven such uses were found. In one of his earliest sermons, "The Image of God," Wesley tries to explain how Adam's eating the fruit would cause his mortality.

> On the contrary, the fruit of that tree alone of whose deadly nature he was forewarned seems to have contained a juice, the particles of which were apt to cleave to whatever they touched. Some of these, being received into the human body, might adhere to the inner coats of the finer vessels; to which again other particles that before floated loose in the blood, continually joining, would naturally lay a foundation for numberless disorders in all parts of the machine. For death in particular; since, more foreign matter cleaving to the former every day, the solid parts of the body would every day lose something of their spring, and so be less able to contribute their necessary assistance to the circulation of the fluids. The smaller channels would gradually fill up, especially those that lie near the extremities, where the current, by reason of its distance from the fountain, was always

more slow and languid. The whole tide, as the force that threw it forward abated, must [also] have abated its swiftness in proportion, till at length that force utterly failing, it ceased to move, and rested in death.[11]

Wesley is here using the physiology of his day; Harvey's proof of the circulation of the blood was just one hundred years old when this sermon was written. Outler notes that this paragraph anticipates "later notions of low-density lipoproteins and atherosclerosis."[12] But the crucial point here is that contemporary science was being employed to understand the truth of Scripture.

There is another place in the sample of material where Wesley appeals to secular science to help interpret Scripture. Matthew 27:45 describes the "darkness over the earth" after the crucifixion, and Wesley comments, "Insomuch, that even an heathen philosopher seeing it, and knowing it could not be a natural eclipse, because it was at the time of the full moon, and continued three hours together, cried out, 'Either the God of nature suffers, or the frame of the world is dissolved.'"[13] Wesley takes it as clear truth that no solar eclipse could occur at the time of the full moon, because it must occur at the time of the new moon.

In a more methodological sense, Wesley takes it as axiomatic that knowledge comes to human beings only through sensory experience. His sermon "On the Discoveries of Faith" begins, "For many ages it has been allowed by sensible men, *Nihil est in intellectu quod non fuit prius in sensu:* that is, 'There is nothing in the understanding which was not first perceived by some of the senses.' All the knowledge which we naturally have is originally derived from our senses."[14] He goes on to dismiss the possibility of innate ideas as "agreed by all impartial persons."[15] Where does Wesley come to such a conclusion? He states that a person blind from birth can have no "knowledge or conception of light or colours." This whole section is an elliptical reference to a long-running argument in Western Philosophy, with important contributions made by Aristotle, Aquinas, Locke, and the Deists. Wesley is here using reason to establish a point that then becomes crucial for his interpretation of Hebrews 11:1. He relies upon a rational argument to show that some sort of sensory experience must be the basis for any particular thought, and so our knowledge of God must have a sensory basis. It is reason, not Scripture, which grounds empirical epistemology.

Reason is good for something else on its own, Wesley says: "It is true, as soon as we came to the use of reason we learned 'the invisible things of God, even his eternal power and godhead,' from 'the things that are made.' From the things that are seen we inferred the existence of an eternal, powerful being that is not seen."[16] While many of Wesley's definitions are taken from Scripture, the definition of reason itself is one given by reason. True, in the sermon "The Case of Reason Impartially Considered," Wesley does use a scriptural example, but only for illustration.[17] His warrant for the definition that is finally used is that it is "another acceptation" where "reason is much the same with *understanding*." He continues, "It means a faculty of the human soul; that faculty which exerts itself in three ways: by simple apprehension, by judgment, and by discourse."[18] This definition has clear echoes of the philosophical discussions of the seventeenth century, and is drawn from the Oxford Aristotelian logical tradition.[19] Clearly it is unreasonable to expect all definitions to be given by Scripture. Wesley is willing to turn to contemporary philosophy to define at least one of his key terms.

Wesley's Negative References to Reason

A key to any understanding of Wesley's use of reason is to be found in his negative references to what reason can do. While there are frequent references to proving doctrines by reason or by Scripture and reason, the reason in question in such references is always reason rightly employed, reason in harmony with Scripture rightly interpreted. The doctrine of original sin, for example, is contrasted with an optimistic view of humanity:

> Nor have heathens alone, men who were guided in their researches by little more than the dim light of reason, but many likewise of them that bear the name of Christ, and to whom are entrusted the oracles of God, spoke as magnificently concerning the nature of man, as if it were all innocence and perfection. Accounts of this kind have particularly abounded in the present century; and perhaps in no part of the world more than in our own country. . . .
>
> But in the meantime, what must we do with our Bibles? For they will never agree with this. These accounts, however pleasing to flesh and blood, are utterly irreconcilable with the scriptural.[20]

Here the emerging view of humankind as good and reasonable is ascribed to "the dim light of reason" and rejected because it does not agree with the scriptural account. In a similar way, the doctrine of Christian perfection is one to be settled on scriptural terms, in opposition to some "rational" opinions based on experience. Wesley understands that reason is useful in interpreting what Scripture means. But only Scripture, in its best interpretation, has the authority to settle the question. He says,

> If any doubt of this privilege of the sons of God, the question is not to be decided by abstract reasonings, which may be drawn out into an endless length, and leave the point just as it was before. . . . "To the law and to the testimony" we appeal. "Let God be true, and every man a liar." By his Word will we abide, and that alone. Hereby we ought to be judged.[21]

In this case, "abstract reasonings" must be understood as those not based on Scripture. Only Scripture is decisive.

Reason Testifies to Scripture

One of Wesley's clearest convictions is that faith and reason are not in conflict. He can say this because he believes that a rational person would find clear proof that the Scriptures are "of God." He presupposes this at points in his writings,[22] and he argues for it in his "Clear and Concise Demonstration of the Divine Inspiration of the Holy Scriptures."[23] In interpreting the story of Dives and Lazarus, he argues that if the Lord said it, it must be true. When Jesus says, "There was a certain beggar named Lazarus," Wesley asks, "Was there, or was there not? Is it not bold enough positively to deny what our blessed Lord positively affirms? Therefore we cannot reasonably doubt but the whole narration, with all its circumstances, is exactly true."[24] Note the use of "reasonably" in this sentence. In many cases, Wesley uses "reason" to justify a conclusion, but the same presupposition, that the Scripture is "of God," is involved.

Wesley is prepared to acknowledge that there are many who reject this presupposition, and therefore would reason in a different manner. While the first part of the *Earnest Appeal* is addressed to those who would accept the presupposition, he turns in §§12-46 to address those who do not. He launches an argument that begins with experience. "You yourself believe there is a God. You have the witness of this in your own breast."[25] He later describes the religion he preaches as

> the religion of love: the law of kindness brought to light by the gospel. . . .
>
> Will you object to such a religion as this that it is not reasonable? Is it not reasonable then to love God? . . .
>
> Is it not reasonable also to love our neighbour: every man whom God hath made? . . .
>
> Is it not reasonable, then, that "as we have opportunity" we should "do good unto all men": not only friends, but enemies; not only to the deserving, but likewise to the evil and unthankful?[26]

For Wesley, salvation depends on more than love—it is salvation by faith, which may appear unreasonable to his audience. But the appearance of irrationality stems from a lack of understanding what faith is. Wesley argues that reason is a faculty which relies upon true judgments:

> You know, likewise that before it is possible for you to form a true judgment of them it is absolutely necessary that you have a *clear apprehension* of the things of God, and that your ideas thereof be all *fixed, distinct,* and *determinate.* And seeing our ideas are not innate, but must all originally come from our senses, it is certainly necessary that you have senses capable of discerning objects of this kind—not those only which are called "natural senses," which in this respect profit nothing, as being altogether incapable of discerning objects of a spiritual kind, but *spiritual* senses, exercised to discern spiritual good and evil.[27]

Wesley says faith is that spiritual sight enabling the person to perceive spiritual things. Only then can the person reason correctly, because he has the data on which to base true judgments, and then to make true inferences. Reason alone cannot get across the "immense chasm" between the visible and invisible worlds.

> This cannot be till the Almighty come in to your succour, and give you that faith you have hitherto despised. Then, upborne as it were on eagles' wings, you shall soar away into the regions of eternity, and your enlightened reason shall explore even "the deep things of God," God himself "revealing them to you by his Spirit."[28]

It is this "enlightened reason" that Wesley sees as congruent with faith. Whereas he here sees it as enlightened by the Holy Spirit, he elsewhere says, "From the whole we may draw that general conclusion, that standing revelation is the best means of rational conviction, far preferable to any of those extraordinary means which some imagine would be more effectual."[29] Wesley is claiming an epistemological privilege for the Christian. Both Scripture and the Holy Spirit, as sources of correct information about spiritual things, can enlighten the mind so that it can reason correctly in these areas. Just as hearing cannot supply sensations of sight to someone born blind, so those without spiritual senses cannot understand spiritual things.

Christian Antiquity

There are fourteen references to Christian antiquity in the sample being analyzed.[30] These references can best be classified under four headings: interpretation of Scripture, warrants in theological arguments, models for current practice, and semantic reference.[31]

On four occasions, Wesley appeals to the Fathers or the primitive church for help in interpreting Scripture. In one, Wesley says that the Apostles' Creed contains "a beautiful summary" of the essential truths contained in Scripture.[32] In another instance, discussed more fully later, he appeals to Theophylact's authority to argue that Lazarus the beggar lived at Jerusalem.[33] In the most significant use of antiquity to interpret Scripture, Wesley is at some pains to refute the suggestion that Paul's "thorn, to the flesh"[34] meant that Paul had committed sin: "Secondly, the ancient Fathers inform us it was bodily pain: 'a violent headache,' saith Tertullian, *(De Pudic)* to which both Chrysostom and St. Jerome agree. St. Cyprian expresses it a little more generally, in those terms 'many and grievous torments of the flesh and of the body.'"[35] Here Wesley is using the Fathers because they are better interpreters of the text, standing closer to the original than we do. While he also argues for his interpretation on the basis of the context, he relies heavily on this argument from antiquity. In another case, Wesley has a long tirade against ecclesiastical censures in both Protestant and Catholic countries. He then continues, "*Whatsoever ye shall loose*—By absolution from that sentence. In the primitive church, absolution meant no more than a discharge from church censure."[36] What he means here is that the ecclesiastical systems of judgment have gone far beyond the practice of Scripture as understood by the primitive church, and ought to be reformed.

The second category of use to which Wesley puts Christian antiquity is that of warrant in theological arguments. In "The Scripture Way of Salvation," Wesley describes his doctrine of salvation. He warns that after the initial joys of justification and sanctification, sin will return and spiritual struggle will continue. He then says, "How exactly did Macarius, fourteen hundred years ago, describe the present experience of the children of God!"[37] Wesley is here using Macarius to support his argument that young Christians who feel that sin is completely conquered need greater experience before they can be certain of this fact. Macarius has "exactly" described what Wesley had seen in the Methodists he was guiding. Another use of the Fathers as a warrant comes in the sermon "The General Spread of the Gospel." There Wesley argues that God's "general manner of working" allows human beings the freedom to resist God's grace. He writes,

> Yea, I am persuaded every child of God has at some time "life and death set before him," eternal life and eternal death, and has in himself the casting voice. So true is that well-known saying of St. Austin (one of the noblest he ever uttered), *Qui fecit nos sine nobis, non salvabit nos sine nobis*—he that made us *without ourselves* will not save us *without ourselves*.[38]

Wesley is here using Augustine as an authority to bolster his argument for both the universality and the resistibility of grace. Augustine is one of the best authorities in this case, since Wesley's opponents were Calvinistic Methodists who could not help knowing that Augustine stood behind Calvin's doctrine of predestination.

The third category of Wesley's use of Christian antiquity is as a model for practice in his own day. Although Campbell's "John Wesley's Conceptions and Uses of Christian Antiquity" notes many more occasions of this use than are contained in my limited sample, one such use does occur. In the sermon "On the Causes of the Inefficacy of Christianity," Wesley is concerned to show that a chief cause is the lack of self-denial among Christians. One example he gives is that of fasting:

> While we were at Oxford the rule of every Methodist was (unless in case of sickness) to *fast* every Wednesday and Friday in the year, in imitation of the primitive church, for which they had the highest reverence. Now this practice of the primitive church is universally allowed. "Who does not know," says Epiphanius, an ancient writer, "that the fasts of the fourth and sixth days of the week (Wednesday and Friday) are observed by the Christians throughout the whole world?"[39]

Wesley believes that the Christian's obligation to fast is established by Scripture. The way in which the primitive Christians carried this out becomes a model for the Oxford Methodists, and by implication, for all Christians if they want Christianity to be more efficacious.

The fourth use of antiquity is that of the semantic reference. Here, ancient sources are used to express thoughts that could easily be expressed in other words. This is the same literary function as that fulfilled by the semantic use of Scripture noted earlier. Three such uses were found in the sample, two of them coming near each other in the sermon "On the Discoveries of Faith." There Wesley suggests that faith shows the soul of the righteous in heaven, "where he converses not only with his former relations, friends, and fellow-soldiers, but with the saints of all nations and ages; with the glorious dead of ancient days; with the noble army of martyrs, the apostles, the prophets, the patriarchs, Abraham, Isaac, and Jacob."[40] The phrase "the noble army of martyrs" is not italicized but is clearly taken from the *Te Deum* in the order for Morning Prayer in the *BCP*. Two paragraphs later he says, "Moreover faith opens another scene in the eternal world, namely the coming of our Lord in the clouds of heaven to 'judge both the quick and the dead.'"[41] Here the phrase is set off with quotation marks, and comes from the Nicene Creed in the order for Communion of the *BCP*. The third such quotation also is from the Nicene Creed, where Wesley uses the phrase, "the Son of God who came down from heaven for us men and for our salvation."[42]

In all of these cases, the same qualities which applied to the semantic use of Scripture can be discerned in Wesley's use of antiquity. Although references to writings from antiquity are sometimes emphasized with quotation marks, often they are not. While they are not always noted with their source, their familiarity would carry

171

with it an added authority. In this case it is the authority of the early church, whose creeds and liturgies were highly respected in the liturgy of the Church of England.

However, there are significant differences between Wesley's conception of antiquity and his use of it. We have seen that Wesley had no positive conception of Christian tradition as a whole. In his stated views, he attributes authority only to Christian antiquity and to the Church of England. In practice, however, Wesley uses the whole scope of Christian tradition. In fact, other portions of Christian tradition function in his theology in many of the ways in which Christian antiquity functions, as the three following examples show.

First, Wesley uses a medieval theologian to interpret Scripture. In the sermon "Dives and Lazarus," Wesley argues that the story of Dives and Lazarus is "real history" rather than a "parable." He quotes Theophylact as saying the Jews had a tradition that Lazarus lived in Jerusalem. What is puzzling is his parenthetical reference to Theophylact as "one of the ancient commentators on the Scriptures,"[43] since Theophylact lived in the eleventh century. On what grounds could Wesley refer to Theophylact as "an ancient commentator"? Nowhere else in the Wesley corpus is the term "ancient" applied to any person or doctrine later than the early church.[44] Most frequently, he uses the term as equivalent to Christian antiquity.[45] Clearly, Theophylact is not part of the primitive church as Wesley defined it. Is it possible that Wesley did not know when Theophylact lived? Wesley had a good grasp of church history and is not likely to have been mistaken on such a simple matter. The most likely conclusion is that Wesley has mistakenly used the term "ancient" to bolster a weak argument, claiming in this case a more elastic meaning than the technical use he normally made of it. Nevertheless, the conclusion remains that this is a quotation from a medieval archbishop used to help interpret Scripture. This does not violate any of Wesley's rules of interpretation; rather, it adds to them by using the information from a medieval source which is otherwise unrecognized in Wesley's stated methodology.

Second, Wesley makes explicit references to parts of tradition that have given him help in the Christian life or in doctrine. Thomas à Kempis, whom Wesley thought of as the author of *The Imitation of Christ*, is described as pious, and his speculations about hell are quoted approvingly.[46] In the sermon "On God's Vineyard," Wesley refers to Martin Luther as being one of the best writers on justification by faith alone, and to "writers of the Romish Church (as Francis Sales and Juan de Castaniza in particular)" as helpful on sanctification.[47] Wesley's point is that Luther and the Roman Catholics are each defective on the other's strong point, and that the Methodists have been graced by God with a clear understanding of both doctrines. However, it is obvious that Wesley learned much from these sixteenth-century sources.

Third, Wesley uses theological concepts that are part of Christian tradition and can be traced back to medieval sources. Albert Outler has found in Wesley "echoes" of various theologians from throughout Christian history. In his notes to the sermon "The Way to the Kingdom," Outler correctly identifies Anselm's arguments in *Cur Deus Homo?* as the background for Wesley's argument in §II.5. Wesley says that "the present and future obedience of all the men upon earth, and all the angels in heaven, would never make satisfaction to the justice of God for one single sin. . . . It costeth far more to redeem one soul than all mankind is able to pay."[48] The similarity between Wesley's formulation and Anselm's ideas of satisfaction, justice, and payment is striking. While it is not clear that Wesley is directly using Anselm, or any particular intermediary source, it is clear that Wesley is using an important theological argument from the broader tradition of Christianity. This is not an explicit use of the tradition outside of Christian antiquity. Rather, it is an unacknowledged dependence on precisely those aspects of Christian history of which Wesley was the most critical in his anti-Catholic polemics. In one instance, Wesley makes explicit reference in a positive way to "casuists, particularly those of the Church of Rome" who provide him with a helpful typology of lies.[49] In quoting *"Nihil est in intellectu quod non fuit prius in sensu,"* Wesley is relying on a scholastic maxim that goes back to Aristotle, but which receives treatment by the schoolmen.[50]

Wesley's acceptance of the Thirty-nine Articles of Religion is another sign of his dependence on the developing tradition of Christian doctrine even after the close of the early church. While the doctrines contained in the Articles were approved by the Church of England, and thus mediated by the church's authority, they were based on centuries of doctrinal development. The doctrine of Christ as one Person with two Natures in Article II stemmed from the Council of Chalcedon in 451. Although one might stretch Wesley's definition of antiquity to cover that council, he never refers to Chalcedon directly. The filioque clause, used in the Nicene Creed and in Article V, first appeared at the Third Council of Toledo in 589.[51] The primacy of Scripture in Article VI was a typically Reformation understanding of scriptural authority, including the relegation of the Apocrypha to secondary status. Other examples could be given of the indebtedness of Anglican doctrine to many points of Christian tradition other than those acknowledged by Wesley. Yet when Wesley edited the Articles for the Methodists in America, he left these parts of the tradition intact.

The unacknowledged use of the *entire* Christian tradition permeates Wesley's writings. The "Bibliographical Index" and "General Index" to Wesley's Sermons contain many references to portions of Christian history that Wesley never categorized as authoritative. His opposition to tradition as an authority in matters of doctrine fails to take into account the ways in which the doctrine of the Church of England is a repository of centuries of tradition. He is insufficiently self-critical on this point.

John Wesley is a highly traditional theologian. He did not seek to create an innovation through the Methodist societies, but sought a revival of true Christianity. While he considered primitive Christianity the best model of purity, he also found other periods to contribute to his understanding of what correct doctrine and faithful practice ought to be. His use of the larger Christian tradition expands his more narrow appeal to the early church. Perhaps the best explanation for the discrepancy between his conception and his use on this point lies with his attitude toward Roman Catholicism. In a period when Roman Catholics were still suspected of disloyalty to their country and still blamed for serious doctrinal errors, Wesley shared the prejudices of his time. Wesley was on the forefront of building bridges to the Roman Catholic community by recognizing the doctrinal areas where they excelled and in noticing the broad areas of agreement between them and Protestants.[52] Nevertheless, there was no group within the sphere of Anglican theology that had good things to say about Roman Catholic doctrine as a whole. More important, Anglican apologetics consistently attacked the perceived Catholic reliance on Scripture and tradition as coequal norms of faith. The theological environment helped shape Wesley's hostile view of the larger Christian tradition. It is clear that he was still too caught up in the polemical debates with Roman Catholics over the proper role of tradition as a whole to make the careful distinctions that were made during later centuries.

The Church of England

Wesley's references to the Church of England usually occur as joint citations with Scripture, antiquity, or both. In his sermon "On Laying the Foundation of the New Chapel," he writes,

> But you will naturally ask, What is Methodism? What does this new word mean? Is it not a new religion? This is a very common, nay, almost an universal supposition. But nothing can be more remote from the truth. It is a mistake all over. Methodism, so called, is the old religion, the religion of the Bible, the religion of the primitive church, the religion of the Church of England.[53]

A few pages later, he describes the Oxford Methodists in similar terms.[54] As noted in the discussion of his conception of the church, it is the Articles, Homilies, and Liturgy that count. In the same sermon he continues,

> And this is the *religion of the Church of England*, as appears from all her authentic records, from the uniform tenor of her liturgy, and from numberless passages in her Homilies. The scriptural primitive religion of love, which is now reviving throughout the three kingdoms, is to be found in her morning and evening service, and in her daily as well as occasional prayers; and the whole of it is beautifully summed up in that one, comprehensive petition, "Cleanse the thoughts of our hearts by the inspiration of thy Holy Spirit, that we may perfectly love thee, and worthily magnify thy holy name."[55]

Wesley's use of the Church of England as an authority reflects his method of discriminating among various types of evidence. Wesley's method, as indicated earlier,[56] was to note that different types of arguments required different types of evidence. Thus, when Wesley was attacked as being disloyal to his church, he appealed to the doctrinal foundations of the Church of England.

Wesley's explicit use of the Church of England as an authority is in strict agreement with his conception. He is a true son of the Church of England, using its own doctrinal standards to justify its renewal. He follows the doctrine of the church not because it is authoritative in its own right, but because he judges it to be "the most scriptural national church" in existence.[57] The form of Christianity it teaches is the same as that taught by the Bible and by Christian antiquity. However, he fails to understand that by relying on the church's liturgy and homilies, he is in fact relying on the larger tradition of the church. The Church of England's doctrine represents a particular version of how Christianity developed over fifteen hundred years, and its debts to postantiquity Christianity are not adequately acknowledged by Wesley.

Experience

As indicated earlier in our discussion of Wesley's doctrine of experience as an authority, Wesley claims a strong reliance on the authority of experience to describe the world as it exists. Matters of fact are the appropriate subject for experiential evidence, he says. His actual uses of experience as an authority can be categorized under three headings. First, he uses it to describe both the physical and moral condition of the world. Second, he appeals to experience for evidence to confirm the teachings of Scripture. Third, he lifts up a certain set of experiences as the goal for Christian life.

Descriptions of the Physical and Spiritual Worlds

For Wesley, matters of fact include both physical and spiritual characteristics of the world. He appeals to experience for evidence about the world as if any unbiased person who examines the matter would come to the same conclusion. Five different types of appeal can be noted.

First, Wesley relies on experience to describe the physical world. He is truly interested in the new sciences that were being developed during his day. In one place Wesley argues from experience about the widespread presence of fire. When discussing how the world might one day be destroyed, he appeals to "a thousand experiments" which show that "we ourselves, our whole bodies, are full of fire, as well as everything round about us."[58] It is not clear what experiments he is referring to, but perhaps his views show a vague awareness that energy is present in many places and in many ways. Experiments are the proper way to ascertain whether "fire" is universally present or not. Wesley concludes that the experiments show it to be so, and this "fact" about fire then takes on a role in showing the plausibility of God's promise to destroy the earth by fire next time.

Second, Wesley occasionally makes a survey of the religious state of the world as part of his argument about the role of Christianity in general and Methodism in particular.[59] His opening paragraph in "The General Spread of the Gospel" says, "In what a condition is the world at present! How does darkness, intellectual darkness, ignorance, with vice and misery attendant upon it, cover the face of the earth!"[60] He takes Brerewood's estimate that most of the world belongs to non-Christian religions as part of the evidence for the sinful state of the world. He then rejects the testimony of Lady Mary Wortley Montagu about the high ethical standards of the Turks, and then surveys the Christian world. He concludes by arguing that the bulk of nominal Christians, both Papists and Protestants, "are as far from [walking as Christ walked] as hell is from heaven."[61] Brerewood's simplistic but scientific analysis of world population serves the theological point Wesley is trying to make. More generally, Wesley appeals to the experience of the reader that humankind as a whole is not very religious.

Third, he appeals to experience to give us knowledge of our own spiritual states. No other source of knowledge can disclose the condition of one's own soul. Scripture may teach that all human beings are sinners, but experience alone can disclose that a particular individual is sinful as well. In "The Marks of the New Birth" he appeals to the reader: "Is the Spirit of adoption now in your heart? To your own heart let the appeal be made. I ask not whether you *was* born of water and the Spirit. But *are* you *now* the temple of the Holy Ghost which dwelleth in you?"[62] In *An Earnest Appeal* he gives an example of his "usual language" addressed to sinners, saying,

> You know your soul is not satisfied. It is still an aching void. Sometimes you find (in spite of your principles) a sense of guilt, an awakened conscience. That grisly phantom religion (so you describe her) will now and then haunt you still. . . . How often are you in fear of the very things you deny? How often in racking suspense? "What if there

be an hereafter? A judgment to come? An unhappy eternity?" Do you not start at the thought? Can you be content to be always thus?[63]

He appeals to the reader's experience of a spiritual void and the fear of God's judgment. This is not a legalistic recitation of rules for human life found in the Bible. Rather, Wesley appeals to the anxieties and uncertainties of individual experience to provide an opening for the gospel. The need for God should be clear to readers once their experience of sin has been brought to their attention.

Fourth, experience describes God's activity in the world. In *An Earnest Appeal* (1743), Wesley writes:

> Behold, the day of the Lord is come. He is again visiting and redeeming his people. . . . Love of all mankind, meekness, gentleness, humbleness of mind, holy and heavenly affections, do take [the] place of hate, anger, pride, revenge, and vile or vain affections. Hence wherever the power of the Lord spreads, springs outward religion in all its forms. . . . All this is plain, demonstrable fact.[64]

In his 1749 open letter to Bishop Lavington, he says,

> You ask, "how I know" so great a work is wrought now? "By inspiration?" No; but by common sense. I know it by the evidence of my own eyes and ears. I have seen a considerable part of it; and I have abundant testimony, such as excludes all possible doubt, for what I have not seen.[65]

Fifth, Wesley uses experience to argue that certain doctrines have certain tendencies in the real world. One of the most interesting facets of the argument in "Free Grace" is the claim that the doctrine of predestination is not a doctrine of God, because "it directly tends to destroy that holiness which is the end of all the ordinances of God."[66] Clearly, this argument is intended to supplement the basic argument which is taken from Scripture. But its implication—that the validity of a doctrine can be assessed, in part, by the effect it has on people—is significant. Wesley argues that the doctrine of predestination "tends to destroy the comfort of religion, the happiness of Christianity,"[67] it "directly tends to destroy our zeal for good works,"[68] and "this doctrine not only tends to destroy Christian holiness, happiness, and good works, but hath also a direct and manifest tendency to overthrow the whole Christian revelation."[69] All these arguments are grounded in a reading of what happens when people preach and teach predestination. They stand alongside the arguments from Scripture, which are also brought to bear on the main contention. In the same category are Wesley's quotation of Thomas Hobbes, "If reason be against a man, a man will always be against reason,"[70] and his contention that reason cannot produce faith.[71] In both cases Wesley is using an observation that is grounded on experience.

Two things are noteworthy about Wesley's appeals to experience. First, he is uncritical in his acceptance of testimony by others. His rejection of Lady Montagu's description of the Turks is based on her perceived lack of religion rather than her reliability as a witness. Instead, Wesley relies on the more numerous accounts of Turks that describe them in subhuman terms. Wesley claims he uses all those accounts that have "any pretence to authenticity," but his standards for authenticity are uncritical. Thus, Wesley stands at the beginning of the age in which a critical use of sources is acceptable. He is aware of the need to distinguish between authentic and inauthentic accounts, but he is not yet applying modern critical standards of truth. Second, Wesley sees experience as objective, that is, commonly shared by all who are exposed to the object. Whether his claims have to do with the presence of fire all around us or with the state of wickedness among humankind, he assumes that the matter is one of "plain, demonstrable fact." Everyone should be able to see the situation in the same way. Thus, once authentic testimony is given, it should be obvious to all that the "day of the Lord is come" and "He is again visiting and redeeming his people." Wesley does not have an understanding of a plurality of perspectives.

Experience Confirms Scriptural Doctrine

The second important role of experience is to confirm the teaching of Scripture. Many of the matters of fact attested by experience also confirm Scripture. However, a question arises here as to just what kind of experience Wesley has in mind. In one case the testimony of experience depends on seeing reality through the eyes of faith. In "Original Sin" Wesley argues that "the whole tenor of the oracles of God" teaches that human beings are sinful:

And this account of the present state of man is confirmed by daily experience. It is true the natural man discerns it not. And this is not to be wondered at. . . . In like manner, so long as men remain in their natural blindness of understanding they are not sensible of their spiritual wants, and of this in particular. But as soon as God opens the eyes of their understanding they see the state they were in before; they are then deeply convinced that "every man living," themselves especially, are by nature "altogether vanity"; that is, folly and ignorance, sin and wickedness.[72]

What is crucial here is the interaction between Scripture and the experience of faith. Wesley acknowledges that unawakened people will not have the "daily experience" which confirms the Scripture. But once God awakens their understanding, presumably by giving them the eyes of faith, then they will see themselves in a new light and acknowledge their sinfulness and the sinfulness of all humanity. At the same time, however, Wesley can claim that, quite apart from faith, experience teaches us about the reality of human sin. For Wesley, the reality that all humanity is sinful is obvious. In the sermon "The Image of God," he describes the change that occurred to human nature in the Fall and then writes,

The consequence of his being enslaved to a depraved understanding and a corrupted will could be no other than the reverse of that happiness which flowed from them when in their perfection. Then were the days of man evil as well as few; then, when both his faculties were decayed, and bitterness poured on their earthly objects, and heavenly ones withdrawn, the mortal, foolish, vicious, enslaved creature was delivered over to his [un]sought-for misery.

How such a creature as this, as every fair inquirer finds by experience himself to be, could come from the hands of the good God, has been the just wonder of all ages.[73]

Note that the experience appealed to here as an authority is available to "every fair inquirer." Wesley frequently refers to "daily experience" in the same manner, assuming it is available to all. With regard to the commandment to love one another,[74] for example, he says, "All men approve of this. But do all men practise it? Daily experience shows the contrary."[75] Again, "daily experience" is the authority which shows that the more appetites are indulged, the more they are increased.[76]

This leads to the deeper question of what kind of experience Wesley is really talking about. He does not make systematic distinctions between different types of experience, and yet it is important for us to know whether he means the religious experience of the believer or the sort of objective experience that is available, in principle, to everyone. The answer is that Wesley is talking about both kinds of experience. First, he believes that there is an objective experience of the world, available to all impartial observers, that reveals many truths of the Bible. Despite what Wesley said about people not seeing their own sinfulness until their eyes are opened, he more frequently appeals to the ills of humankind as something generally observed. His note on Romans 3:10 is a case in point; it reads "That all men are under sin appears from the vices which have raged in all ages."[77] Further, there are aspects of self-knowledge which all persons share. In *An Earnest Appeal* he says, "The oracles of God bear thee witness in every page (and thine own heart agreeth thereto) that thou wast made in the image of God, an incorruptible picture of the God of glory."[78] That kind of experience within each person is available to all. Every person, simply on the basis of experience, can know the realities of sin and of the divine model for human nature.

To those who love God, there is a different sort of experience that confirms Scripture in a different way. For these persons, the promises of Scripture have become real in their lives, and they *know* by their own self-knowledge the truth of the gospel. Later in the same work Wesley says,

> But what need have we of distant witnesses? You have a witness in your own breast. For am I not speaking to one that loves God? How came *you* then to love him at first? Was it not because you knew that he loved you? Did you, could you love God at all, till you "tasted and saw that he was gracious," that he was merciful to you a sinner? What avails then controversy or strife of words? "Out of thy own mouth"! You own you had no love to God till you was sensible of his love to you.[79]

Thus, it is clear that, as the Christian progresses, different kinds of experience become available and serve to confirm Scripture in different kinds of ways.

Experience as the Goal of the Christian Life

This confirmation of Scripture leads to a third role played by experience in Wesley's theology. Because Scripture is understood as guiding the individual to salvation, which can be experienced, those experiences which confirm Scripture's teaching also serve as the goal for the Christian life. For Wesley, Christianity can be seen as a system of doctrines or as a set of experiences—the doctrines made real in the lives of believers.

Indeed, faith itself is a kind of experience. Defining it as a set of spiritual senses makes faith a kind of experience that gives us knowledge. In the sermon "On the Discoveries of Faith," he says, "Faith, on the other hand, is the 'evidence of things not seen,' of the *invisible world;* of all those invisible things which are revealed in the oracles of God. But indeed they reveal nothing, they are a mere 'dead letter,' if they are 'not mixed with faith in those that hear them.'"[80] A little later he writes,

> By faith I know "there are three that bear record in heaven, the Father, the Word, and the Holy Spirit," and that "these three are one";[a] that "the Word," God the Son, "was made flesh,"[b] lived, and died for our salvation, rose again, ascended into heaven, and now sitteth at the right hand of the Father. By faith I know that the Holy Spirit is the giver of all spiritual life; of righteousness, peace, and joy in the Holy Ghost;[c] of holiness and happiness, by the restoration of that image of God wherein we are created. Of all these things faith is the evidence, the sole evidence to the children of men.[81]

Note that in these paragraphs there are three quotations from Scripture and echoes of several creeds from the early church. Yet Wesley says he knows these things by faith, earlier defined as a spiritual sense, and that this is the "sole evidence to the children of men." Yet, it seems that even the appropriation of Scripture is a kind of experience that helps us know the truth.

While Wesley recognized that experience had certain key limitations, his usual practice was to treat its evidence as positive. In two cases, however, his usage of experience is specifically designed to show that an appeal to experience must be negated by higher authorities or other experiences. In the first instance, Wesley notes that just because some people are mistaken about their being in God's favor does not mean that others are always mistaken as well.

In the sermon "The Witness of the Spirit, II," he first poses an objection and then answers it:

> "But madmen, French prophets, and enthusiasts of every kind have imagined they experienced this witness." They have so, and perhaps not a few of them did, although they did not retain it long. But if they did not, this is no proof at all that others have not experienced it: as a madman's *imagining* himself a king does not prove that there are no *real* kings.[82]

Here Wesley is arguing that while some may be mistaken about their experience, such mistakes do not mean that all are always mistaken about their experience. The second instance is much like the first. In the sermon "Christian Perfection" Wesley argues that it is possible for some to "suppose they do not commit sin when they do, but this proves nothing either way."[83]

Conclusion

For the most part, Wesley's use of the four nonscriptural authorities—reason, Christian antiquity, the Church of England, and experience—is in agreement with his conception of them. It is clear that all of these are intertwined with Scripture so that it is most accurate to describe them as one single locus of authority in Wesley's theology. We have seen that reason testifies to Scripture, interprets Scripture, and in scientific matters even limits Scripture's range of meaning. Similarly, Christian antiquity and experience are used to interpret Scripture, and yet Scripture governs how they are to be applied to Christian faith and practice.

However, two significant elements appeared in our analysis of Wesley's use of these authorities that go beyond his conception of how they are properly to function. First, Wesley's negative view of reason in some circumstances is in tension with his statements about religion and reason going hand in hand. When Wesley advises people not to reason but to have faith in God and God's saving grace in their lives, he appears to be going against his own admonition that the only true religion is a rational religion. Here he has abandoned reason altogether for an apparently fideist position of trusting in God without thinking. Note that Wesley's advice is not to think more carefully. Nor is it to use correct reason or a higher reason. Rather, he urges believers to abandon it completely because of its misuse by the devil. Wesley's valiant effort to hold together reason and religion begins to show its difficulties here. He is not yet challenged by the developments of modern science that severely question the biblical worldview. Rather, he is challenged by a rational approach to human experience.

The second element in Wesley's use of these authorities that goes beyond his conception of them appears in his appeals to aspects of Christian tradition other than Christian antiquity and the Church of England. In some cases, he is simply making implicit use of developments which had been deposited in the Church of England's doctrine. These Wesley took for granted, and he failed to give adequate recognition to their medieval and Reformation sources. However, we also find cases in which Wesley uses these sources in the same ways in which he uses Christian antiquity. While these instances are relatively rare, they are significant because Wesley's fivefold conception of authority makes no allowance for them at all. Wesley is a traditional theologian. His conception of the different epochs of Christianity and of their purity or impurity is far too simplistic and breaks down when he actually employs the ideas and words of later Christian teachers. Thus, a Wesley who appears highly rational and narrowly biased toward early Christianity is in reality less rational and more dependent on the whole Christian tradition than he would admit.

CHAPTER 7

Interpretation of Scripture

Purpose

Wesley's use of Scripture is a direct consequence of the overall purpose which he believes Scripture should serve. Despite the wide variety of types of literature within the corpus of his written work, most of his writings directly serve the end of saving souls. The bulk of his theological writings takes the form of sermons, both homiletical and theoretical. There are also polemical writings, designed to justify his theology and his practice. His few doctrinal treatises are either explanations of his theology or discussions of points directly relevant to soteriology. Even the letters to his followers relate to the management of the Methodist movement or offer spiritual advice.

In all of these literary forms, Wesley employs Scripture in accordance with what he understood to be its central purpose—the salvation of souls. His writings were decidedly practical, and he self-consciously avoided speculative theology as a waste of his time. For him, any use of the Bible should conduce to people knowing "one thing, the way to heaven."[1] The pattern of citations that we found in Wesley's writings emphasizes those texts that deal most explicitly with the order of salvation. His understanding of the wholeness of Scripture centers on that topic, and the doctrine of salvation plays a significant role in his practice of interpretation.

Three examples will illustrate his concern for the practical purposes of scriptural interpretation. The sermon "On Laying the Foundation of the New Chapel" has as its text Numbers 23:23, "According to this time it shall be said . . ., What hath God wrought!" He opens the sermon with an explanation of how that text will be considered: "We need not now inquire in what sense this was applicable to the children of Israel. It may be of more use to consider in what sense the words are applicable to ourselves; how far the people of England have reason to say, 'According to this time, what hath God wrought!'"[2] There are several occasions where Wesley uses the text for a sermon as the springboard to launch his sermon rather than as the subject of an exposition. This is one of the few cases in which he explicitly declines to consider the context of the passage and simply uses it as a convenient phrase for the message he is trying to proclaim. In a sense, the practical import of his message is more important than following his own rules of interpretation. He knows what needs to be said, and there is a connection, however weak, between the text and his subject. Just as Balaam's message announced the wonderful deeds God had wrought through the Hebrews, so Wesley was prepared to announce the wonderful deeds done by God through the Methodists. Wesley's concern is not careful exegesis of this text, but the proclamation of God's saving activity in his own day and time.

The second example of Wesley's practical concern is his unusually harsh condemnation of those who differ from his interpretation of John 5:39. Although this text will be examined more fully later, it should be made clear that his practical view of the text controls his translation of it. He demands that Ἐρευνᾶτε τὰς γραφάς be translated as an imperative and calls the other possible translation "shamelessly false." Wesley fully knows that ἐρευνᾶτε is both the imperative and indicative form of the verb, and could be translated either way. While the Authorized Version uses the imperative, modern translations use the indicative, presumably because of the context. However, searching the Scriptures is one of the three primary means of grace described by Wesley. It was important in Wesley's understanding of how to guide the spiritual journeys of those in the Methodist Societies. His practical concern overrode his concern for accuracy in translation.

The third example of Wesley's practical concern is that he follows through on his design to make the *Explanatory Notes upon the New Testament* "as plain as possible."[3] While there are echoes and brief statements of complex doctrinal positions therein, by and large the notes are practical. Some of the longest notes are those most hortatory in purpose. Consider the note on Matthew 16:24, "If any man be willing to come after me, let him deny himself, and take up his cross, and follow me":

Should we not consider all crosses, all things grievous to flesh and blood, as what they really are,—as opportunities of embracing God's will at the expense of our own; and, consequently, as so many steps by which we may advance toward perfection? We should make a swift progress in the spiritual life, if we were faithful in this practice. . . . Let us bear these little things, at least for God's sake, and prefer his will to our own in matters of so small importance and his goodness will accept these mean oblations; for he despiseth not the day of small things.[4]

The entire note is hortatory. There is no discussion of the significance of crosses in Palestinian justice, or whether Jesus was predicting his own death on a cross, or any other historical explanation. Rather, Wesley is concerned with making the text's application clear to his readers.

Prerequisites

Wesley's prerequisites for the interpretation of Scripture are extremely hard to measure by his use of them. Prayer before Bible reading, and the influence of the Spirit on the reader, cannot be measured by the output of the reader's study. However, the use of prayer can be measured by Wesley's diary in conjunction with at least one of the sermons in the sample being analyzed. To publish the sermon "Free Grace" in 1739 was difficult for him. The dispute about predestination was dividing the English Evangelicals, and separated the Wesley brothers from their Oxford colleague George Whitefield. Wesley's account of his struggle is contained in a letter to James Hutton and the Fetter Lane Society, written April 30, 1739. He had determined not to preach against predestination, but found himself doing so anyway: "I was led, I know not how, to speak strongly and explicitly of predestination, and then to pray that if I spake not the truth of God he would stay his hand, and work no more among us; if this was his truth, he would 'not delay to confirm it by signs following.'"[5] "Brother" Purdy was pressing him to preach on predestination. He and Wesley cast lots and received an answer from the Lord to "preach and print." Wesley continued preaching. His Diary for April 29 states, "5.30 Prayed; writ" and then he preached at 7:00 A.M. on "Free Grace."[6] The result was the printing of the sermon "Free Grace" with the preface which claimed Wesley was "indispensably obliged to declare this truth to all the world."[7]

In this situation, Wesley clearly follows his rule of seeking the inspiration of the Spirit concerning his interpretation of Scripture. He prayed, cast lots, and sought the advice of Christian friends both concerning content and concerning manner of presentation. This pattern is repeated with other sermons. The Diary entries frequently show prayer and the writing of a sermon linked together.[8] For March 26, 1790, the Diary entry reads "4[:00 A.M.] Prayed, sermon, prayer." On that day he finished "On the Wedding Garment."[9] It is possible, however, that by "sermon" Wesley meant preparation for the sermon he preached at 9:00 that day. Also, he twice entered "sermon" without the notation "prayed." Further, there is no way to ascertain the subject of Wesley's prayers and no way to show that he noted every prayer time in his Diary. However, given the only available evidence, namely, the Diaries, we have strong indications that Wesley did couple prayer with his scriptural interpretation.

Wesley also noted that a wide range of knowledge in various disciplines was extremely helpful if not necessary to correct interpretation of Scripture. The five areas of knowledge that he identifies are all ones in which he demonstrated competence. He knew "the original tongues" and relied on his knowledge of Greek and Hebrew for arguments at key points.[10] He was well educated in classical literature and world history and sought to relate the Bible to those ideas and events where appropriate.[11] His interest in the sciences shows up at key points.[12] He used the Fathers as resources for his interpretation.[13] The description of the ideal minister Wesley gave in *An Address to the Clergy* was one that Wesley himself largely fulfilled.[14] Wesley's vast learning in history, science, and theology, his reasoning ability, and his knowledge of the original biblical languages are frequently illustrated in the citations used in part 2 of this study.

Rules of Interpretation

Wesley usually does not make explicit appeal to one of his rules of interpretation in his use of Scripture. Once the rules have been identified, however, it is possible to see many places in which they have been applied or broken. We will examine each of Wesley's seven rules in turn.

Speak as the Oracles of God

We have noted earlier the large number of scriptural quotations found in Wesley's sermons, and to a lesser but still significant extent, in the polemical writings. This is the clearest evidence that Wesley was indeed following his own rule of interpretation by adopting the very words of Scripture wherever he could. Some of his sermons make less use of Scripture than others. "On Laying the Foundation of the New Chapel," for instance, has only twenty-four scriptural quotations compared with one hundred fifty-nine in "Christian Perfection." In the former, he is reviewing the history of the Methodist Revival, whereas in the latter he is trying to provide scriptural arguments to support one of his most controversial tenets.

It was precisely to support his most controversial points that Wesley most often appealed to his rule of speaking as the oracles of God. In his *Earnest Appeal*, he writes, "Have you not another objection nearly allied to this, namely that we preach perfection? True, but what perfection? The term you cannot object to, because it is scriptural. All the difficulty is to fix the meaning of it according to the Word of God."[15] Thus, Wesley is prepared to stand his ground on the argument that if a term is found in Scripture, it can be used without objection. The only difficulty is to "fix its definition" according to the Bible.

On the other hand, Wesley once notes that he avoids words that bring about controversy when they occur infrequently in Scripture. However, he makes this comment in regard to the word "conversion," because, he says, "it rarely occurs in the New Testament."[16] Strictly speaking, Wesley is right. In the AV, "conversion" occurs only once in the New Testament, at Acts 15:3. However its cognates occur nine times in the New Testament,[17] rendering Wesley's claim somewhat suspect. It is more likely that he is concerned about reducing controversy, and avoids scriptural words on occasions when he feels that the controversy would not be helpful.

In the sermon "The Witness of the Spirit, II," he makes a similar point. Arguing that he is generally satisfied with his earlier sermon on the same topic, he says, "Neither do I conceive how any of these expressions may be altered so as to make them more intelligible. I can only add, that if any of the children of God will point out any other expressions which are more clear, and more agreeable to the Word of God, I will readily lay these aside."[18] The use of the very words of Scripture is, in Wesley's view, the best way to be "agreeable to the Word of God." He understands that there are several such possibilities and expresses openness to change. He is convinced, however, of the rightness of his own terminology because it is found in the Bible itself. Presumably any other words that are more agreeable would be biblical phrases as well.

The concatenation of scriptural quotations discussed at length earlier[19] is one clear instance of using Scripture in accordance with the rule "speak as the oracles of God." Wesley believed the message of Scripture was plain, and he sought to use those plain words to enforce scriptural truth. Another illustration of this rule is Wesley's use of Scripture as the dictionary for defining key terms. The definition from Scripture he quotes most often is that of "faith" from Hebrews 11:1. This text is quoted twenty-six different times in the sermons, and in eleven instances it serves as an explicit definition.[20] One of the most explicit of these definitional uses of Scripture comes in "The Scripture Way of Salvation." Wesley writes,

> Faith in general is defined by the Apostle, ἔλεγχος πραγμάτων οὐ βλεπομένων—"an evidence," a divine "evidence and conviction" (the word means both), "of things not seen"—not visible, not perceivable either by sight or by any other of the external senses. It implies both a supernatural *evidence* of God and of the things of God, a kind of spiritual *light* exhibited to the soul, and a supernatural *sight* or perception thereof.[21]

Wesley takes this definition as the authoritative one. He does not contrast it with others; rather, he considers other Scripture passages to refine it and explain it more fully. For example, he quotes Ephesians 1:18 ("'the eyes of' our 'understanding being opened'") and Galatians 2:20 (Christ "loved *me*, and gave himself for *me*")[22] to indicate the manner and the content of this spiritual sight. But "faith" is not the only key term for which Wesley seeks a scriptural definition. In the *Earnest Appeal*, as we have already seen, Wesley argues that the only question was to fix the meaning of "perfection" according to the word of God. Again, in his note on Matthew 5:9, Wesley suggests "Peace, in the Scripture sense, implies all blessings, temporal and eternal."[23] In his sermon "The Means of Grace," he writes,

It has been, secondly, objected, "This is seeking salvation by works." Do you know the meaning of the expression you use? What is "seeking salvation by works"? In the writings of St. Paul it means either seeking to be saved by observing the ritual works of the Mosaic law, or expecting salvation for the sake of our own works, by the merit of our own righteousness.[24]

In each of these instances, Wesley uses Scripture as a dictionary to define key terms.

Two possible purposes of such usage should be considered, however briefly. First, we saw in chapter 4 that Wesley's desire for simplicity reflects the spirit of his age. Nothing could be more simple and pure than the original words of the text. Wesley's implementation of his rule to "speak as the oracles of God" illustrates the larger concern to curb dogmatic additions to the authority of Scripture. He sought to let the text plainly speak for itself. There is thus a significant relationship between this rule and interpretation according to the literal sense, which will be considered later. Second, the suggestion that this is possibly a type of sanctified speech showing the speaker to be a mature Christian must be taken seriously. It would appear that the context of the Revival, with its concern to transform nominal Christians into more deeply committed Christians, would lend credence to this interpretation.

However, one would then expect Wesley's pattern of speech to change when addressing an audience more cultured than his typical working-class Methodists. In such a setting, demonstrating his piety by quantity of scriptural quotation would not improve his credibility at all. Wesley's one sermon *ad magistratum*[25] shows the same patterns of scriptural quotation as the others. On the one hand, this might indicate that the hypothesis of sanctified speech is not accurate, because Wesley used it where it did not matter in that regard. On the other hand, it could be that he did not alter an established habit for a noble audience, or that he thought this method of citing Scripture would carry authority there as well.

Use the Literal Sense Unless It Contradicts Another Scripture or Implies an Absurdity

Wesley's strongest instinct in interpreting Scripture is to read it as it is and take its most literal, direct meaning. His sermon "The Means of Grace" poses the question "whether there are any means of grace."[26] He proposes to answer that question by consulting "the oracles of God," because it is impossible to conceive "that the Word of God should give no direction in so important a point."[27] Wesley then answers the question by quoting biblical commands about prayer, searching the Scriptures, and partaking of the Lord's Supper. To support these as being commanded and binding on Christians, he describes Scripture's statement as "express," "plain," "full and express," "clear," "plain and clear," "peremptory," "clear explicit," and "evident."[28] What makes this claim of clarity even more striking is that Wesley's second means of grace is built upon a translation of the Greek that is at best ambiguous. With regard to John 5:39, which reads "Search the Scriptures" in the AV, Wesley says,

> The objection that this is not a command, but only an assertion that they did "search the Scriptures," is shamelessly false. I desire those who urge it to let us know how a command can be more clearly expressed than in those terms, ἐρευνᾶτε τὰς γραφάς. It is as peremptory as so many words can make it.[29]

Wesley knows his Greek better than this. He knows that the second person plural indicative and imperative forms are exactly the same, and that the judgment about translation must rely on the context. It is true that the English translations prior to his time agree with his view here.[30] However, Wesley's unwillingness to see the possibility of another translation illustrates the *a priori* conviction that the Scripture is clear and plain.[31]

On this same understanding, Wesley often attacks those who interpret the Scripture in anything other than its "plain, indisputable" meaning.[32] His exegesis of 1 John 3:9 forms part of his argument for Christian perfection. In the sermon "The Marks of the New Birth," he writes,

> But some men will say, "True; 'whosoever is born of God doth not commit sin' *habitually*." *Habitually!* Whence is that? I read it not. It is not written in the Book. God plainly saith, he "doth not commit sin." And thou addest, "habitually"! Who art thou that *mendest* the oracles of God? That "addest to the words of this Book"? Beware, I beseech thee, lest God "add to thee all the plagues that are written therein"! Especially when the comment thou addest is such as quite swallows up the text: so that by this μεθοδεία πλάνης, this artful method of deceiving, the precious promise is utterly lost; by

this κυβεία ἀνθρώπων, this tricking and shuffling of men, the Word of God is made of none effect.[33]

Two points need to be emphasized with respect to this quotation. First, Wesley says he is opposed to any altering of the text at all. He is not prepared to depart from what is written there. One is not to "mend" the text. Second, this mending is especially wrong when it "swallows up the text" and the "precious promise is lost" and the Word is rendered ineffectual. This is a case where Wesley has a key text that plays an important role in establishing the whole tenor of Scripture, and it must not be watered down so that its meaning is less strong than a plain and literal interpretation. Wesley is concerned that the message of the text be allowed its full force so that it supports the pattern of doctrine he calls the analogy of faith. Similar attacks on altering the text can be found in several places.[34]

However, there are other places where Wesley does precisely what he condemns, inserting words into the text. Sometimes he quotes a biblical passage and inserts "explanatory" words into the verse. At one point he interrupts his quotation of Hebrews 10:26-27 to insert "experimental" before "knowledge of the truth."[35] In the conclusion of "The Witness of the Spirit, II," he quotes both Romans 8:15 and Philippians 4:7, inserting an explanatory phrase in the middle of the latter: "But when we have once received this 'Spirit of adoption,' that 'peace which passes all understanding,' and which expels all painful doubt and fear, will 'keep our hearts and minds in Christ Jesus.'"[36] Doubtless, Wesley would argue that such "mending" does not "swallow up the text" or lose the "precious promise" or render the Word "ineffective."

In the *Notes* Wesley frequently adds to the text by inserting words in the middle. He consciously mends the text of 1 John 2:20 to make it read "Ye know all things *that are needful for your soul's health.*"[37] He argues for this emendation on the grounds that not mending the text would leave it in contradiction to Matthew 10:24 and, on the basis of the context, that without the added words the following verses would be contradicted. However, his comment on Matthew 26:52 mends the text by adding what is simply not there: "*All they that take the sword*—Without God's giving it to them; without sufficient authority." For this addition, no argument is given, no other Scriptures cited. Perhaps Wesley sees these as obvious qualifications to the meaning of the text. But it appears to be precisely the sort of "mending" of which he accused his opponents.

When the content of the text gets even more uncomfortable for Wesley, there is a more explicit "mending." In Wesley's translation, Romans 11:8 reads "God hath given them a spirit of slumber, eyes that they should not see, and ears that they should not hear, unto this day." Such a verse poses distinct problems for Wesley, who argues strongly against this kind of predestination and for the free grace of God working to save everyone. Thus Wesley's note reads "*God hath* at length withdrawn his Spirit, and so *given them* up to *a spirit of slumber;* which is fulfilled *unto this day.*" Wesley here mends the text in a way that does violence to this verse and to Paul's meaning.

The key to understanding Wesley on this point is the rule about interpretation according to the analogy of faith. For him, mending the text is interpretation that violates its true meaning. The true meaning of any text must be consistent with the general tenor of Scripture. Thus, to interpret according to that general tenor is not mending, but explanation that brings out the true meaning. This point is made in the sermon "The Signs of the Times." There Wesley rejects one obvious meaning because it is blasphemous. He begins by quoting John 12:40, alluding to Isaiah 6:10:

> "He hath blinded their eyes, and hardened their hearts; that they should not see with their eyes, nor understand with their hearts, and be converted, and I should heal them." The plain meaning is, not that God did this by his own immediate power—it would be flat blasphemy to say that God in this sense hardens any man—but his Spirit strives with them no longer, and then Satan hardens them effectually.[38]

The point to notice here is that the "plain" meaning is the result of interpretation and not the one that is most literally obvious. Perhaps Wesley has in mind here his rule that any Scripture where the literal sense contradicts another Scripture or leads to an absurdity must be interpreted according to a different sense. We have already seen how Wesley argues in "Free Grace" that no Scripture can be used to prove a Calvinist understanding of predestination—better it be left as meaningless than given that meaning.

The last half of Romans 8 is another instance of a passage difficult for Wesley to annotate. It is a *locus classicus* for the doctrine of predestination, and in his *Notes* Wesley takes pains to put an Arminian gloss on it. In the course of the argument he suggests that the passage cannot be taken literally:

> The works of providence and redemption are vast and stupendous, and therefore we are apt to conceive of God as deliberating and consulting on them, and then decreeing to act according to "the counsel of his own will"; as if, long before the world was made, he had been concerting measures both as to the making and governing of it, and had then writ down his decrees, which altered not, any more than the laws of the Medes and Persians. Whereas, to take this consulting and decreeing in a literal sense, would be the same absurdity as to ascribe a real human body and human passions to the ever-blessed God.
>
> This is only a popular representation of his infallible knowledge and unchangeable wisdom.[39]

Here Wesley is arguing that the predestinarian conception of God relies on a literal reading of the text which is absurd inasmuch as it cannot do justice to God's attributes.[40]

It is not always clear what Wesley suggests when the literal meaning is not the correct interpretation. Within the sample of material analyzed for this study, there is no place where Wesley simply rejects the literal interpretation and substitutes an allegorical or "figurative" sense. Robin Scroggs suggests that the interpretation of Matthew 3:12 is allegorical.[41] There John the Baptist says (in Wesley's translation), "Whose fan *is* in his hand, and he will throughly cleanse his floor, and gather the wheat into the garner; but will burn up the chaff with unquenchable fire." Wesley's note says that the fan is the "word of the gospel," the floor is the church, and the wheat are those who are truly good. Wesley does not introduce this as figurative interpretation. Rather, he would understand this as the literal meaning of the metaphor John is using. The same argument could be made about Scroggs' view that the interpretation of the parable of the ten virgins (Matthew 25:1-13) is allegorical. Wesley would again maintain that this must have been Jesus' intent in telling the parable and such interpretation is the only way to give the literal meaning of the text.

In one setting he claims that both literal and "figurative" interpretations are valid. In the sermon "The New Creation," he writes the following about the new heaven and the new earth:

> Nay, no creature, no beast, bird, or fish, will have any inclination to hurt any other. For cruelty will be far away, and savageness and fierceness be forgotten. So that violence shall be heard no more, neither wasting or destruction seen on the face of the earth. "The wolf shall dwell with the lamb" (the words may be literally as well as figuratively understood) "and the leopard shall lie down with the kid."[42]

Here the meaning of "figuratively" seems to be that the text in question is a metaphor for a comprehensive peace between God's creatures and not simply between wolves and lambs. This understanding also holds for the interpretation of Jesus' being spared from the slaughter of the innocents in Matthew 2:16-18. Wesley's note suggests that the preservation of Jesus "may be considered as a figure of God's care over his children in their greatest danger."[43]

In another place, Wesley consciously interprets a text in a "spiritual sense" that goes beyond the literal. In "The Signs of the Times," he asks whether there are any signs that God's power is approaching:

> I appeal to every candid, unprejudiced person, whether we may not at this day discern all those signs (understanding the words in a spiritual sense) to which our Lord referred John's disciples. "The blind receive their sight." Those who were blind from their birth, unable to see their own deplorable state, and much more to see God and the remedy he has prepared for them in the Son of his love, now see themselves, yea, and "the light of the glory of God in the face of Jesus Christ."[44]

Wesley continues by arguing that spiritual lameness, spiritual deafness, and the leprosy of sin have been cured in many. When it comes to the poor having the gospel preached to them, he takes that in the literal meaning of the word "poor." Wesley's interpretation does not show many signs of using different senses of Scripture other than this metaphorical application of the literal sense.

One other aspect of Wesley's use of the literal sense of Scripture appears in his concern for the historical circumstances of the original writers of the Bible. It was discussed earlier that he often takes scriptural phrases out of context. But throughout the *Explanatory Notes upon the New Testament* he points out customs, currencies, relevant Jewish sayings, and other parts of the historical background that help the reader to understand the meaning of the text. At Matthew 10:14, he explains "Shake off the dust from your feet" by saying:

> The Jews thought the land of Israel so peculiarly holy, that when they came home from any heathen country, they stopped at the borders, and shook or wiped off the dust of it from their feet, that the Holy Land might not be polluted with it. Therefore the action here enjoined was a lively intimation, that those Jews who had rejected the gospel were holy no longer, but were on a level with heathens and idolaters.[45]

One need not agree with this understanding of the context or what it implies for interpretation in order to appreciate Wesley's concern to discover what the action meant at the time of the writing of the text.

However, this concern for the historical context of the Bible highlights the crucial difference between Wesley and historical-critical interpretation. Here Wesley understands that the literal sense is that sense which the author intended when writing. On such a definition, interpretation according to the literal sense requires the highest understanding possible of the original context. The ultimate extension of this view sees Scripture as a purely human document to be understood completely in the light of its historical circumstances.

While Wesley is interested in the human side of Scripture, his primary emphasis falls on the divine authorship of the text. For Wesley, the Bible's unity stems from the fact that it has a single ultimate author. Thus, for Scripture to be interpreted according to the intent of the author, one must consult the entire Book, because that is the only key we have to what the author is trying to say. Thus, the exceptions to the rule of literal interpretation become critically important. The literal sense cannot be contradictory to other Scriptures, because that would charge God with self-contradiction. The literal meaning of a text must be one that coincides with the general tenor of Scripture, which is determined by the analogy of faith.

Interpret the Text with Regard to Its Literary Context

One of the clearest uses of this rule in Wesley's writing comes in "The Means of Grace." The objectors are said to quote Exodus 14:13, "Stand still and see the salvation of God":

> Let us examine the Scriptures to which you refer. The first of them, with the context, runs thus: "And when Pharaoh drew nigh, the children of Israel lifted up their eyes . . ., and they were sore afraid. [. . .] And they said unto Moses, Because there were no graves in Egypt, hast thou taken us away to die in the wilderness? And Moses said unto the people, Fear ye not: stand still, and see the salvation of the Lord. [. . .] And the Lord said unto Moses, [. . .] Speak unto the children of Israel that they go forward. But lift thou up thy rod, and stretch out thine hand over the sea, and divide it. And the children of Israel shall go on dry ground through the midst of the sea."
>
> This was the "salvation" of God which they "stood still" to see—by "marching forward" with all their might![46]

Here Wesley adroitly uses the context to reverse the intended meaning of the objector.

In another instance, Wesley begins "The Use of Money" with reference to the context. The text for the sermon is Luke 16:9. Wesley begins by not only reciting the parable for which this is the concluding lesson, but also noting the audience to whom the parable was first told, and that the previous parable was addressed to a different audience.[47] However, Wesley is also capable of deserting the context, especially when the passage serves as the text of the sermon. This rule is not applied to the texts for "The Means of Grace," "On Laying the Foundation of the New Chapel," and "Causes of the Inefficacy of Christianity."[48] In each of these cases, however, he makes some reference to the literary context before he departs from it.

In extended interpretation there are many occasions where Wesley takes into account the context of the verse for its proper understanding. In his sermon "The Marks of the New Birth," Wesley argues that one such mark is power over sin. He quotes 1 John 3:1-2 for support, and then suggests, "Suffer we the Apostle to interpret his own words by the whole tenor of his discourse. In the fifth verse of this chapter he had said, 'Ye know that he (Christ) was manifested to take away our sins; and in him is no sin.' What is the inference he draws from this?"[49] He then continues by quoting other verses from the same chapter and arguing his view of 1 John's whole train of thought.

Wesley's interpretation according to the first rule, "speak as the oracles of God," frequently violates this rule about using the literary contexts. Wesley's habit of using scriptural phrases without reference or explanation also ignores the context from which they were taken. Wesley might argue that this was not a matter of extended interpretation, but simply using the words of Scripture the way they were intended to be used.

Scripture Interprets Scripture, According to the Analogy of Faith and by Parallel Passages

Interpretation according to the analogy of faith has already been seen to play a key role in Wesley's understanding of the literal sense of Scripture. By "analogy of faith," he means "the general tenor of [the oracles of God] . . . that grand scheme of doctrine which is delivered therein, touching original sin, justification by faith, and present, inward salvation."[50] Thus, no particular part of Scripture can be fully understood without reference to the whole of Scripture. Wesley's use of this rule can be traced under three different headings: the wholeness of the Bible, the use of parallel passages, and the use of counterpoint texts.

We have already discussed at some length the ways in which Wesley's use of Scripture relates to his understanding of its wholeness, as seen in the pattern of citations for Scripture's authority. It will suffice here simply to argue again that for Wesley, all interpretation must be according to the whole message of the Bible. Thus, in the sermon "On Laying the Foundation of the New Chapel," he defends Methodism from the charge of being new by saying,

> This is the *religion of the Bible,* as no one can deny who reads it with any attention. It is the religion which is continually inculcated therein, which runs through both the Old and New Testament. Moses and the prophets, our Blessed Lord and his apostles, proclaim with one voice, "Thou shalt love the Lord thy God with all thy soul, and thy neighbour as thyself."[a] The Bible declares, "Love is the fulfilling of the Law,"[b] "the end of the commandment,"[c] of all the commandments which are contained in the oracles of God.[51]

Here Wesley argues for a particular theme and then quotes several different parts of the Bible to make his point. This habit of citing many different passages from different parts of Scripture to make the same point occurs regularly throughout Wesley's writings.[52]

In the *Notes* at Matthew 11:28, Wesley interprets the words "Come to me all ye that labour and are heavy laden, and I will give you rest." His interpretation treats the burden of the "heavy laden" as "the guilt and power of sin." "Rest" is thus justification (resting from the guilt) and sanctification (rest from the power of sin). While such an interpretation is not implausible, Wesley's commitment to interpretation according to his version of the analogy of faith gives a sharp focus to these words.

One of the perennial problems for defenders of scriptural wholeness comes in the interpretation of the apparently conflicting emphases of Romans and James. In his *Notes* Wesley recognizes the difficulty and then attempts to harmonize the two epistles. However, it is significant that he does so by introducing a concept of double justification. His note on James 2:21 says,

> St. Paul says he [Abraham] was justified by faith, Rom. iv. 2, etc.: yet St. James does not contradict him; for he does not speak of the same justification. St. Paul speaks of that which Abraham received many years before Isaac was born, Gen. xv. 6; St. James, of that which he did not receive till *he had offered up Isaac on the altar*. He was justified, therefore, in St. Paul's sense, (that is, accounted righteous,) by faith, antecedent to his works. He was justified in St. James's sense, (that is, made righteous,) by works, consequent to his faith. So that St. James's justification by works is the fruit of St. Paul's justification by faith.[53]

Clearly Wesley has a problem here. His normal discussions of the order of salvation refer to sanctification which follows justification. One might suggest that Wesley has interpreted James' "justification" as equivalent to "sanctification." But in his sermon "The Scripture Way of Salvation," he makes the argument that human beings are sanctified (that is made righteous) by faith. Works are necessary only remotely and conditionally, as they are necessary to a continuing and lively faith.[54] Therefore, this problem is not a case of mistaken terminology.

The passage in question is one of several references to a doctrine of double justification, which Wesley held but did not emphasize.

Harald Lindström discusses the issue at some length, arguing that "sanctification has its place between present justification or present salvation on the one hand and final justification or final salvation on the other."[55] John Deschner agrees with Lindström that there is a twofold justification in Wesley. He uses Wesley's *Notes* on Matthew 12:37 and the polemical writings of 1772–73 as evidence. Deschner concludes, "Final justification remains, nevertheless, a justification by faith, although works are then adduced to prove the existence of living faith."[56] Wesley is here resolving a problem of consistency between books of the Bible by reference to the analogy of faith, the Bible's general tenor.

A second way of looking at this rule of interpretation is to consider Wesley's suggestion that the interpreter consider "parallel passages." There is a sense in which concatenations of scriptural quotations are really "parallel" passages. In many of these, Wesley finds texts that carry the same message and uses them in sequence to make the point he wishes to make. However, there are places where Wesley is explicitly looking for a passage that is "parallel" to one under more lengthy consideration. One purpose of seeking parallels is to clarify the meaning of terms by finding how they are used in other places. In the sermon "On Working Out Our Own Salvation" Wesley writes,

> But how are we to "work out" this salvation? The Apostle answers, "With fear and trembling." There is another passage of St. Paul wherein the same expression occurs, which may give light to this: "Servants, obey your masters according to the flesh," according to the present state of things, although sensible that in a little time the servant will be free from his master, "with fear and trembling." This is a proverbial expression, which cannot be understood literally. For what master could bear, much less require, his servant to stand trembling and quaking before him? . . . It is easy to see that these strong expressions of the Apostle clearly imply two things: first, that everything be done with the utmost earnestness of spirit, and with all care and caution—perhaps more directly referring to the former word, μετὰ φόβου, "with fear"; secondly, that it be done with the utmost diligence, speed, punctuality, and exactness—not improbably referring to the latter word, μετὰ τρόμου, "with trembling."[57]

Another purpose of examining parallel passages however, has to do with reinforcing the content of a passage. In "Upon Our Lord's

Sermon on the Mount, IV," Wesley quotes Matthew 5:13, part of his text,

> "If the salt have lost its savour, wherewith shall it be salted? It is thenceforth good for nothing but to be cast out, and trodden under foot of men." . . . If ye had never known the Lord there might have been hope—if ye had never been "found in him." But what can you now say to that his solemn declaration, just parallel to what he hath here spoken? "Every branch in me that beareth not fruit, he (the Father) taketh away. . . . He that abideth in me, and I in him, bringeth forth much fruit. . . . If a man abide not in me" (or, do not bring forth fruit) "he is cast out as a branch, and withered; and men gather them" (not to plant them again, but) "to cast them into the fire." (John 15:2, 5-6)[58]

Here Wesley is reinforcing the uncomfortable message of Matthew 5:13 with the same point made in John 15:5-6. Wesley is using a parallel passage to support his interpretation.

But there is an interesting variation of this "parallel passage" rule. On many occasions, Wesley turns to a related passage not to support but rather to pose a potential objection to the point he wants to make. In this counterpoint use, he introduces a text that seems to bear a contrary meaning and then disposes of the objection by reconciling the two texts. In the sermon "Upon Our Lord's Sermon on the Mount, IV," Wesley is concerned to prove that Christianity is a social religion[59] and should not be hidden by a solitary life. Wesley devotes §III of the sermon to answering objections. He writes,

> "But 'God is a Spirit, and they that worship him must worship him in spirit and in truth.' And is not this enough? Nay, ought we not to employ the whole strength of our mind herein? Does not attending to outward things clog the soul, that it cannot soar aloft in holy contemplation? . . . Whereas St. Paul would have us 'to be without carefulness,' and to 'wait upon the Lord without distraction.'"
>
> I answer, "God is a Spirit, and they that worship him must worship him in spirit and in truth." Yea, and this is enough: we ought to employ the whole strength of our mind therein. But then I would ask, "What is it to worship God, a Spirit, in spirit and in truth?" Why, it is to worship him with our spirit; to worship him in that manner which none but spirits are capable of. . . . Consequently one branch of the worshipping God in spirit and in truth is the keeping his outward

commandments. To glorify him therefore with our bodies as well as with our spirits, to go through outward work with hearts lifted up to him, to make our daily employment a sacrifice to God, to buy and sell, to eat and drink to his glory: this is worshipping God in spirit and in truth as much as the praying to him in a wilderness.[60]

Note that here Wesley provides a different interpretation of the apparently conflicting verse from the one attributed to his opponent. He explicitly asks what the other verse means and then shows that it really does not conflict with the point he made earlier.

Many other examples of this counterpoint use exist in Wesley's writings. In general they should be taken as an indication of two things. First, theology was often written in a controversial form during the eighteenth century, and Wesley is no exception. Some of his sermons, like "The Means of Grace" and "Free Grace," are highly controversial in form. Others, like "Catholic Spirit" and the series "Upon Our Lord's Sermon on the Mount," do not have an explicitly controversial form but yet take up controversies that rest on different interpretations of key texts. In many of these cases Wesley puts words and Scripture texts into the mouths of his opponents and then refutes them.

Second, this counterpoint use of Scripture must be seen as another way in which Wesley took seriously the wholeness of Scripture. He is bound to consider all of the texts that bear on a particular subject and not just those favorable to his view. By proposing a conflicting text and then showing that the conflict is only apparent, he strengthens his argument that the whole tenor of Scripture points in a particular direction.

The wholeness of Scripture is a strong element in Wesley's hermeneutics. We have seen that it affects the literal sense of Scripture for Wesley, and that he insists on interpretation according to the analogy of faith as a primary rule. Further, we have seen that the rule is one which did indeed play an important role in his use of Scripture. Why does Wesley see the wholeness of Scripture as constituted by the order of salvation? There is no firm evidence to which one can point for a certain answer. Wesley nowhere argues for this as the general tenor of the Bible. It is obvious to him that it is so. In his note on 1 Peter 4:11, he simply says, *"The oracles of God* teach that men should repent, believe, obey. He that treats of faith and leaves out repentance, or does not enjoin practical holiness to believers, does not speak as the oracles of God: he does not preach Christ, let him think as highly of himself as he will."[61] Here Wesley summarizes the contents of the Bible with the familiar triad of the order of salvation. The thrust of his message is to condemn incompleteness. Alternative lists of what the Bible teaches are not in question.

Several points may be suggested here. First, it was a widely shared assumption among Wesley's contemporaries that the Bible's main point was individual salvation. For example, Baxter's writings were directed to that point. Tillotson was concerned with it. Even Locke's exegesis was an attempt to uncover the simple message of the Bible to determine the true conditions for individual salvation. Within this context, it is not surprising that Wesley should come to the Bible "to find the way to heaven."[62]

Second, Wesley continues the Puritan appeal to the entire Scripture as a single voice with a single theme. Compared with these three leading theologians, Wesley's emphasis on the wholeness of Scripture fits in well with Baxter's conception and use, but is completely missing in Tillotson. Locke's concern for simplicity led to an approach that prevented such an appeal to the general tenor of the whole Bible.

Third, Wesley saw in Scripture an answer to the question of the individual's experience of God. The advances made in scientific method gave great credibility to reasoned interpretation of observed phenomena. Over and over Wesley made reference to "experimental" religion—a faith that could be observed, that is, felt, by the individual who was experiencing it. Further, while faith and commitment could not be directly observed, one could trust the testimonies given by individuals about their experiences and test their authenticity by observing the individuals' behavior in the path toward entire sanctification.

Albert Outler was correct in asserting that Wesley's distinctiveness in the Christian tradition lies in his holistic understanding of the Christian life.[63] He drew upon the traditions of "faith alone" and holy living to formulate a distinctive theology. This theology was grounded in an interpretation of Scripture that read it as answering the question of the individual's search for salvation. The cultural process that gave rise to Deism emptied traditional Anglicanism of its power to move the common people. Wesley was a child of the age of reason. His appeal to experience as the goal of the Christian life was the theological counterpart of the natural philosophers who rejected speculative science for observable phenomena. Given that cultural milieu, Wesley's formulation of the analogy of faith as the individual's experience of grace—prevenient, justifying, and sanctifying—is understandable.

Commandments Are Covered Promises

Wesley reads Scripture as a book of promises that will be fulfilled. In *An Earnest Appeal* he quotes Matthew 5:11-12 and says, "Do not you know that this (as well as all other Scriptures) must needs be fulfilled? If so, take knowledge that this day also it is fulfilled in your ears."[64] Wesley says in "The Means of Grace" that "I do expect that he will fulfil his Word, that he will meet and bless me in this way."[65] Further he says, "A sincere desire to receive all his promises" should be part of every Christian's preparation for the Lord's Supper.[66] It should be noted that Wesley's definition of "fulfillment" may differ from what a modern reader would expect. His note on Matthew 2:17 reads, "A passage of scripture, whether prophetic, historical, or poetical, is in the language of the New Testament fulfilled when an event happens to which it may with great propriety be accommodated."[67] Thus, words spoken in the Bible with one purpose in their original use can be said to be "fulfilled" by later events. Wesley's own translation of Matthew 21:32 reads, "For John came to you in a way of righteousness, and ye believed him not: but the publicans and the harlots believed him: and ye, seeing *it*, repented not afterward, that ye might believe him."[68] He then comments, "O how is this scripture fulfilled at this day!"[69] In another case, the beatitude "Blessed are they that mourn, for they shall be comforted" is "fulfilled" by those who are born again.[70] Many other examples can be found, including one where prophecies in Isaiah are referred to as "glorious promises made to the Christian church."[71]

What is critical to notice here is Wesley's reliance on the prophesies and statements in Scripture as promises to be "fulfilled" also in his own day. Crucial to this is his understanding that "as God is one, so the work of God is uniform in all ages. May we not then conceive how he *will* work on the souls of men in times to come by considering how he *does* work *now*? And how he *has* wrought in times past?"[72]

This usage of Scripture as a book of promises is one aspect of Wesley's implementation of his rule that commandments are "covered promises." Only one specific instance of interpreting a commandment in that way was contained in the sample studied. In the *Notes* his translation of Matthew 5:48 is, "Therefore ye shall be perfect, as your Father who is in heaven is perfect." The Authorized Version uses the imperative form "Be ye therefore perfect."[73] This translation is permitted by the ambiguity of the Greek Ἔσεσθε οὖν ὑμεῖς τέλειοι. However, it is important that Wesley's translation preserves the ambiguity of the Greek. "Ye shall" can be taken as future indicative or present imperative. His note, however, stresses the future promise of perfection:

> So the original runs, referring to all that holiness which is described in the foregoing verses, which our Lord in the beginning of the chapter recommends as happiness, and in the close of it as perfection.
>
> And how wise and gracious is this, to sum up, and as it were seal, all his commandments with a promise; even the proper promise of the gospel, that he will "put" those "laws in our minds, and write them in our hearts!"[74]

Wesley here makes explicit appeal to his principle of interpretation. He translates the imperative as a future indicative, and thereby insists on God's grace which will bring about what he has commanded. Wesley's principle covers more ground, however, than this ambiguity of Greek tenses. He intends it to mean that all biblical commandments are also promises. This claim must also be understood against his use of Scripture as a book of promises that can be fulfilled.

Interpret Literary Devices Appropriately

Wesley is conscious of issues of literary style. The introduction to his *Sermons on Several Occasions* says, "Nothing here appears in an elaborate, elegant, or oratorical dress."[75] He saw himself as writing *"ad populum*—to the bulk of mankind—to those who neither relish nor understand the art of speaking."[76] However, Wesley was himself aware of that art as it was studied and practiced in his day. This made him capable of interpreting literary devices in the Scriptures even if he disdained their use in his own prose. He notes various stylistic uses such as that the apostles rarely addressed people by name but rather used titles like "brethren" or "beloved."[77] He believes that Scripture's great literary merit is shown in many ways. At one point, for instance, Wesley notes that the examples presented in Romans 4 "are selected and applied with the utmost judgment and propriety."[78] Specifically, there are seven literary devices to which Wesley refers in his interpretation.

The first of these devices occurs when Wesley argues that "figurative" language must be interpreted properly. While some metaphors can be interpreted figuratively and literally,[79] others should be taken only figuratively. At one point Wesley argues that interpreters read Ecclesiastes 3:18 "in a more literal sense than ever Solomon meant it."[80] This point plays an important role in his comment on Matthew 26:26. The comment on the Last Supper reads,

> *This* bread *is*, that is, signifies or represents, *my body*, according to the style of the sacred writers. Thus, Gen xl.12, "The three branches are three days." Thus, Gal iv. 24, St. Paul, speaking of Sarah and Hagar, says, "These are the two covenants." Thus, in the grand type of our Lord, Exod. xii.11, God says of the paschal lamb, "This is the Lord's passover." Now Christ, substituting the holy communion for the passover, follows the style of the Old Testament, and uses the same expressions the Jews were wont to use in celebrating the passover.[81]

Two points are noteworthy here. First, the earlier conclusions about the unity of Scripture are borne out here. There is a "style of the sacred writers" that includes Paul, Jesus, and the Old Testament. Second, Wesley argues that the phrase "This is my body" can best be understood as symbolic on the same basis as other examples in the Bible. Two of the biblical examples are not parallel with the one under consideration. The Genesis passage is the interpretation of a dream, and the Galatians passage is an explicitly allegorical interpretation of Scripture. However, one reading of Exodus 12:11 could construe "This is the Lord's passover" as being a symbol of the Lord's passing over the people. Wesley suggests that the best reason for a symbolic interpretation of this passage is the similarity of style with these other passages.

The second literary device Wesley notes is transposition. His comment on Matthew 5:29 suggests that the 29th verse might refer to verses 27 and 28, and verse 30 refer to verses 21 and 22.[82] A third literary device he notes is the parallel structure of verses 38 and 34 in Romans 8.[83] A fourth literary device is synecdoche, using a part to represent the whole.[84] A fifth literary device is the use of "proverbial expressions," as in Matthew 6:3, "Let not thy left hand know what thy right hand doeth."[85] A sixth literary device is that of gradation, or the movement from a lower level of subject matter to a higher level.[86]

Perhaps the most controversial literary device Wesley notes is the use of another voice by the author. Wesley argues that Romans 7:7-25 cannot apply to the apostle himself:

> This is a kind of digression, to the beginning of the next chapter, wherein the apostle, in order to show in the most lively manner the weakness and inefficacy of the law, changes the person and speaks as of himself, concerning the misery of one under the law. This St. Paul frequently does, when he is not speaking of his own person, but only assuming another character, Rom. iii.5, 1 Cor. x. 30, iv.6. The character here assumed is that of a man, first ignorant of the law, then under it and sincerely, but ineffectually, striving to serve God. To have spoken this of himself, or any true believer, would have been foreign to the whole scope of his discourse; nay, utterly contrary thereto, as well as to what is expressly asserted, Rom. viii.2.[87]

In a similar way the "we" in James 3:1-3 must be a "figure of speech" since common sense shows that apostles could not offend in the ways described.[88] Note that in both cases it is not the literary form that suggests a different interpretation. Rather, the different interpretation is required by the content, the absurdity of a literal reading. But note that the absurdity of the literal reading lies in its relation to the general tenor of Scripture as understood by Wesley. Here again the concept of Scripture's wholeness determines the interpretation by governing what is absurd and what is not. Wesley cannot accept that Paul would have spoken the words of Romans 7:7-25, and so a literary device is assumed and the passage interpreted accordingly.

Wesley sometimes does rely on literary analysis to interpret Scripture. However, literary devices do not play a large role in his interpretation, but serve as ways of helping understand particular texts when needed. His use of them is dependent on his understanding of the divine authorship of Scripture, because he sees a unified literary style throughout all of Scripture.

Seek the Most Original Text and the Best Translation

Wesley's judgments about the correct text of the Bible must be measured against the background of his time. Textual criticism got its modern start with the work of Erasmus during the 1500s. Slow progress had been made, and by Wesley's time significant work was being done. Among other pioneers in the field, Johannes Bengel was a significant contributor; most of Wesley's understanding of textual criticism was derived from him. Bengel's influence was also felt on the content of Wesley's exegesis. Wesley took Bengel's *Gnomon of the New Testament* as the basis for his own *Explanatory Notes upon the New Testament*.

We have seen that Wesley is committed to the idea that establishing the best text is important, and he knows that the texts used by the translators of the Authorized Version could be improved upon. His translation of the New Testament is full of emendations that have a textual basis. For example, the AV of Matthew 9:13 ends, "For I am not come to call the righteous, but sinners to repentance." The Greek words εἰς μετάνοιαν are included in many manuscripts, but are now not included in the modern Nestle text.[89] Wesley's text reads, "For I am not come to call the righteous, but sinners" along with the NRSV and NIV and other modern translations. For many such corrections Wesley makes no justifying comment.

In four places, however, Wesley provides reasons for the textual changes that he makes. From the AV of Matthew 5:22, "But I say unto you, That whosoever is angry with his brother without a cause shall be in danger of the judgment," Wesley drops the words "without a cause." He offers this note on the verse:

> Some copies add, "without a cause": But this is utterly foreign to the whole scope and tenor of our Lord's discourse. If he had only forbidden the being angry without a cause, there was no manner of need of that solemn declaration, "I say unto you"; for the scribes and pharisees themselves said as much as this. Even they taught, men ought not to be angry "without a cause." So that this righteousness does not "exceed" theirs. But Christ teaches, that we ought not for any cause to be so angry as to call any man *Raca*, or *Fool*.[90]

Note that no external manuscript evidence is cited here. Wesley simply notes that some copies have the extra words. The arguments he advances are internal and appeal to the whole Sermon on the Mount, suggesting that the revised text is more consistent with the whole.

In a similar way, the content of the text is decisive in the case of 1 John 5:7-8. Modern critical editions delete a large section of verse 7 and part of verse 8. Wesley's text transposes the two verses but retains all of the traditional wording. His text reads, "[7] For there are three that testify on earth, the Spirit, and the water, and the blood: and these three agree in one. [8] And there are three that testify in heaven, the Father, the Word, and the Holy Ghost: and these three are one." His comment on the text appeals to Bengel, his favorite authority on such matters. He then gives his exposition of the two verses and concludes,

> It must now appear, to every reasonable man, how absolutely necessary the eighth verse is. St. John could not think of the testimony of the Spirit, and water, and blood, and subjoin, "The testimony of God is greater," without thinking also of the testimony of the Son and Holy Ghost; yea, and mentioning it in so solemn an enumeration. Nor can any possible reason be devised, why, without *three testifying in heaven*, he should enumerate *three*, and no more, *who testify on earth*. . . .
>
> The seventh verse, therefore, with the sixth, contains a recapitulation of the whole economy of Christ, from his baptism to pentecost; the eighth, the sum of the divine economy, from the time of his exaltation.
>
> Hence it farther appears, that this position of the seventh and eighth verses, which places those who testify *on earth* before those who testify *in heaven*, is abundantly preferable to the other, and affords a gradation admirably suited to the subject.[91]

Wesley did not have the research materials needed to make a detailed manuscript analysis of these verses. He did know, however, how to analyze the content of a text and had learned from Bengel that some internal arguments might be marshaled for or against a certain position.[92] Wesley's insistence on the doctrine of the Trinity in the face of Deist criticisms made this verse a critical one to retain in the Scriptures. Going even farther with this content criticism, Wesley argues for retaining the words "of God" in 1 John 3:16. He knows they are not in the original text, but argues that they belong there by implication. For this he suggests parallels with John 20:15 and Song of Solomon 1:2.

Perhaps Wesley's most serious mistake, from the viewpoint of modern textual criticism, is his argument for deleting the word "Jeremy" in Matthew 27:9. The main English versions in use before his time agreed in naming Jeremy as the prophet who spoke the words which followed. Wesley's text simply says, "Then was fulfilled what was spoken by the prophet, saying. . . ." He then comments, "The word Jeremy, which was added to the text in later copies, and thence received into many translations, is evidently a mistake: for he who spoke what St. Matthew here cites, or rather paraphrases, was not Jeremy, but Zechariah."[93] Many things are at stake in this conclusion for Wesley. His understanding of the infallibility of the text requires an explanation. The emerging science of textual criticism provides a helpful answer he can use. The fact that he has no manuscript evidence is not nearly as important as his conviction that the original texts could not have made this kind of mistake.

These four examples taken together do not show Wesley as a great text critic. Almost all of his conclusions are based on Bengel. However, his openness to this new understanding of the Bible shows that he is willing to consider these kinds of issues so long as they do not contradict his theology. Where textual issues threaten to disrupt his reading of the whole message of Scripture, he abandons critical interpretation for the best traditional arguments he can find.

More pervasive for Wesley were questions of the proper translation of the biblical text from the original languages. Here Wesley was more at home and could argue the issues more forcefully on the basis of his own knowledge. Most important, he was aware of the difficulties of good translation and of the issues involved. In his sermon "The Marks of the New Birth," he writes,

> This hope (termed in the Epistle to the Hebrews πληροφορία πίστεως [Hebrews 10:22], and elsewhere πληροφορία ἐλπίδος [Hebrews 6:11] —in our translation, the "full assurance of faith," and the "full assurance of hope"; expressions the best which our language could afford, although far weaker than those in the original). . . .[94]

Wesley's translation of the New Testament was a significant revision of the text. He used the Authorized Version as his base, but made numerous alterations.[95] For example, in the book of Matthew, only 181 of the 1,070 verses did not have some change made to them. The changes can be grouped into five categories. First, there are changes which result from a revised Greek text. These were discussed earlier. George Croft Cell, in his introduction to *John Wesley's*

New Testament, argues that this reason explains a large number of the changes. Robin Scroggs suggests otherwise on the grounds that not many textual changes had been made even by Bengel and other scholars.[96] A resolution of how many such changes were for what reasons must await the publication of the definitive text in the Bicentennial Edition of Wesley's *Works*.

Second, there are changes that result from shifts in the English language. In almost every place where the AV uses "unto" Wesley uses "to."[97] He frequently changed the AV's "of" to "by,"[98] and the AV's "that" to "which" as a pronominal conjunction.[99] Many of Wesley's emendations are of this type, without substantive meaning but making the text clearer to eighteenth-century readers. Scroggs counts this as the most important reason.

Third, there are changes which result from a better understanding of Greek grammar. In most of the places where the AV has "answered and said," Wesley uses "answering said," which is a better translation of the Greek.[100] Such revisions rest on an understanding of the process of translation as attempting to capture the literal meaning of the original grammar without the wooden repetition of the Greek forms. In much the same way, Wesley omits many of the words italicized in the AV because they are not in the Greek text. He also does not italicize others on the grounds that they were legitimate parts of a good translation of the Greek text. These changes result from improvements in the scholarly understanding of Greek syntax made between 1611 and Wesley's time.

Fourth, Wesley prints the text in thematic paragraphs, abandoning the one paragraph to a verse that was characteristic of the AV. He was not alone in doing so. Other eighteenth-century translations did the same.[101] Among others, John Locke had argued that the division of the text into chapters and verses was an external cause of the obscurity of Scripture.[102]

Fifth, there are changes which result from Wesley's choice of a different word to provide what he thinks is a better translation of the Greek. These are substantive changes that often carry theological implications. For example, where the Greek text has μακάριοι Wesley uses "happy" instead of "blessed." Thus, in his translation Matthew 5:3-4 reads "Happy *are* the poor in spirit: for theirs is the kingdom of heaven. Happy *are* they that mourn: for they shall be comforted."[103] This supports Wesley's dictum that holiness and happiness are two names for the same thing.

Questions about translation sometimes play important parts in his sermons as well. In his sermon "Original Sin" he writes, "We see, when God opens our eyes, that we were before ἄθεοι ἐν [τῷ] κόσμῳ—'without God,' or rather, 'atheists in the world.'"[104] None of the leading English translations before Wesley's time used "atheists," although Outler's footnote tells us that the Geneva Bible used it in a marginal note.[105] Wesley's note on the passage paraphrases the text as "wholly ignorant of the true God, and so in effect atheists."[106] Thus, the transliteration is an acceptable translation as well. However, the word "atheist" carried pejorative connotations in the eighteenth century, and sharpened the distinction between the stages of being sinner and justified. Another case of translation that carried theological import was Wesley's insistence on the correct tense of σεσωσμένοι in Ephesians 2:8. Without printing the Greek word, he makes reference to the translation:

> And first let us inquire, What is *salvation?* The salvation which is here spoken of is not what is frequently understood by that word, the going to heaven, eternal happiness. It is not the soul's going to paradise, termed by our Lord "Abraham's bosom." It is not a blessing which lies on the other side death, or (as we usually speak) in the other world. The very words of the text itself put this beyond all question. "Ye *are* saved." It is not something at a distance: it is a present thing, a blessing which, through the free mercy of God, ye are now in possession of. Nay, the words may be rendered, and that with equal propriety, "Ye *have been* saved." So that the salvation which is here spoken of might be extended to the entire work of God, from the first dawning of grace in the soul till it is consummated in glory.[107]

Here Wesley argues for the present experience of salvation by insisting that it is something that happens in this life and not something to be expected in the future.

Scroggs concludes that "it can be said that the translation of John Wesley was a highly successful one for his day, based on the soundest learning at his disposal. While there are a few mistakes and some visible influences of his theology, his revision as a whole can be verified from the text itself."[108] From the limited sample studied here, Scroggs appears to be correct. Wesley did seek the most original text and best translation for the most part. His theological bias did affect his results in some key places, and should be considered in any overall evaluation of his translation work.

Conclusion

Three significant conclusions can be drawn from the evidence discussed in this chapter. First, Wesley's use of Scripture largely agrees with his conceptions of Scripture. Wesley applies each of the seven rules in a way that serves the purpose of interpretation as he understood it—the salvation of souls. He himself fulfills many of the prerequisites of good interpretation, and he interprets Scripture in ways that do not violate his own rules of interpretation. However, his interpretation sometimes shows a greater freedom than his stated conceptions would suggest. Frequently, this freedom results from conflicting rules of interpretation. Faced with such conflicts, Wesley picks that rule which best fits the purpose of interpretation in general. For example, he insists that people not "mend the text." Yet, if the text needs additional words in order to be interpreted in accordance with the general tenor of Scripture, Wesley freely makes additions.

Second, the principle that Scripture is to be interpreted as a whole dominates all the others. Nowhere in his conception of hermeneutics does Wesley rank his rules of interpretation in any way. Indeed, his explicit hermeneutics is so undeveloped that rarely does he relate any one rule to another. It would be characteristic of Wesley to deny that there were any conflicts between them at all. However, in his practice Wesley continually refers to the general tenor of Scripture to justify breaking one of the rules. For example, he follows the textual criticism of his day, except where it denies the validity of verses key to the analogy of faith. The doctrine of the Trinity is a necessary presupposition to the analogy of faith, so Wesley will not accept any emendation of 1 John 5:7 as found in the AV. Wesley's rule that biblical passages are to be interpreted with regard to their context is broken by his application of the rule to "speak as the oracles of God." His frequent use of scriptural phrases ignores the context altogether. The rule about interpretation according to the literal sense carries with it an explicit exception for contradicting other Scriptures. Wesley exploits this exception when dealing with passages that relate to the doctrine of predestination. His sermon

"Free Grace" indicates the lengths to which he is prepared to go to appeal to the general tenor of Scripture in opposition to the literal sense of a particular verse.

Third, Wesley has a serious problem in his hermeneutics. The tension between interpretation according to the literal sense and interpretation according to the general tenor of Scripture is never adequately addressed. To Wesley, it is obvious that the general tenor of Scripture consists of the doctrine of salvation applied to the experience of the individual. The purpose of biblical interpretation is salvation, and the general tenor is expressed in those doctrines which compose the order of salvation. Further, Wesley understands this to be the literal sense of the text when taken as a whole. However, many particular texts, when taken literally, do not support the general tenor Wesley has found.

The problem for Wesley is that this tension is never recognized. Nowhere is his view of the general tenor of Scripture defended in any general way. There are many different texts that are adduced to support particular points, but nowhere does Wesley make a systematic survey of the whole Scripture and show good reasons why the salvation of the individual soul is the main theme. Nowhere are alternative readings of Scripture examined so that this reading is shown to be the best possible one. If by "literal" Wesley means "faithful to the author's intent," and if the role of different human beings as participants in the creation of the Bible is acknowledged, then Wesley must resolve the problem between his understanding of the general tenor and other versions of the "literal" sense of the whole Bible.

Despite his failure adequately to resolve this tension, Wesley has shown the fruits of an exegesis that seeks to take seriously the general tenor of Scripture in the interpretation of each of its parts. The attraction of Wesley's hermeneutics is its holistic approach, which provides a fruitful interpretative tool. One must decide if Wesley's understanding of the analogy of faith is indeed a faithful and correct reading of the text. Further, one must decide if one can share Wesley's assumption that the biblical text can and should be read as a whole. But if one answers yes to those questions, then a very interesting and helpful hermeneutics opens up new pathways to understanding the Bible.

Conclusion

Wesley and the Authority of Scripture

Wesley's stated theological method is complex. We have seen that one must take into account the five different authorities that he both acknowledges and uses in his writings. We have seen that on different occasions Wesley formulates his position in seemingly contradictory ways, providing ample opportunities for his critics to accuse him of inconsistency. Yet, when Wesley is read carefully and attention is paid to the whole body of his writings, a consistent view of Scripture appears. The primacy of Scripture in his understanding of authority is clear. For Wesley, the Bible is the supreme authority for Christian teaching, indeed for sound thinking as such. It must be followed in preference to any other authority. Wesley holds a strong position on its inspiration; God is the author of Scripture. He understands that the very nature of God means that he cannot be ignorant and cannot lie. Since Scripture is divinely authored, it cannot make mistakes. Wesley's position on infallibility is uncompromising: there are no mistakes in the Bible. Wesley sees Scripture as sufficient, clear, and whole. Its wholeness is constituted by the analogy of faith, which he characterizes as "that grand scheme of doctrine which is delivered therein, touching original sin, justification by faith, and present, inward salvation."[1] The analogy of faith, for Wesley, constitutes at once the general theme of Scripture and the primary rule for the right interpretation of Scripture.

Once the authority of Scripture is clearly affirmed, the subordinate roles of other authorities become clear. Reason, Christian antiquity, the Church of England, and experience are all important to the method of determining Christian doctrine. For Wesley, these five form a single witness to the truth when they are rightly used. Scripture's message is reasonable; it is best interpreted by the early church; its teachings are clarified by the Church of England; and its principles are experienced in the lives of believers. Each authority has its own area of competence; more important, they all give the same message.

However, the strength of this affirmation is limited by the fact that Wesley defines the terms so that they are mutually interdependent. Of the five, Scripture depends least on the others. It is to be taken in its "plain, obvious meaning." However, we have seen that when Scripture implies a contradiction or absurdity, thereby contravening the standards of reason, one must depart the literal sense for a figurative one. Wesley had learned from Bengel that the Greek text of Scripture was not certain. He knew that in many cases a careful determination had to be made before one even knew what the text said. His arguments for textual revision are usually internal and governed by the basic tenets of Christian orthodoxy. Indeed, whatever the sense of Scripture might be, it could never be interpreted so as to portray God as the author of double predestination. That argument in "Free Grace" is so framed that it sometimes appeals to the general tenor of Scripture and sometimes to theological convictions.

The other terms depend on Scripture and each other for their definition. Concerning reason, Wesley defines it according to contemporary philosophy. But it is inconceivable to him that a "reasonable" person would not accept the divine authority of Scripture. Thus Scripture's content comes to determine what "reason" teaches. Christian antiquity, defined as the purest age of the church, is delimited by how faithful the Christians then living were to the teachings of Scripture. Wesley appeals to the Church of England not as an organizational hierarchy, but in terms of its Articles, Homilies, and Liturgy, which he deems to be scriptural. General human experience is important evidence in many matters of fact. For theological issues, it is only the Christian experience of real believers that counts.

Wesley's use of Scripture is generally consistent with his conception thereof. Scripture is clearly the dominant authority in practice as well as in theory, cited more often than all the other authorities combined and given the decisive role to play. We have seen that Wesley's doctrines of assurance and perfection are based mainly on "the plain sense of Scripture." Other arguments are brought in to reinforce the exegetical arguments, but Wesley thinks he is reading Scripture's clear meaning on these matters. Furthermore, Wesley's interpretation is controlled by his practical interest. Doctrinal speculation rarely occurs. Rather, Wesley interprets Scripture according to the analogy of faith and its soteriological focus. This is made clear both in the pattern of citation of his texts and in the way he handles difficult problems.

However, Wesley's use of Scripture points to a greater flexibility in three areas. First, his conception of inspiration gives a significant role to the human authors when he is actually commenting on key texts. While not admitting an error in the text, he explains why an error in the genealogical tables of Matthew 1 would be part of God's plan in writing for the Gospel's first audience.

Second, he makes a much greater use of the whole Christian tradition than his conception would suggest. To take Wesley's statements about tradition at face value, one would expect to find references only to the primitive church and the Church of England. Instead, we have found explicit references to several figures from Medieval and Reformation periods. We have also found uses of ideas and phrases taken directly from creeds and theologians during the "dark" periods of Christianity. From a twentieth-century point of view, Wesley is insufficiently self-critical about his use of tradition. One might argue that all Christian churches are the inheritors of centuries of Christian tradition and therefore are inescapably bound up in using it. Whereas some churches might seek to curb that influence, the Church of England provides explicit warrants for traditional influence in its Articles and Liturgy. In depending on the Church of England, Wesley is depending on the whole of Christian tradition more than he would admit. Whereas his conception of a fivefold but unified locus of authority is clear, his use indicates a fourfold but unified locus of authority. Christian antiquity and the Church of England are included in the broader category of tradition. He would never attribute to the whole of tradition an authority sui generis, but we have seen that he came to deny that type of authority to Christian antiquity as well. Wesley's use of tradition is subject to the similar qualification that only scriptural aspects of tradition are authoritative.

Third, Wesley's rules of interpretation occasionally conflict. Interpretation according to the analogy of faith dominates all the others, and even the literal sense of Scripture is to be abandoned if it conflicts with this general tenor. This conflict gives Wesley a great deal of freedom in his handling of texts. The tensions that are inevitably present in this freedom are not adequately addressed by Wesley's conception of Scripture. Nevertheless, the holistic approach to Scripture represented here has been seen to be a fruitful hermeneutic tool.

Wesley's theology was grounded in a reading of Scripture that holds to the authority of Scripture as primary within a complex but unified locus of authority. Wesley emphasizes the simplicity of Scripture while simultaneously acknowledging the usefulness of other authorities. Critics could argue that Wesley does not believe in Scripture alone, if a strict definition of that term is being used. However, no one does. Implicit in Wesley's method is the conviction that Scripture alone is our authority, yet Scripture is never alone. By acknowledging a fivefold locus of authority, Wesley makes clear the matrix of theological authority which is usually at work in Christian theology. The authority of particular churches is construed differently within those churches, and the authority of Christian antiquity, however defined, varies among different churches as well. However, some form of reason, tradition, and experience is usually authoritative in Christian theology, implicitly if not explicitly.

The Wholeness of Scripture

Wesley's reading of Scripture emphasizes the wholeness of the Bible as the key to its interpretation. Although his conception does not provide a hierarchy for the rules of interpretation, it is clear from his use that interpretation according to the analogy of faith is the controlling idea. Wherever different principles seem to clash, it is to the "general tenor" of the text that Wesley appeals.

It is his understanding of the "general tenor" of Scripture that is at once the most appealing and most puzzling aspect of Wesley's conception and use of Scripture. Modern biblical interpretation has analyzed Scripture, breaking it down into component parts. For example, the study of different authors within the canon of the New Testament often takes place in isolation and the problems pertaining to one author are seen as not necessarily related to those of another author. Wesley's claim that there is a general theme of Scripture which binds it together is appealing precisely because of its synthetic approach. Following Kelsey, it is clear that any Christian theologian must at some level discern a wholeness to the Bible. Wesley offers a clear view of what that wholeness is and proceeds to follow it in his interpretation. The analogy of faith really does function as the hermeneutical guide to the Scriptures. Within the analogy of faith, it is the doctrine of holiness that serves as his canon within the canon. While Wesley is not sufficiently self-critical to make that claim explicitly, holiness does function as the center of the interpretative framework. Such a framework is intriguing to modern interpreters precisely because it unifies many disparate elements in Scripture.

The puzzling aspect of his view of the general tenor of Scripture is the reasoning which justifies this particular formulation rather than another. We saw that Wesley nowhere argues for this understanding and has no conception that other, competing formulations might exist. To him, this is the plain, literal meaning of the whole Bible and any unbiased reader should see it clearly. We have seen that a partial explanation of how Wesley came to see the wholeness of Scripture in this way lies in his spiritual biography. As his theology and personal faith changed during 1738–39, so did his understanding of Scripture. Yet, Wesley would not have suggested an experiential basis for this new view of Scripture; when he asked to be shown scriptural proof for the crucial changes, the Moravians showed him.[2] To Wesley, the argument about how the general tenor of Scripture should be summarized would have to be based on the text itself.

Modern readers of Wesley do not have the luxury of presuming that any unbiased reader would see the three-part doctrine of salvation as the obvious way to characterize the wholeness of Scripture. Modern critical study has challenged any characterization of wholeness, and the diversity of voices within the Christian church has offered many views about what Christianity is all about. Any modern defender of Wesley's view would have to argue in very detailed ways that this particular view of Scripture is the best way to characterize what is going on in the text when considered as a whole.

Unfortunately, Wesley himself offers very little help in assembling the arguments needed to justify that thesis. In defense of his most controversial doctrines, assurance and perfection, Wesley offers detailed exegetical arguments that show the scriptural basis for his position. While one does not have to accept his views as the best interpretation of those texts, surely one must respect his engagement with the text and one can understand how he got from the texts in question to the position advocated. It is different with his construal of the wholeness of Scripture. His view of what the whole Scripture is about is clear. In a variety of ways he describes it as the restoration of the human being away from sin, through justification by faith back to the holiness which was God's original intent. But nowhere does Wesley correlate that view of Scripture's wholeness with the entirety of Scripture itself. Although individual verses are quoted, he does not offer an account of how the full span of Scripture, from Genesis to Revelation, is best construed in this way.

In fairness to Wesley, such arguments about the wholeness of Scripture would have been foreign to him. They are not common in the history of theology, and we are perhaps asking him to provide an argument for which he does not see any need. Further, an argument about the wholeness of Scripture will not be conclusive in any event. Like the sum of the meaning of a work of art, any construal of Scripture's wholeness will inevitably rest finally on an intuitive grasp that this is indeed binding it all together. Wesley saw that thread in the story of individual salvation, and pursued it wherever it went. More elucidation of why others should see that wholeness would have been helpful, but ultimately the convincing quality of his view lies in the attractiveness of the view itself when compared with the whole Bible.

The Unity of Authority, Scripture, and the Christian Life

Wesley's whole relationship to Scripture is bound up in his understanding of the unity of authority, Scripture, and the Christian life. When Wesley speaks of each of these alone, he appeals to their unitary character. But there is also a deeper unity that ties all three together in his thought.

We have seen that religious authority in Wesley's thought is unitary, with five parts each defined as interdependent with the others. It is inconceivable to Wesley that any one of the five, when properly used, would contradict any of the other four. This unity allows Wesley to appeal to any one of the five or any combination of them as a warrant in theological argument. Within this unity, Scripture is primary. The other four are subordinate to it, even though they influence its conclusions. Wesley is *homo unius libri* in the sense that Scripture is the starting point and primary standard for Christian faith and practice. Whatever rational or traditional interpretation is made must have in view the better elucidation of its message.

The unity of Scripture is the dominant theme of Wesley's hermeneutics. Other principles function in his thought, but they are abandoned if they conflict with interpretation according to the analogy of faith. Wesley is convinced that all of Scripture has one message—the salvation of the individual. Doubtful Scriptures are best understood with reference to this whole.

The unity of the Christian life is Wesley's practical concern. He eschews speculative theology. His focus is on the experience of grace by the individual. He not only seeks salvation for the individual, but teaches that one should expect to experience it in an identifiable manner. The order of salvation thus gives an integrated plan for a Christian's journey. The beginning point is applicable to all human beings. The intermediate stages are clear. The destination is desired by everyone. Wesley's answers to the basic religious questions about the meaning and goal of human life have integrity and appeal to the common person. Wesley puts these practical questions at the forefront of interpretation. He comes to the Bible seeking the message of salvation for himself and for others. He is willing to follow the new sciences for understanding the physical world because the Bible is not authoritative in those areas. Further, he is not interested in finding biblical justification for speculative theology. Rather, he seeks the plain, simple message that the Bible has to offer about the meaning of an individual's life in the sight of God.

For Wesley all three of these—authority, Scripture, and the Christian life—are then unified by their mutual relationship. The locus of authority is held together by its dominant member Scripture, which in turn is seen as having the theme of salvation as its unifying center. The unity of Scripture is expressed in its testimony to the justifying and sanctifying grace of God. The other parts of the fivefold locus of authority carry the same message. Together, these authorities describe a system of doctrine that was meant to become real in the experiences of believers. Wesley's distinction between Christianity as a system of doctrine and as an inward principle is crucial. What the Scripture teaches and the authorities confirm is made real in the lives of believers.

Whether Wesley's view of the Christian life, of Scripture, and of religious authority can make new contributions to the witness of the Christian church remains to be seen. A genuinely Wesleyan understanding of Scripture would meet at least five criteria. First, it would uphold a high view of the authority and inspiration of Scripture, taking the position that in the Bible God has chosen to reveal himself to humankind in a way that is dependable and certain. Second, it would provide proper places for other authorities and constantly seek a unified view of truth, constantly seeking the correlation of Scripture with all other approaches to knowledge. Third, it would seek the whole message of the Bible, listening carefully to its individual parts but also seeking to understand the entire book as concerning the saving activity of God, reconciling humanity to himself and restoring them to the image in which they were created. Fourth, it would utilize the best critical tools available, using any means possible to elucidate the message of the Bible. Fifth, and most important, a Wesleyan understanding of Scripture would not be narrowly Wesleyan, but rather a genuine attempt to articulate the best understanding of the whole Christian church. Methodism from its inception has sought to be "the old religion, the religion of the Bible, the religion of the primitive church."[3] If a genuinely Wesleyan view of Scripture could be articulated for our times, its contribution to Christian witness would be significant.

Representative Sample of Wesley's Works Used in Part Two

The following sample from Wesley's works was used in part 2 of this study. In the process of making a selection that would be a balanced representation of the entire corpus, attention was paid to the type of work, the year of its composition, and whether the text (of the sermon) was from the Old or New Testament.

Sermons, Year, Text

"The Image of God," 1730, Gen. 1:27
"The Circumcision of the Heart," 1733, Rom. 2:29
"Salvation by Faith," 1738, Eph. 2:8
"Free Grace," 1739, Rom. 8:32
"Christian Perfection," 1741, Phil. 3:12
"The Means of Grace," 1746, Mal. 3:7
"The Marks of the New Birth," 1748, John 3:8
"Upon Our Lord's Sermon on the Mount, IV," 1748, Matt. 5:13-16
"Catholic Spirit," 1750, 2 Kings 10:15
"The Law Established Through Faith, I," 1750, Rom. 3:31
"The Great Assize," 1758, Rom. 14:10
"Original Sin," 1759, Gen. 6:5
"The Use of Money," 1760, Luke 16:9
"The Scripture Way of Salvation," 1765, Eph. 2:8
"The Witness of the Spirit, II," 1767, Rom. 8:16
"On Laying the Foundation of the New Chapel," 1777, Num. 23:23
"The Case of Reason Impartially Considered," 1781, 1 Cor. 14:20
"The General Spread of the Gospel," 1783, Isa. 11:9
"On Working Out Our Own Salvation," 1785, Phil. 2:12-13
"The New Creation," 1785, Rev. 21:5
"The Signs of the Times," 1787, Matt. 16:3
"On the Discoveries of Faith," 1788, Heb. 11:1
"Dives and Lazarus," 1788, Luke 16:31

"Causes of the Inefficacy of Christianity," 1789, Jer. 8:22
"On the Wedding Garment," 1790, Matt. 22:12

Exegetical

Explanatory Notes Upon the New Testament, Matthew, Romans, James, 1 John, 1755

Polemical Writings

An Earnest Appeal to Men of Reason and Religion, 1743
A Letter to the Author of "The Enthusiasm of Methodists and Papists Compared," 1750

Wesley's Scriptural References in the *Sermons* Compiled by Book

The following is a compilation of the scriptural references found in Wesley's *Sermons* from "Index of Scriptural References" in *Works*, 4:651-87. The Index is generally quite reliable. It does, however, depend on the footnotes in the text. In some cases the editors had to use their judgment to decide between two or more possible references for the same words. Two drawbacks to the quality of the data should be noted. First, the references include citations made by the editors in the footnote even where the text is not directly referred to in Wesley's text. Because these are not differentiated in the Index, they have simply been included. Second, where more than one of the Gospels could have been cited, the editors frequently cite Matthew and "etc." Thus, footnote 15 at *Works*, 1:205 could have cited Deuteronomy 6:5, Luke 10:27, and Mark 12:30. The footnote reads "Matthew 22:37, etc." Thus, the predominance of Matthew over Luke and Mark in the following list may be less pronounced than is indicated. Given these problems in the database, the list is still sufficiently accurate for the general conclusions reached in this study. Following are the names of the books of the Bible and the number of times each is cited in the *Works* Index, listed in order of frequency.

Matthew, 947	Galatians, 269	Jeremiah, 97
Romans, 907	Revelation, 248	1 Thessalonians, 94
Psalms, 750	Philippians, 232	Deuteronomy, 89
Luke, 507	Mark, 199	Exodus, 86
Hebrews, 501	Genesis, 195	Ecclesiastes, 75
John, 487	James, 185	2 Samuel, 48
1 Corinthians, 478	1 Timothy, 178	1 Samuel, 43
Ephesians, 440	Colossians, 177	Daniel, 43
1 John, 438	Job, 176	2 Thessalonians, 42
Acts, 387	2 Timothy, 148	Leviticus, 34
2 Corinthians, 329	2 Peter, 123	Numbers, 29
Isaiah, 306	Ezekiel, 120	Jude, 26
1 Peter, 284	Proverbs, 111	2 Kings, 24

Zechariah, 22

Malachi, 20

Joshua, 19

1 Kings, 19

Micah, 19

Habakkuk, 19

Song of Solomon, 15

Hosea, 15

Judges, 12

2 Chronicles, 12

Joel, 11

1 Chronicles, 10

Lamentations, 10

Amos, 10

Jonah, 8

Philemon, 5

2 John, 4

Ezra, 2

Nehemiah, 2

Esther, 1

Nahum, 1

Zephaniah, 1

Haggai, 1

Ruth, 0

Obadiah, 0

Titus, 0

3 John, 0

Abbreviations

Whenever possible, citations of Wesley's works refer to the Bicentennial Edition of *The Works of John Wesley*. If the relevant volumes have not yet been published, then older editions are used. To facilitate the use of multiple editions, I have cited the section number as provided by Wesley in some writings, notably the *Sermons* and *Appeals*, and provided dates for letters and *Journal* entries. References to *Explanatory Notes upon the New Testament* will be given only by book, chapter, and verse since most editions are unpaginated. The following abbreviations are used to refer to these editions and other frequently cited works.

Appeals   *An Earnest Appeal to Men of Reason and Religion*, and *A Farther Appeal to Men of Reason and Religion, Parts I, II, and III*, ed. Gerald R. Cragg, vol. 11 in *Works*. They will be referred to separately as *Earnest Appeal* and *Farther Appeal*.

AV   Authorized Version of the Bible, commonly known as the King James Version.

BCP   *The Book of Common Prayer . . . According to the Use of the Church of England* (Oxford: University Printers, 1710).

Curnock   *The Journal of the Rev. John Wesley, A.M.*, ed. Nehemiah Curnock, 8 vols. (London: Epworth Press, 1909–16).

Jackson   *The Works of John Wesley*, ed. Thomas Jackson, 14 vols. (London: Wesleyan Conference Office, 1872; repr., Grand Rapids, Mich.: Zondervan, 1958–59).

Journal   *The Journal of John Wesley*, in either Curnock or *Works*.

Letters   *The Letters of the Rev. John Wesley*, in either Telford or *Works*.

NIV   New International Version of the Bible.

Notes   John Wesley, *Explanatory Notes upon the New Testament* (London: William Bowyer, 1755; repr. London: Wesleyan-Methodist Book Room, n.d.).

NRSV   New Revised Standard Version Bible.

RSV   Revised Standard Version of the Bible.

Sugden   *Wesley's Standard Sermons,* ed. Edward H. Sugden, 2 vols. (London: Epworth Press, 1921).

Sermons   John Wesley, *Sermons,* ed. Albert C. Outler, in *Works.*

Telford   *The Letters of the Rev. John Wesley, A.M.,* ed. John Telford, 8 vols. (London: Epworth Press, 1931).

Works   *The Works of John Wesley;* begun as "The Oxford Edition of the Works of John Wesley" (Oxford: Clarendon Press, 1975–1983); continued as "The Bicentennial Edition of the Works of John Wesley" (Nashville: Abingdon Press, 1984–); 14 of 35 vols. published to date.

Wesley   When this term is used without further qualification, it refers to John Wesley.

Notes

Introduction

1. See Werner Georg Kümmel, *The New Testament: The History of the Investigation of Its Problems*, trans. S. McLean Gilmour and Howard C. Kee (Nashville/New York: Abingdon Press, 1972), 20. Kümmel notes the Diet of Augsburg as a key point where a fundamental observation leading to the modern view of Scripture was made. Although there were significant steps taken earlier, after 1518 the question of Scripture's authority and interpretation is clearly at the center of the theological agenda.

2. Richard P. Heitzenrater, *Mirror and Memory: Reflections on Early Methodism* (Nashville: Kingswood Books, 1989), 213.

3. It is certainly the case that this study would not have been possible in its present form without the new critical edition of Wesley's *Works* now being published. The "Index of Scriptural References" to the Sermons in *Works*, 4:651-87, and the footnotes in each volume have been enormously helpful.

4. John Deschner, *Wesley's Christology: An Interpretation* (Dallas: Southern Methodist University Press, 1960), 7-10; Wilbur H. Mullen, "John Wesley's Method of Biblical Interpretation," *Religion in Life* 47 (1978): 99; and Larry Shelton, "John Wesley's Approach to Scripture in Historical Perspective," *Wesleyan Theological Journal* 16 (Spring 1981): 23, chose to limit their consideration to the Wesleyan "Standards"—either 44 or 53 sermons and the *Explanatory Notes upon the New Testament*. There is some justification for this on the grounds that in the Model Deed of 1763 Wesley himself commended these as standards by which to judge Methodist preaching. However, this study is interested in the *whole* of Wesley's thought, including those sermons written after 1763 and other types of material both published and unpublished.

5. Albert Outler, "A New Future for Wesley Studies: An Agenda for Phase III," in *The Future of the Methodist Theological Traditions*, ed. M. Douglas Meeks (Nashville: Abingdon Press, 1985), 48.

6. Cf. "Some Remarks on Mr. Hill's 'Review of All the Doctrines Taught by Mr. John Wesley,'" §I.1, Jackson, 10:382: "The plain inference is, If there are a hundred passages in the 'Christian Library' which contradict any or all of my doctrines, these are no proof that I contradict myself. Be it observed once for all, therefore, citations from the 'Christian Library' prove nothing but the carelessness of the correctors."

7. For example, within *The Doctrine of Original Sin*, Jackson, 9:191-464, the material on pp. 353-431 and 434-64 is borrowed from other authors. In this case, Wesley acknowledges his debt. Other times, as in the sermon "The Duty of Constant Communion," *Works*, 3:427-39, he does not.

8. Cf. §§7-8 of the Preface to the *Notes* where Wesley acknowledges his debt.

9. The entire deed is printed in "The Large Minutes," Jackson, 8:330-31.

10. Frank Baker, "John Wesley, Biblical Commentator," *Bulletin of the John Rylands Library* 71 (1989): 114. The entry in the *Journal* can be found in *Works*, 21:236, which has "correcting or enlarging."

11. *Works*, 4:651-87.

Chapter 1: The Authority of Scripture Alone

1. Preface to *Sermons on Several Occasions*, §3, *Works*, 1:104. On the sources for Wesley's thought, see Albert C. Outler, Introduction in *Works*, 1:66-96.

2. *Notes*, Preface, §10.

3. *Notes*, Rev. 1:11.

4. *Notes*, Rev. 1:20.

5. Telford, 7:252.

6. *Notes*, 1 Cor. 7:25.

7. *Notes*, Jude 14.

8. See *Notes*, Matthew 1:1, where Wesley refers to "Jewish tables" which the evangelists would have consulted. There Wesley says that any "difficulties" in the genealogies in Matthew and Luke would have originated from those tables and not from a fault in the revelatory process.

9. *Notes*, 1 Cor. 14:32.

10. *Notes*, Phil. 1:20.

11. *Notes*, Acts 15:7.

12. *Notes*, preface to 1 Tim.

13. Preface in *Notes*, §12. This is a prime case of the methodological point made earlier about how to handle material Wesley borrowed from someone else. In §§10-13 of the Preface to the *Notes*, Wesley added only the last three sentences of §12 and the first sentence of §13. All of the material quoted here is taken, with minor changes and significant deletions, from the Preface in John Albert Bengel, *Gnomon of the New Testament*. Cf. it with the translation ed. M. Ernest Bengel and J. C. F. Steudel, trans. James Bandinel et al., 5 vols., 3rd ed. (Philadelphia: Smith, English, and Co.; and New York: Sheldon, 1860), 1:5-6, 43. Wesley gave no indication that this material was not original. As argued in the introduction, I am treating this material as if Wesley had written it himself, because of the way in which he took responsibility for the *Notes*.

14. Jackson, 11:484. It is possible that Wesley borrowed the logical outline of this argument from *Richard Baxter's Saints' Everlasting Rest*, 7th rev. ed. (London: Thomas Underhill and Francis Tyton, 1658), 239-41. See appendix 2 in Scott Jones, "John Wesley's Conception and Use of Scripture" (Ph.D. diss., Southern Methodist University, 1992), 298-300, for comparison of the texts. Whether Wesley adapted the argument directly from Baxter or used an intermediary source is not presently known. While the similarity is clear, the editors of the Bicentennial Edition of *Works* treat it as an original work of Wesley's. I am indebted to Frank Baker for this information, given to me in a letter prior to the publication of "A Clear and Concise Demonstration" in *Works*.

15. For Woolston, see Leslie Stephen, *History of English Thought in the Eighteenth Century*, 3rd ed., 2 vols. (New York: Peter Smith, 1949 repr.), 1:228-33. See David Hume, "Of Miracles," chap. 10 in *An Inquiry Concerning Human Understanding*, ed. Charles W. Hendel, The Library of Liberal Arts (Indianapolis: Bobbs-Merrill, 1955).

16. The logical status of such conclusions is made clear in Henry Aldrich's *Artis Logicae Compendium*, which Wesley abridged and translated, publishing it as *A Compendium of Logic*. There, an axiom is defined as "a proposition which needs not, and cannot, be proved." The following are given as examples: "From natural divinity. 1. God cannot deceive, or be deceived. Whence flow these certain and evident conclusions: 2. Absolute faith is due to the testimony of God: 3. Revelation never contradicts either sense or reason. It may indeed transcend both. But it cannot possibly contradict either, rightly employed about its proper object" (Jackson,

14:179). Regarding the abridgment, Rex D. Matthews, "'Religion and Reason Joined': A Study in the Theology of John Wesley" (Ph.D. diss., Harvard University, 1986), 151, says, "Wesley adds nothing to the original, he only condenses and occasionally rewrites slightly for clarity and concise expression, following the organization of Aldrich's Latin original exactly."

17. Matthews, "Religion and Reason Joined," 184.

18. *Works*, 25:175-76.

19. Matthews, "Religion and Reason Joined," 192, who refers to Cell, *The Rediscovery of John Wesley* (New York: Henry Holt, 1935), 84-86.

20. See *A Compendium of Logic*, Jackson, 14:178: "To assent to testimony is the same as to believe; and such an assent is termed faith. Divine faith depends on the testimony of God: Human faith, on the testimony of man."

21. See the disparaging quotation about believing anything, even Voltaire or the *Shastah*, below.

22. See the 1734 letter to Richard Morgan, Sr., *Works*, 25:380; and *The Principles of a Methodist Farther Explained*, §V.8, *Works*, 9:222.

23. Curnock, 6:117.

24. January 6, 1756, Telford, 3:345.

25. To Penelope Maitland, May 12, 1763, Telford, 4:212.

26. §II.9, *Works*, 3:527.

27. §3, *Works*, 2:100.

28. §II.3, *Works*, 4:249.

29. Klaus Scholder, *The Birth of Modern Critical Theology: Origins and Problems of Biblical Criticism in the Seventeenth Century*, trans. John Bowden (London: S.C.M. Press; and Philadelphia: Trinity Press International, 1990), 2.

30. Barbara J. Shapiro, *Probability and Certainty in Seventeenth-Century England: A Study of the Relationships Between Natural Science, Religion, History, Law, and Literature* (Princeton: Princeton University Press, 1983), 117.

31. Gerald R. Cragg, *Reason and Authority in the Eighteenth Century* (Cambridge: Cambridge University Press, 1964), 1.

32. Hans W. Frei, *The Eclipse of Biblical Narrative: A Study in Eighteenth and Nineteenth-Century Hermeneutics* (New Haven and London: Yale University Press, 1974).

33. *Works*, 18:214-15.

34. §III.5, *Works*, 2:483.

35. §II.10, *Works*, 2:531.

36. "An Account of the Brothers' Steps," Jackson, 11:500.

37. "The Unity of the Divine Being," §§19-20, *Works*, 4:69.

38. Letter to the editor of *Lloyd's Evening Post*, November 28, 1774, Telford, 6:123. The *Compact Edition of the Oxford English Dictionary*, 2 vols. (Oxford: Oxford University Press, 1971), 2:2772, (s.v. "shaster") defines *"Shastah"* as "any one of the sacred writings of the Hindus." Wesley specifically refers to Madame Guyon as somebody who fell into error by trusting "inward impressions" rather than "the written word" (Preface to *An Extract of the Life of Madame Guion*, Jackson, 14:277).

39. Peter Gay, *The Enlightenment: An Interpretation: The Rise of Modern Paganism* (New York: Alfred A. Knopf, 1966), 378.

40. Anthony Collins, *A Discourse of Free-Thinking, Occasion'd By the Rise and Growth of a Sect Call'd Free Thinkers* (London: n.p., 1713; repr., New York: Garland, 1984), 51.

41. Ibid., 20-24.

42. Ibid., 37-38.

43. Frei, *Eclipse of Biblical Narrative*, 76.

44. Ibid., 79.

45. Chapter 3 of this study will argue that Scripture, reason, Christian antiquity, the Church of England, and experience form a unified locus of authority in Wesley's conception of Scripture.

46. Preface to the 1746 edition of *Sermons on Several Occasions, Works*, 1:105.

47. "On God's Vineyard," §I.1, *Works*, 3:504.

48. "Bible-bigot" is also used in *Journal*, June 5, 1766, *Works*, 22:42.

49. June 22, 1763, Telford, 4:216. The "little help from men" is a reference to his discussions with the Moravians in February, March, and April of 1738. Cf. *Journal*, April 27, 1738, *Works*, 18:233-35.

50. *The Nature, Design, and General Rules of the United Societies, Works*, 9:73.

51. §II.1, *Works*, 1:381.

52. §V.1, *Works*, 1:393-94.

53. "Christian Perfection," §2, *Works*, 2:99-100.

54. §I.5, *Works*, 2:37. For the quotation, see Matthew 28:20.

55. Preface in *Notes*, §10.

56. "On Faith (Hebrews 11:6)," §I.8, *Works*, 3:496. A similar point is made in *Popery Calmly Considered*, Jackson, 10:141.

57. Jackson, 10:142.

58. *Works*, 26:145.

59. September 28, 1745, §5, *Works*, 26:155.

60. See *Works*, 9:219, 25:664, 25:343; Telford, 5:80; *Notes* on 1 John 4:1, 1 Thess. 5:21; and Jackson, 10:285 and 10:178, for similar uses of Isaiah 8:20.

61. *Advice to the People Called Methodists with Regard to Dress*, §V.1, Jackson, 11:472. See also *Predestination Calmly Considered*, §67, ibid., 10:242.

62. September 28, 1745, §4, *Works*, 26:155.

63. Preface to *Sermons on Several Occasions*, §§5, 10, *Works*, 1:105, 107.

64. "Minutes of Some Late Conversations Between the Rev. Mr. Wesley and Others," Jackson, 8:315.

65. Cf. *An Address to the Clergy*, Jackson, 10:482-85, where a large number of acquired gifts and areas of knowledge are described as important to the ministry.

66. William Baird, *History of New Testament Research, Vol. One: From Deism to Tübingen* (Minneapolis: Fortress Press, 1992), 88-90. See chapter 2 for the discussion of Wesley's treatment of the analogy of faith as the key to the wholeness of Scripture.

Chapter 2: The Characteristics of Scripture

1. *BCP*.

2. John Wesley, *The Sunday Service of the Methodists in North America with Other Occasional Services* (London, 1784), reprinted as *John Wesley's Sunday Service of the Methodists in North America*, Quarterly Review Reprint Series (Nashville: United Methodist Publishing House and United Methodist Board of Higher Education and Ministry, 1984), 307.

3. All Church of England priests had to subscribe to the *BCP* and the Articles as conditions of their ordination. For details on the form commonly used during Wesley's day, see Edgar C. S. Gibson, *The Thirty-nine Articles of the Church of England*, 2nd rev. ed. (London: Methuen, 1898), 62.

4. Letter to "John Smith," September 28, 1745, §5, *Works*, 26:155.

5. §3, Jackson, 10:141.

6. John Sergeant, *Sure Footing in Christianity, or Rational Discourses on the rule of Faith. With . . . Animadversions on Dr. Pierce's Sermon* (London, 1665).

7. John Tillotson, *Rule of Faith, or an Answer to the Treatise of Mr. J. S. entitled Sure-Footing, &c.*, 11th ed., corrected (London, 1720). In *The Works of the Most Reverend Dr. John Tillotson . . . Containing 54 Sermons . . . together with the Rule of Faith.* 8th ed. (London: T. Goodwin et al., 1720), 567, 568.

8. See *A Dissuasive from Popery*, part II, book 1, §2, in *The Whole Works of the Right Rev. Jeremy Taylor*, ed. Charles Eden and Reginald Heber (London: Longman Green, 1861–65), 6:380-82, quoted in Paul Elmer More and Frank Leslie Cross, eds., *Anglicanism: The Thought and Practice of the Church of England, Illustrated from the Religious Literature of the Seventeenth Century* (London: S.P.C.K., 1957), 91-92. "That the Scripture is a full and sufficient rule to Christians in faith and manners, a full and perfect declaration of the Will of God, is therefore certain, because we have no other. For if we consider the grounds upon which all Christians believe the Scriptures to be the Word of God, the same grounds prove that nothing else is."

9. See Gilbert Burnet, *An Exposition of the Thirty-Nine Articles of the Church of England*, rev. ed. James Page (New York: Appleton, 1842), 90-91.

10. See William Chillingworth, *The Religion of Protestants, a Safe Way to Salvation*, 3rd ed. (London: J. Clark, 1664), 47, 49: "Scripture is the sole rule for men to judge controversies by," and the meaning of Scripture as a perfect Rule is that "the Scripture, to them which presuppose it Divine, and a Rule of Faith, as Papists and Protestants do, contains all the material objects of Faith, is a compleat and total and not only an imperfect and a partial Rule."

11. *A Letter to the Rev. Dr. Conyers Middleton*, §15, Jackson, 10:14. See also his 1773 letter to James Creighton (May 24, 1773), where he says "Revelation is complete: yet we cannot be saved unless Christ be *revealed* in our hearts," Telford 6:28.

12. §I.8, *Works*, 3:496.

13. *Notes*.

14. §II.2, *Works*, 3:299.

15. John Wesley, *A Survey of the Wisdom of God in Creation: or a Compendium of Natural Philosophy*, 2 vols., 1st ed. (London, 1763), 2:22-23. Wesley's Preface to this work, Jackson 14:301, states that "it is now, I believe, not only pure, containing nothing false or uncertain; but as full as any tract can be expected to be, which is comprised in so narrow a compass." In interpreting Wesley's editorial work, we must be cautious and not attribute too much of the content to him directly. In this case, however, he has taken responsibility for the whole text. The position expressed here is confirmed in other places. Several references in Wesley's sermons touch on the issues of the earth's motion around the sun and the new theory of gravitation.

16. Ibid., 23.

17. "On Divine Providence," §20, *Works*, 2:545.

18. "The Promise of Understanding," §I.1, *Works*, 4:283.

19. "Spiritual Worship," §I.6, *Works*, 3:93.

20. See More and Cross, *Anglicanism*, for a useful selection of writings on the sufficiency of Scripture.

21. Frederick W. Farrar, *History of Interpretation* (New York: E. P. Dutton, 1886; repr., Grand Rapids: Baker Book House, 1961), 187. He also footnotes references from Chrysostom and Basil. Farrar takes a dim view of the Fathers' teaching on this point, regarding it as one of the errors that gave rise to allegorical interpretation.

22. John Calvin, *Institutes of the Christian Religion*, ed. John T. McNeill, trans. Ford Lewis Battles, vols. 20-21, The Library of Christian Classics (Philadelphia: Westminster Press, 1960), §I.v.1, 1:52. See also §I.xvii.13, 1:227.

23. Ibid., I.xiv.3, 1:162.

24. §II.2, *Works*, 3:585.

25. §2, *Works*, 4:162.

26. §4, *Works*, 2:536. The parenthetical comment is also an appeal to accommodation of the revelation to human capacities. See n. 22 above.

27. July 2, 1772, Telford, 5:327.

28. N. H. Keeble, *Richard Baxter: Puritan Man of Letters* (Oxford: Clarendon Press, 1982), 50. He is quoting *A Christian Directory* (London, 1673), II.xx.579.

29. Keeble, *Richard Baxter*, 40.

30. Tillotson, *Rule of Faith*, 585.

31. March 28, 1768, §II.6, *Works*, 9:378.

32. I am indebted to Professor William Babcock for this observation.

33. §15, Jackson, 10:14.

34. September 28, 1745, §19, *Works*, 26:160. Wesley refers to Part I of the *Farther Appeal*.

35. Preface to *Notes*, §10.

36. *Advice to the People Called Methodists with Regard to Dress*, §I.2, Jackson, 11:466. Cf. *Notes*, 2 Timothy 2:15, for an exhortation to explain and to apply the "whole scripture."

37. Jackson, 11:431.

38. "Free Grace," §20, *Works*, 3:552, emphasis added.

39. *A Farther Appeal*, Part II, §II.1, *Works*, 11:214.

40. *Notes*, Matt. 5:22.

41. *The Doctrine of Original Sin*, Jackson, 9:334.

42. *Some Remarks on Mr. Hill's "Farrago Double-Distilled,"* Jackson, 10:426.

43. David H. Kelsey, *The Uses of Scripture in Recent Theology* (Philadelphia: Fortress Press, 1975), 106.

44. *Notes*, Romans 12:6.

45. Luther A. Weigle, *The New Testament Octapla: Eight English Versions of the New Testament in the Tyndale-King James Tradition* (New York: Nelson, n.d.), 902-3.

46. Modern Roman Catholic scholars such as Bertrand de Margerie argue that the rule of faith in Irenaeus is the same as the analogy of faith in the decree *Dei Verbum* of Vatican II. See Margerie, *Introduction à l'Histoire de l'Éxegèse*, vol. 1, *Les Pères Grecs et Orientaux* (Paris: Éditions du Cerf, 1980), 66 n. 10.

47. Calvin, *Institutes*, "Prefatory Address," §2, 1:12-13, and IV.xvii.32, 2:1404.

48. In Heinrich Schmid, *The Doctrinal Theology of the Evangelical Lutheran Church*, trans. Charles A. Hay and Henry E. Jacobs, 3rd rev. ed. (Philadelphia: Augsburg Publishing House, 1899, repr.), 76-77.

49. In Heinrich Heppe, *Reformed Dogmatics: Set Out and Illustrated from the Sources*, rev. ed. Ernst Bizer, trans. G. T. Thomson (Grand Rapids: Baker Book House, 1978, repr.), 35. A different translation, given in a footnote in Calvin, *Institutes*, 1:13, includes the phrase "the general sentences and axioms of every main point of divinity."

50. *The Arte of Prophesying*, p. 652 of *Workes* (London, 1616), quoted in John R. Knott, Jr., *The Sword of the Spirit: Puritan Responses to the Bible* (Chicago and London: University of Chicago, 1980), 36.

51. *Prose Works*, v. 2, 82, 338, and *Christian Doctrine*, 6:582-83, quoted in Knott, *Sword of the Spirit*, 115.

52. Δὸς ποῦ στῶ or, *An Answer to Sure Footing* . . . (Oxford, 1666), 28-30, quoted in More and Cross, *Anglicanism*, 116.

53. Jeremy Taylor, *The Liberty of Prophesying*, in *The Whole Works*, 5:424-25.

54. John Locke, *A Paraphrase and Notes on the Epistles of St. Paul to the Galatians, 1 and 2 Corinthians, Romans, Ephesians,* ed. Arthur W. Wainwright, 2 vols. (Oxford: Clarendon Press, 1987), Preface, 1:113. Wainwright's footnote (p. 395), says, "Locke may be using *Analogy* in the sense of 'analogue,' or he may be alluding to beliefs formulated by reasoning from analogy." This completely misses the point. "Analogy of faith" is a technical term in the history of biblical interpretation.

55. Ibid., 2:585.

56. *Works,* 25:180.

57. "On Guardian Angels," III.[1], *Works,* 4:231.

58. The eleven places, some found by the editors of the Bicentennial Edition and others in my research, are as follows:

a. "Justification by Faith," §2, *Works,* 1:183.

b. "The End of Christ's Coming," §III.5, *Works,* 2:483.

c. "The New Creation," §2, *Works,* 2:501.

d. "Causes of the Inefficacy of Christianity," §6, *Works,* 4:89.

e. "On Guardian Angels," §III.[1], *Works,* 4:231.

f. *Notes,* Romans 12:6.

g. *Address to the Clergy,* Jackson, 10:490.

h. Preface to *Explanatory Notes upon the Old Testament,* §3, Jackson, 14:247.

i. §18, ibid, p. 253.

j. *The Principles of a Methodist,* §13, *Works,* 9:55.

k. *Farther Thoughts on Christian Perfection,* quoted in *A Plain Account of Christian Perfection,* Jackson, 11:431.

Outler has two footnotes on the term in *Works,* 1:183, 473. The first one interprets Wesley's view of the analogy of faith as "the general and true sense of Scripture (both the truths revealed in Scripture and solid inferences drawn from them, as in the creeds and biblically grounded theology)." The second restates the analogy of faith as "one's sense of the whole."

59. *Notes,* Romans 12:6. The scriptural references are to 1 Peter 4:11 and Jude 3.

60. §III.5, *Works,* 2:483.

61. *Notes,* Romans 12:6.

62. Preface to *Explanatory Notes upon the Old Testament,* Jackson, 14:253.

63. On pp. 101-2, Kelsey *(Uses of Scripture)* recapitulates his conclusions from earlier chapters. The theologians he examines appeal to the doctrines taught in scripture, concepts proposed by scripture, narratives in scripture, biblical images or symbols, and biblical theological statements. He further notes that some of these patterns are construed in logically diverse ways themselves.

64. Jackson, 14:253.

65. §6, *Works,* 4:89.

66. "The End of Christ's Coming," §III.5, *Works,* 2:482.

67. *Notes,* Romans 12:6. Reference is to Jude 3.

68. For example, the doctrine of the Trinity fits this description, as discussed later. Cf. Colin Williams, *John Wesley's Theology Today* (Nashville/New York: Abingdon Press, 1960), 16-17, for a helpful summary of Wesley's essential doctrines. Williams isolates several key texts, but he includes "the work of the Holy Spirit" instead of mentioning the new birth and sanctification specifically.

69. April 19, 1764, *Works,* 21:456, and Telford, 4:237.

70. §VI.4, *Works,* 9:226-27.

71. Jackson, 14:247.

72. §13, *Works,* 9:55.

73. "The New Creation," §2, *Works,* 2:501.

74. Jackson, 10:490.

75. *Earnest Appeal*, §46, *Works*, 11:62.

76. Jackson, 13:411.

77. §I.8, *Works*, 4:398. Of all the themes of "the whole Scripture," holiness receives the most frequent mention by Wesley. Cf. *Works*, 3:405, 4:336, 25:382, Jackson, 9:244, 308, 10:203, and 364.

78. "On Divine Providence," §4, *Works*, 2:536.

79. Jackson, 10:211.

80. *Notes*.

81. *Notes*, 1 John 5:8.

82. §17, *Works*, 2:384.

83. Locke, *Paraphrase and Notes*, 2:585.

84. Preface to *Sermons on Several Occasions*, *Works*, 1:105-6.

85. §III.[1], *Works*, 4:231.

86. §II.1, *Works*, 4:336.

87. March 15, 1733/34, *Works*, 25:382.

88. November 22, 1725, letter to Susanna Wesley, *Works*, 25:188. See also Rex D. Matthews, "'Religion and Reason Joined': A Study in the Theology of John Wesley" (Ph.D. diss., Harvard University, 1986), 184-92.

89. See *The Compact Edition of the Oxford English Dictionary*, s.v. "temper, *sb.*," 2:3254, §II.9. A 1777 usage defines "temper" as "the disposition which remains after these emotions are past; and which forms the habitual propensity of the soul."

90. *Journal*, September 1, 1778, Curnock, 6:209. See Outler's introduction to the sermon in *Works*, 1:398-400.

91. Timothy Smith, "John Wesley and the Wholeness of Scripture," *Interpretation* 39 (1985): 246-47, 260-61. Smith says this theme shows up in a 1725 sermon, that it was reinforced by the changes of 1738 and 1739, and that it continued until 1791. He thus argues that Wesley holds a "hermeneutic of holiness," the view that "the living center of every part of inspired Scripture was the call to be holy, and the promise of grace to answer that call." Smith's argument is not carefully nuanced in that he appears to take "holiness" to stand for the whole order of salvation in Wesley's thinking. Further, Smith fails to distinguish between Wesley's conception and use of Scripture in his discussion. He is, however, correct in discerning that in Wesley's use of Scripture the goal of holiness was the living center by which the rest of Scripture was to be interpreted.

92. See "The Scripture Way of Salvation," §III.13, *Works*, 2:167, where Wesley builds an argument using two types of necessity. Faith is unconditionally and immediately necessary for sanctification, while good works are conditionally and remotely necessary.

93. "Free Grace," §20, *Works*, 3:552.

94. §26, *Works*, 3:556.

95. §13, *Works*, 9:55.

96. §I.11, *Works*, 2:25.

97. John Deschner, *Wesley's Christology: An Interpretation* (Dallas: Southern Methodist University Press, 1960), 87.

98. Ibid., 86.

99. "Free Grace," §29, *Works*, 3:558.

100. See "The Reward of the Righteous," §I.6, *Works*, 3:405; "The Repentance of Believers," §II.2, *Works*, 1:347; "On Laying the Foundation of the New Chapel," §II.2, *Works*, 3:585; "A Plain Account of the People Called Methodists," §I.5, *Works*, 9:256; and "A Letter to the Rev. Dr. Conyers Middleton," §II.2-3, Jackson, 10:72.

101. *Notes*, Romans 8:33.

102. §4, *Works*, 2:536. Outler notes that the idea expressed by the "fine writer" "informs the whole of Jonathan Edwards," but that the phrase is not found in his writings.

103. "The Means of Grace," §III.9, *Works*, 1:388.

104. §II.11, *Works*, 2:110.

105. §V.2, Jackson, 11:472.

106. To "Dean D—— ," 1785, Telford, 7:252.

107. *Notes*.

108. Deschner, *Wesley's Christology*, 87.

109. Jackson, 11:414. The history of dividing the Old Testament law into political, moral, and ceremonial parts is not clear. Henning Graf Reventlow, *The Authority of the Bible and the Rise of the Modern World*, trans. John Bowden (Philadelphia: Fortress Press, 1985), 240, says it "is traditionally a Reformation insight." However, it is at least as old as Irenaeus and Justin Martyr. R. P. C. Hanson, *Allegory and Event: A Study of the Sources and Significance of Origen's Interpretation of Scripture* (Richmond: John Knox Press, 1959), 289-90, notes "early Christians almost all agreed that the moral commandments could be distinguished from the ritual." He refers to Irenaeus, *Adversus Haereses*, IV.24.1. He also indicates that the rabbis made the same distinction. Margerie (*Les Pères Grecs et Orientaux*, 41), says that Justin made the distinction also, referring to *Dialogues with Trypho*, xxvii, 5, and xxviii, 3.

110. *Works*, 2:511-12. The reference to Peter comes from Acts 15:10. Wesley held the same position in 1745 when he wrote *A Second Dialogue Between an Antinomian and His Friend*.

111. *Notes*.

112. *Notes*.

113. *Notes*.

114. April 5, 1758, Telford, 4:11.

115. "The Righteousness of Faith," §1, *Works*, 1:202-3.

116. *A Letter to the Rev. Dr. Conyers Middleton*, §II.2, Jackson, 10:72.

117. "The Westminster Confession of Faith," in John Leith, ed., *Creeds of the Churches: A Reader in Christian Doctrine from the Bible to the Present*, rev. ed. (Richmond: John Knox Press, 1973), 202-3.

118. Deschner, *Wesley's Christology*, 112-14. Deschner raises the question about Wesley's imprecise use of the terms and suggests that it may point to the "two-sidedness" of Wesley's doctrine of salvation.

119. *BCP*, "Articles of Religion," Article VI.

120. §4, Jackson, 10:141.

121. F. L. Cross and E. A. Livingstone, eds., *The Oxford Dictionary of the Christian Church*, 2nd ed. (London: Oxford University Press, 1974), s.v. "Laodicea, Canons of."

122. *Notes*, Rev. 22:18-19.

123. July 19, 1731, *Works*, 25:293.

124. See the essays contained in the collection *Aldersgate Reconsidered*, ed. Randy L. Maddox (Nashville: Kingswood Books, 1990), esp. Maddox's Introduction.

125. Locke argues that "faith and repentance, i.e., believing Jesus to be the Messiah, and a good life, are the indispensable conditions of the new covenant, to be performed by all those who would obtain eternal life," *The Reasonableness of Christianity*, ed. and abr. I. T. Ramsey (Stanford, Calif.: Stanford University, 1958), §172, 44-45.

126. Kelsey, *Uses of Scripture*, 100.

Chapter 3: The Authority of Scripture in Tension with Other Authorities

1. Ted Campbell, "The 'Wesleyan Quadrilateral': The Story of a Modern Methodist Myth" in Thomas A. Langford, ed., *Doctrine and Theology in the United Methodist Church* (Nashville: Kingswood Books, 1991), 155-59.

2. Colin Williams, *John Wesley's Theology Today* (Nashville/New York: Abingdon Press, 1960), 23-38.

3. Albert C. Outler, "The Wesleyan Quadrilateral in John Wesley," in Langford, *Doctrine and Theology,* 86.

4. Donald A. D. Thorson, *The Wesleyan Quadrilateral: Scripture, Tradition, Reason, and Experience as a Model of Evangelical Theology* (Grand Rapids: Zondervan, 1990), 21-24.

5. Campbell, "Wesleyan Quadrilateral," 160-61.

6. "Thoughts Upon a Late Phenomenon," §3, *Works,* 9:535. Cf. *Notes,* Matthew 16:18: "There hath been a small remnant [of the church] in all ages."

7. §3, Jackson, 10:141.

8. Latin and English text of the decree given in Philip Schaff, *The Creeds of Christendom, with a History and Critical Notes,* vol. 2 (New York: Harper & Bros., 1896), 80. The debate at Trent used "tradition" with subtle nuances which were subsequently lost on the interconfessional debates and wars of the seventeenth and eighteenth centuries. For an account of the Tridentine discussion, see Hubert Jedin, *A History of the Council of Trent,* trans. Dom Ernest Graf, 2 vols. (London: Thomas Nelson and Sons, 1957), 2:58-64, 73-87.

9. §12, *Works,* 2:456.

10. §26, *Works,* 2:462.

11. §§27-28, *Works,* 2:462-64.

12. Ted A. Campbell, *John Wesley and Christian Antiquity* (Nashville: Kingswood Books, 1991), 51. Campbell argues that Wesley still uses the early church in various ways, despite this view of decline.

13. It must be signaled at this point that here Wesley's conception and his practice diverge significantly. So far we are only discussing Wesley's *conception* of authority. In chapter 6 we will analyze his *use* of antiquity and the Church of England, and see that his use of tradition belies his refusal to acknowledge its influence in his thought.

14. For the use of the word "vivified" in this way, see *The Book of Discipline of The United Methodist Church, 1988* (Nashville: United Methodist Publishing House, 1988), 51, 80.

15. March 10, 1762, Telford, 4:175.

16. "To George L. Fleury," May 18, 1771, §12, ibid., 5:247.

17. §I.2, *Works,* 2:590. See Matthews, "Religion and Reason Joined," 125, who says that these three definitions of reason correspond to those given in Samuel Johnson's *Dictionary of the English Language.*

18. *Journal,* June 15, 1741, *Works,* 19:201; "The General Deliverance," §I.5, *Works,* 2:441; and *A Word to a Drunkard,* Jackson, 11:169.

19. Matthews, "Religion and Reason Joined," 157-58. One place where Wesley uses "reason" as equivalent to inference occurs in "What Is Man?" §5, *Works,* 4:21.

20. To John Valton, April 9, 1781, Telford, 7:57.

21. *Journal,* April 16, 1758, *Works,* 21:141.

22. "Thoughts on the Writings of Baron Swedenborg," §13, Jackson, 13:432; *Journal*, February 27, 1747, *Works*, 20:160; February 28, 1770, Curnock, 5:355; and January 25, 1738, *Works*, 18:212 n. 95, §3.

23. To Samuel Sparrow, October 9, 1773, Telford, 6:49.

24. Jackson, 10:276.

25. March 28, 1768, §III.4, *Works*, 9:382.

26. December 1, 1760, Telford, 4:118.

27. §II.6, *Works*, 4:338.

28. *A Short History of the People Called Methodists*, §131, *Works*, 9:502.

29. §22, *Works*, 11:370. To Freeborn Garrettson, the American Methodist preacher, he writes, "If I have plain Scripture or plain reason for doing a thing well. These are my rules, and my only rules. . . . I wish to be in every point, great and small, a scriptural, rational Christian" (January 24, 1789, Telford, 8:112).

30. "To 'Amicus Veritatis,'" January 12, 1750, §10, *Works*, 26:401. Cf. his November 17, 1759, letter to John Downes: "Then by your own account I am no enthusiast, for I resolve none of my notions into immediate inspiration. I have something to do with reason—perhaps as much as many of those who 'make no account of my labours.' And I am ready to give up every opinion which I cannot by calm, clear reason defend." §14, *Works*, 9:361.

31. "The Case of Reason Impartially Considered," §1.6, *Works*, 2:592.

32. §1.7, *Works*, 2:592.

33. §I.1, Jackson, 10:481.

34. §II.3, *Works*, 2:177. The reference is to Romans 1:20.

35. §1, *Works*, 3:400. References are to Hebrews 11:6 and Psalms 58:10.

36. The complete list is given in Gordon Rupp, *Religion in England, 1688–1791* (Oxford: Clarendon Press, 1986), 261.

37. §I.3, Jackson, 10:486.

38. §II.10, *Works*, 2:598.

39. "Farther Thoughts on Christian Perfection," quoted in *A Plain Account of Christian Perfection*, §25, Jackson, 11:414-15.

40. Ibid., 415.

41. *The Doctrine of Original Sin*, ibid., 9:223.

42. Ibid., 293.

43. "Of the Gradual Improvement of Natural Philosophy," §24, ibid., 13:487. The same point is made in a letter to Mary Bishop, February 7, 1778, Telford, 6:298.

44. See Matthews, "Religion and Reason Joined," 173-83.

45. The earliest usage in a publication is in 1733 in his *Collection of Forms of Prayer*, Jackson, 11:226. For early usages, see his *Journal*, November 7, 1739, *Works*, 19:120, and the Preface to *Hymns and Sacred Poems* (1740), in Jackson, 14:327. The last occurrence in a published work comes in his *Thoughts on a Single Life*, §10, Jackson, 11:460, published in 1763. However, there are numerous references in his private correspondence, the last of which is in 1789.

46. October 13, 1764, Telford, 4:270.

47. August 31, 1784, ibid., 7:233.

48. December 21, 1776, ibid., 6:243; December 23, 1780, ibid., 7:44; and "Thoughts on a Single Life," Jackson, 11:460.

49. To Jane Hilton, July 22, 1766, Telford, 5:24; To Peggy Dale, February 8, 1766, ibid., 4:321; and To Ann Bolton, April 15, 1771, ibid., 5:238. Matthews, "Religion and Reason Joined," 180, has searched for the origin of the phrase "reasoning devil" in the works of Milton, Shakespeare, Blake, Bunyan, Cowper, Herbert, Dryden, and Pope with no results.

50. To William Minethorp, November 29, 1776, Telford, 6:241.
51. §I.43, *Works*, 11:502.
52. To Dr. Rutherforth, March 28, 1768, §III.4, *Works*, 9:382.
53. Matthews, "Religion and Reason Joined," 178-79.
54. *Farther Appeal, Part III*, §III.29, *Works*, 11:311.
55. December 12, 1760, Telford, 4:124. See also ibid., 5:247.
56. *A Farther Appeal, Part III*, §III.28, *Works*, 11:310. See also *The Principles of a Methodist Farther Explained*, §V.7, *Works*, 9:220, and a letter to the editor of *Lloyd's Evening Post*, November 17, 1760, Telford, 4:111.
57. §22, *Works*, 11:370.
58. Cf. the letter to Freeborn Garrettson, January 24, 1789, Telford, 8:112.
59. §II.17, *Works*, 4:186.
60. November 5, 1769, Telford, 5:154.
61. "On Divine Providence," §20, *Works*, 2:545.
62. §I.6, *Works*, 3:92-93. His argument with Newton is that inert matter cannot exert a force like gravity. Rather, he suggests, God must be the prime mover. While he favors Hutchinson's idea of a "subtle matter" which impels things toward each other, his main concern is that God be seen as the prime mover.
63. §§7, 10, *Works*, 2:379-80, 381-82.
64. *A Farther Appeal, Part III*, §III.29, *Works*, 11:311.
65. §9, *Works*, 1:474.
66. *A Farther Appeal, Part III*, §III.28, *Works*, 11:310; and *The Principles of a Methodist Farther Explained*, §V.7, *Works*, 9:220.
67. *Letter to the Author of "The Enthusiasm of Methodists and Papists Compared,"* §22, *Works*, 11:370.
68. January 24, 1789, Telford, 8:112.
69. November 5, 1769, ibid., 5:154.
70. §10, Jackson, 8:254-55.
71. §§23-26, *Works*, 2:54-55.
72. "The Case of Reason Impartially Considered," §I.6, *Works*, 2:592.
73. John Andrew Quenstedt, quoted in Heinrich Schmid, *The Doctrinal Theology of the Evangelical Lutheran Church*, trans. Charles A. Hay and Henry E. Jacobs, 3rd rev. ed. (Philadelphia: Augsburg Publishing House, 1899, repr.), 36.
74. "Of the Church," §II.24, *Works*, 3:54.
75. July 5, 1768, Telford, 5:96.
76. September 28, 1745, §14, *Works*, 26:158.
77. §II.5, *Works*, 4:337. For another early statement of this rule, see also "On the Sabbath," §II.1, *Works*, 4:273.
78. §I.12, *Works*, 3:50.
79. John Locke, *An Essay Concerning Human Understanding*, ed. Peter H. Nidditch (Oxford: Clarendon Press, 1975), 687, IV:xvii:23.
80. Ibid., 693, IV:xviii:6.
81. Ibid., 704, IV:xix:14.
82. Anthony Collins, *An Essay Concerning the Use of Reason in Propositions, The Evidence Whereof Depends upon Human Testimony*, repr. (New York and London: Garland, 1984), 8.
83. Ibid., 24-25.
84. Ibid., 38.
85. See Locke, *Essay*, 694, IV:xviii:7.
86. Ted Allen Campbell, "John Wesley's Conceptions and Uses of Christian Antiquity" (Ph.D. diss., Southern Methodist University, 1984), 149.

87. In Philip P. Wiener, *Dictionary of the History of Ideas: Studies of Selected Pivotal Ideas* (New York: Scribner's, 1968–74), s.v. "Primitivism," George Boas, 577b.

88. Theodore Dwight Bozeman, *To Live Ancient Lives: The Primitivist Dimension in Puritanism* (Chapel Hill and London: University of North Carolina Press, 1988), 9.

89. Ibid., 29. He quotes Thomas Cartwright as saying, "Those that came nearest unto the apostles' times, because they were nearest the light, did see best."

90. Geoffrey F. Nuttall, *Richard Baxter* (London: Nelson, 1965), 124.

91. Richard Baxter, *The Saints' Everlasting Rest*, 7th ed. (London: Thomas Underhill and Francis Tyton, 1658), 14.

92. N. 95, *Journal*, January 25, 1738, *Works*, 18:212-13, §5.

93. See *Journal* for February 21, 1736, *Works*, 18:150, where he writes, "Mary Welch, aged eleven days, was baptized according to the custom of the first church and the rule of the Church of England, by immersion. The child was ill then, but recovered from that hour."

94. *Works*, 18:171.

95. *Works*, 18:213.

96. §II.3, *Works*, 2:69-70.

97. *Notes*, 2 Thessalonians 2:3.

98. §14, *Works*, 3:469-70. See esp. "The Mystery of Iniquity" §§23-24, 28, *Works*, 2:460-61, 464; but also "Thoughts Upon a Late Phenomenon," *Works*, 9:534-37; "The Wisdom of God's Counsels," §8, *Works*, 2:555; *Notes*, Acts 6:1; "Prophets and Priests," §8, *Works*, 4:77; and *The Advantage of the Members of the Church of England*, §12, Jackson, 10:137. See also Campbell, "Conceptions and Uses," 157-58.

99. Letter to Joseph Benson, February 22, 1782, Telford, 7:106.

100. "On Laying the Foundation of the New Chapel," §II.3, *Works*, 3:586.

101. §II.3, 11, Jackson, 14:224-25.

102. July 25, 1755, *Works*, 26:575.

103. §II.3, *Works*, 3:586.

104. November 27, 1738, *Works*, 25:593. The material in brackets is supplied by the editors of the Bicentennial Edition of *Works*, as a conjecture where the manuscript is unclear.

105. *A Letter to the Rev. Dr. Conyers Middleton*, §III.11-12, Jackson, 10:79.

106. August 5-8, 1740, §V.14, *Works*, 26:29.

107. *Journal*, October 21, 1735, *Works*, 18:138.

108. June 25, 1746, §9, *Works*, 26:203.

109. §6, *Works*, 9:368.

110. *Journal*, September 13, 1736, *Works*, 18:171.

111. February 22, 1782, Telford, 7:106.

112. §III.28, *Works*, 11:310. Cf. *The Principles of a Methodist Farther Explained*, §V.7, *Works*, 9:220.

113. §15, Jackson, 10:14.

114. Letter to William Dodd, March 12, 1756, §13, Telford, 3:172.

115. §III.22, Jackson, 10:38.

116. §4, ibid., 10:134.

117. *Journal*, January 25, 1738, *Works*, 18:212-13.

118. For a more complete treatment of Wesley's relationship to the Church of England, see Frank Baker, *John Wesley and the Church of England* (Nashville/New York: Abingdon Press, 1970). However, Baker's purpose there is not primarily to treat Wesley's use of the Church and its doctrine and liturgy as theological authorities.

119. November 27, 1738, *Works*, 25:593.
120. December 1, 1738, *Works*, 25:595.
121. *A Short History of Methodism*, §15, *Works*, 9:371. See also Part I of the *Farther Appeal*, §V.24, *Works*, 11:166.
122. §VI.11, *Works*, 11:185.
123. May 24, 1773, Telford, 6:28.
124. Wesley notes that ministers of the Church of England were bound by this oath in "On God's Vineyard," §I.4, *Works*, 3:505. See Edgar C. S. Gibson, *The Thirty-nine Articles of the Church of England*, 2nd rev. ed. (London: Methuen, 1898), 58-62.
125. §3, December 30, 1745, *Works*, 26:176.
126. September 24, 1755, *Works*, 26:594-95.
127. §VI.12, *Works*, 11:186.
128. May 22, 1750, *Works*, 26:426.
129. September 28, 1745, *Works*, 26:156.
130. July 31, 1747, *Works*, 26:255.
131. §1, *Works*, 9:538.
132. *BCP*, Article VI, "Of the Sufficiency of the Holy Scriptures for Salvation."
133. September 18, 1756, Telford, 3:201.
134. December 1, 1760, ibid., 4:115.
135. Preface to *A Collection of Forms of Prayer*, Jackson, 14:270-71.
136. *Farther Thoughts on Separation from the Church*, §1, *Works*, 9:538.
137. §II.8, *Works*, 3:526. Cf. also "Remarks Upon Mr. Locke's 'Essay on Human Understanding,'" Jackson, 13:462.
138. "The Love of God," §I.3, *Works*, 4:333.
139. *Journal*, November 5, 1766, *Works*, 22:66.
140. §I.1, *Works*, 1:271. Cf. "The Witness of the Spirit, II," §V.1, *Works*, 1:296-97.
141. §II.1, *Works*, 3:204.
142. §III.5-6, *Works*, 3:208.
143. "On Sin in Believers," §V.1, *Works*, 1:333. See also the note on 1 Thessalonians 2:14 in *Notes*.
144. August 14, 1766, Telford, 5:24.
145. "The Witness of the Spirit, II," §V.1, *Works*, 1:296-97.
146. Ted Runyon makes the point well in saying that "Creation/recreation—these are the bookends of Wesley's theology, the framework and structure within which his more familiar soteriological doctrines of prevenient grace, justification, new birth and sanctification, must be set in order to be properly understood." "A New Look at Experience" *Drew Gateway* 57 (1987): 48.
147. George Croft Cell, *The Rediscovery of John Wesley* (New York: Henry Holt, 1935), 45.
148. Ibid., 72.
149. §§15-16, *Works*, 25:403-4.
150. *Works*, 18:511. This is from Wesley's manuscript journal and was not included in the published version.
151. *Works*, 18:208-9.
152. §I.11, *Works*, 1:276.
153. §§II.12-III.4, Jackson, 10:75-76.
154. See above, the *Journal* for January 8, 1738, *Works*, 18:208-9.
155. §21, *Works*, 11:399.
156. See Jackson, 10:75-76.
157. §I.1, *Works*, 1:285.

158. §III.6, *Works*, 1:290.
159. §IV.1, *Works*, 1:293.
160. *Journal*, June 22, 1739, *Works*, 19:73.
161. *Works*, 19:295-96.
162. §II.14, *Works*, 2:111.
163. §19, Jackson 11:406.
164. "On Laying the Foundation of the New Chapel," §II.1, *Works*, 3:585.
165. §II.15, *Works*, 3:590.

Chapter 4: Interpretation of Scripture

1. §5, *Works*, 1:105-6.
2. "The New Birth," §II.3, *Works*, 2:191.
3. *A Plain Account of Christian Perfection*, §27, Jackson, 11:444.
4. §II.1, *Works*, 1:381.
5. In this, Wesley was following the AV text and defended this translation, even when he should have known it was less preferable than "You search the Scriptures."
6. "The New Birth," §II.2, *Works*, 2:191.
7. §18, Jackson, 14:253. For the source of the quotation, see the next note.
8. *A Letter to the Right Reverend The Lord Bishop of Gloucester*, §II.10, *Works*, 11:509. Gerald Cragg has identified the quotation as being a variant of *Imitatio Christi*, I. v, which is quoted also in the Preface to *Explanatory Notes upon the Old Testament* and an undated letter to Dean William Digby.
9. "The Means of Grace," §V.4, *Works*, 1:396. The same point is made in Charles Wesley's hymn, "Scripture Alone," in *The United Methodist Hymnal: Book of United Methodist Worship* (Nashville: United Methodist Publishing House, 1989), #595:

> Whether the Word be preached or read,
> no saving benefit I gain
> from empty sounds or letters dead;
> unprofitable all and vain,
> unless by faith thy word I hear
> and see its heavenly character.

10. §8, Jackson, 14:213.
11. Reprinted in Albert C. Outler, ed., *John Wesley*, Library of Protestant Thought (New York: Oxford University Press, 1964), 124. The exact text is "And in another place Chrysostom saith that man's human and worldly wisdom or science is not needful to the understanding of Scripture but the revelation of the Holy Ghost who inspireth the true meaning unto them that with humility and diligence do search therefor."
12. *Notes*.
13. Larry Shelton, "John Wesley's Approach to Scripture in Historical Perspective," *Wesleyan Theological Journal* 16 (Spring 1981): 37-38.
14. Duncan S. Ferguson, "John Wesley on Scripture: The Hermeneutics of Pietism," *Methodist History* 22 (1984): 242-43.
15. George Lyons, "Hermeneutical Bases of Theology," *Wesleyan Theological Journal* 18 (1983): 71.
16. Timothy Smith, "John Wesley and the Wholeness of Scripture," *Interpretation* 39 (1985): 251.
17. Colin Williams, *John Wesley's Theology Today* (Nashville/New York: Abingdon Press, 1960), 26. Calvin, *Institutes*, §I, viii, 4, 1:79, says, "The same Spirit, therefore, who has spoken through the mouths of the prophets must penetrate into

our hearts to persuade us that they faithfully proclaimed what had been divinely commanded."

18. "The Nature of Enthusiasm," §12, *Works*, 2:50.

19. §21, *Works*, 2:54.

20. §25, *Works*, 2:55.

21. Richard Baxter, *Saints' Everlasting Rest*, 7th rev. ed. (London: Thomas Underhill and Francis Tyton, 1658), 173.

22. N. H. Keeble, *Richard Baxter: Puritan Man of Letters* (Oxford: Clarendon Press, 1982), 31.

23. Ibid., 33.

24. Baxter, *Saints' Everlasting Rest*, 209.

25. November 27, 1750, *Works*, 26:447.

26. February 24, 1786, Telford, 7:319.

27. July 5, 1768, ibid., 5:96.

28. September 28, 1745, §14, *Works*, 26:158. Cf. also his letter to Amicus Veritatus, January 12, 1750 (§13 *Works*, 402), where he says, "I desire to be guided by right *reason*, under the influence of the Spirit of God."

29. §4, *Works*, 4:30.

30. §III.10, *Works*, 1:388.

31. §V.1, *Works*, 393-94.

32. §I.2, Jackson, 10:482-84.

33. Ibid., 483.

34. "A Letter to the Rev. Dr. Rutherforth," §II.6, *Works*, 9:378-79.

35. William Arnett, "John Wesley—Man of One Book: An Investigation of the Centrality of the Bible in the Life and Works of John Wesley with Special Emphasis on His Labours as an Interpreter of the New Testament" (Ph.D. diss., Drew University, 1954), 89-96, lists six rules:

1. Emphasizing the literal sense.
2. The importance of the context.
3. Comparing Scripture with Scripture.
4. The importance of Christian experience.
5. The use of reason as the "handmaid of faith, the servant of revelation."
6. Practicality—eliminating the elaborate, the elegant, and the oratorical.

The quotation about reason as the "handmaid of faith" is from William R. Cannon, *The Theology of John Wesley* (Nashville/New York: Abingdon-Cokesbury, 1946), 159, not from Wesley. In what follows a number of areas of similarity will be seen. Arnett's formulation agrees with mine about the use of the literal sense, interpretation in context, and Scripture interpreting Scripture. His last three "rules" are not actually rules of interpretation but aspects of how Wesley interpreted the Bible. Each of them has been covered elsewhere. Further, Arnett fails to cover a number of other rules that Wesley mentions, so his list is incomplete.

36. To "John Smith," September 28, 1745, §6, *Works*, 26:155.

37. §7, *Works*, 26:155.

38. "On God's Vineyard," §I.1, *Works*, 3:504; and a letter to Mrs. Barton, February 19, 1777, Telford, 6:256.

39. "Farther Appeal," §V.30, *Works*, 11:174; and Preface to *The Doctrine of Original Sin*, §6, Jackson, 9:195.

40. *Predestination Calmly Considered*, §29, Jackson, 10:220; "On Knowing Christ After the Flesh," §9, *Works*, 4:102; *Journal*, July 18, 1765, *Works*, 22:13; and letter to Ann Bolton, January 29, 1773, Telford, 6:14, where he notes that "in the oracles of God there is no improper expression. Every word is the very fittest that can be."

41. *Notes*, 1 Peter 4:11. Note the reference to the doctrinal core of Scripture, what he elsewhere calls "the analogy of faith" as the teaching of the oracles of God.

42. §9, *Works*, 4:102.

43. *Works*, 22:13.

44. To "John Smith," §19, *Works*, 26:160.

45. March 12, 1756, §7, Telford, 3:169.

46. §I.5, *Works*, 2:102.

47. Sermon 21, "Upon Our Lord's Sermon on the Mount, I" §6, *Works*, 1:473; "Of the Church," §12, *Works*, 3:50; "A Call to Backsliders," §I.2(4), *Works*, 3:215; "On the Sabbath," §II.1, *Works*, 4:272; "The Love of God," §II.5, *Works*, 4:337; letter to Lady Cox, March 7, 1738, *Works*, 25:533; and letter to Samuel Furly, May 10, 1755, *Works*, 26:557.

48. *Works*, 3:50.

49. *Works*, 25:533.

50. §I.2(4), *Works*, 3:215. Although Wesley does put these words in the mouth of the backslider, they have the character of an appeal to a commonly accepted rule to which all would agree. Therefore it represents his true position whereas other things in the backslider's speech might not.

51. See "Thoughts on the Writings of Baron Swedenborg," §13, Jackson, 13:432, "plain, obvious meaning"; "On Corrupting the Word of God," §II.[2], [III].1, *Works*, 4:249-50, where he refers to explanation in "the most natural, obvious way" and to the "common, obvious sense"; "The Marks of the New Birth," §2, *Works*, 1:417, "the plainest manner"; "The Witness of the Spirit, II" §§III.1, V.1, *Works*, 1:288, 296, "the plain, natural meaning of the text"; and "Christian Perfection," §II.14, *Works*, 2:111, "plain, natural, obvious meaning."

52. Jackson, 11:429.

53. Robert M. Grant, *A Short History of the Interpretation of the Bible*, rev. ed. (London: Adam and Charles Black, 1965), 102, argues that the reformers differed from Aquinas and other medieval exegetes in their insistence on "the right of the text, as literally interpreted, to stand alone."

54. John Gerhard, quoted in Heinrich Schmid, *The Doctrinal Theology of the Evangelical Lutheran Church*, trans. Charles A. Hay and Henry E. Jacobs, 3rd rev. ed. (Philadelphia: Augsburg Publishing House, 1899, repr.), 78. The Reformed Scholastics argued that "the strict literal sense" is to be followed "unless it is false," with Turrentin basing this upon, among other reasons, the perspicuity of Scripture (Heinrich Heppe, *Reformed Dogmatics: Set Out and Illustrated from the Sources*, rev. ed. Ernst Bizer, trans. G. T. Thomson [Grand Rapids: Baker Book House, 1978, repr.], 37-38).

55. John R. Knott, Jr., *The Sword of the Spirit: Puritan Responses to the Bible* (Chicago and London: University of Chicago, 1980), 5-6, discusses Richard Sibbes, Richard Baxter, Gerrard Winstanley, John Milton, and John Bunyan. He suggests that despite their differences, all five illustrate this commitment to plainness.

56. Baxter, *Saints' Everlasting Rest*, 186.

57. Quoted in Robert E. Sullivan, *John Toland and the Deist Controversy* (Cambridge, Mass., and London: Harvard University Press, 1982), 62.

58. John Locke, *The Reasonableness of Christianity*, ed. and abr. I. T. Ramsey (Stanford, Calif.: Stanford University, 1958), 67.

59. Locke, *A Paraphrase and Notes on the Epistles of St. Paul to the Galatians, 1 and 2 Corinthians, Romans, Ephesians*, ed. Arthur W. Wainwright, 2 vols. (Oxford: Clarendon Press, 1987), 1:114.

60. "On the Fall of Man," §II.6, *Works*, 2:409.

61. "The Reward of the Righteous," §1, *Works*, 3:401.

62. *Journal* for May 19, 1738, §12, *Works*, 18:248. Cf. "The Witness of the Spirit, I," §I.2, *Works*, 1:271, where he refers to "those numerous texts of Scripture which describe the marks of the children of God; and that so plain that he which runneth may read them."

63. §11, *Works*, 4:197. Cf. also "An Israelite Indeed," §II.3, *Works*, 3:285, where he quotes Romans 3:7 saying, "One passage is so express that there does not need any other."

64. Cf. "The Marks of the New Birth," §I.5, *Works*, 1:420-21; *Notes*, John 6:63-64, Mark 4:2, 2 Cor. 3:6, Rom. 7:6; *An Address to the Clergy*, §I.2, Jackson, 10:482-83; Preface to *A Short Exposition of the Ten Commandments, Extracted from Bishop Hopkins*, ibid., 14:241; and "The Law Established Through Faith, II," §I.3-4, *Works*, 2:35-36. Some of these refer to the "law" being dead unless interpreted spiritually.

65. *An Address to the Clergy*, §I.2, Jackson, 10:482-83.

66. *Notes*.

67. *Notes*.

68. "The Marks of the New Birth," §I.5, *Works*, 1:420-21.

69. *Notes*.

70. May 10, 1755, *Works*, 26:557.

71. §III.1, *Works*, 1:321.

72. §IV.2, *Works*, 1:327.

73. §II.5, *Works*, 4:337. See also "Upon Our Lord's Sermon on the Mount, I," §6, *Works*, 1:472-73, for another reference to absurdity as a grounds for leaving the literal sense.

74. *The Compact Edition of the Oxford English Dictionary* gives two definitions of the term that correspond to this. S.v. "Absurdity," I:11, nos. 2 and 3.

75. §II.5, *Works*, 4:337.

76. §II.1, *Works*, 4:272-73.

77. See *Notes*, Rev. 20:3, where he asks, "How far these expressions are to be taken literally, how far figuratively only, who can tell?" See also *Notes*, Rev. 5:1, 16:2, and 16:18.

78. *Notes*, Rev. 21:15.

79. *Notes*, Luke 18:34.

80. *Notes*, Gal. 4:24.

81. §12, Jackson, 10:137.

82. *Minutes of Several Conversations Between the Rev. Mr. Wesley and Others from the Year 1744, to the Year 1789*, ibid., 8:317.

83. Q. 76, ibid., 336.

84. In addition to the two cited below, it is found in "The Wilderness State," §III.8, *Works*, 2:218, and *A Letter to the Right Reverend the Lord Bishop of Gloucester*, §I.12, *Works*, 11:478.

85. Jackson, 11:429.

86. Ibid., 10:490.

87. John Andrew Quenstedt, quoted in Schmid (*Doctrinal Theology*, 76), says, "The more obscure passages, which need explanation, can and should be explained by other passages that are more clear, and thus the Scripture itself furnishes an interpretation of the more obscure expressions when a comparison of these is made with those that are more clear; so that Scripture is explained by Scripture." *The Westminster Confession*, chapter 1, section IX (in John Leith, ed., *Creeds of the Churches: A Reader in Christian Doctrine from the Bible to the Present*, rev. ed. [Richmond: John Knox Press, 1973], 196), says, "The infallible rule of interpretation of Scripture is the

Scripture itself; and therefore, when there is a question about the true and full sense of any Scripture (which is not manifold, but one), it must be searched and known by other places that speak more clearly."

88. §[III].1-2, *Works*, 4:250.

89. §2, *Works*, 2:501.

90. *An Address to the Clergy*, Jackson, 10:490.

91. In addition to the two cited next, see "On Corrupting the Word of God," §II.[2.], *Works*, 4:249.

92. *An Address to the Clergy*, Jackson, 10:490-91.

93. §5, *Works*, 1:106.

94. §III.4, *Works*, 1:289. While there are many places Wesley cites parallel passages, another is in "A Call to Backsliders," §II.2(3), *Works*, 3:220.

95. July 31, 1737, §4, *Works*, 18:531-32.

96. May 24, 1738, §12, *Works*, 18:248.

97. May 10, 1755, *Works*, 26:557.

98. In addition to the one quoted next, see "On Perfection," §II.1, 2, 11, *Works*, 3:76-77, 80; and *A Letter to the Rev. Dr. Conyers Middleton*, §II.4, Jackson, 10:73.

99. "Upon Our Lord's Sermon on the Mount, V," §II.2-3, *Works*, 1:554-55.

100. §V.3-4, *Works*, 1:297-98.

101. §II.4, *Works*, 4:337.

102. *Notes*, Rev. 21:15.

103. Preface to *Notes*, §4.

Chapter 5: The Function of Scripture as an Authority

1. See Appendix 1 for a complete list of the works used in Part 2.

2. For example, see "The Marks of the New Birth," §I.5, *Works*, 1:420, where he makes two such references.

3. "The Marks of the New Birth," §II.5, *Works*, 1:424.

4. "The Scripture Way of Salvation," §III.15, *Works*, 2:168.

5. "Dives and Lazarus," §I.3, *Works*, 4:7.

6. "The Marks of the New Birth," §II.1, *Works*, 1:422.

7. "The Apostle" can refer to Peter, Paul, James, or John. Cf. *An Earnest Appeal*, §49, *Works*, 11:63, where it refers to Paul, whom Wesley believed to be the author of Hebrews.

8. See the discussion later of Wesley's use of the Apocrypha.

9. §II.3, *Works*, 1:382; (a) See Psalm 74:13, *BCP*; (b) 1 John 3:22; (c) See Galatians 4:9; (d) Matt. 22:29.

10. See E. D. Hirsch, Jr., *Cultural Literacy: What Every American Needs to Know* (Boston: Houghton Mifflin, 1987), 2. Hirsch defines cultural literacy as "the network of information that all competent readers possess. It is the background information, stored in their minds, that enables them to take up a newspaper and read it with an adequate level of comprehension, getting the point, grasping the implications, relating what they read to the unstated context which alone gives meaning to what they read." Hirsch then goes on to establish what Americans ought to know to be literate. The idea of cultural literacy could be used as a tool to investigate historically the level of knowledge that could be presumed about a person in any given historical setting. Rather than being tied to literacy, the act of reading, it could be tied simply to any use of language. That every functioning culture has a shared "network of information" which all communicators in that culture possess is clear.

Precisely what is included in that network is a matter of historical investigation, and may vary widely between different groups in that culture.

11. George Rudé, *Hanoverian London, 1714–1808* (Berkeley and Los Angeles: University of California Press, 1971), 116, notes that the charity schools intended "to inculcate elementary Christian values, and prepare them for 'service of the lowest kind.'" While he suggests that they did not stress reading, he quotes a sermon preached at the Orphan Working School at Hoxton (near London) in 1760 as saying the children should have "so much reading as every Christian who values his Bible would wish them to have." Evidence about the level of literacy would be helpful to have, not only for the urban poor but for the entire country.

12. Letter from Susanna Wesley to John, July 24, 1732, reprinted in *Journal,* August 1, 1742, *Works,* 19:288.

13. *Works,* 19:290.

14. *Works,* 2:121; (a) 2 Cor. 7:1; (b) cf. Heb. 4:1, 10; (c) cf. Phil. 3:13-14; (d) cf. Rom. 8:21.

15. *Works,* 11:71; (a) Rom. 1:16; (b) cf. 1 Cor. 12:4, 6; (c) cf. John 5:25; (d) Gen. 1:3; (e) cf. Ps. 33:9; (f) cf. Gen. 2:1; (g) Ecclus. 2:18; (h) Matt. 7:7, etc.; (i) Eph. 2:9; (j) cf. Rom. 4:5. Note the use of the Apocryphal passage at note (g). See what follows for Wesley's usage of this material.

16. Hans W. Frei, *The Eclipse of Biblical Narrative: A Study in Eighteenth and Nineteenth-Century Hermeneutics* (New Haven and London: Yale University Press, 1974), 1-3.

17. One such example is the use of Malachi 3:7 as the text for the sermon "The Means of Grace," *Works,* 1:378. This text is nowhere mentioned in the body of the sermon. Its chief role is to provide the word "ordinances," part of the question with which the sermon opens.

18. *Works,* 2:172.

19. §III.1, *Works,* 1:286-88.

20. §2, *Works,* 4:6. Wesley regards Luke 16:19-31 as a true story, not a parable.

21. §19, *Works,* 11:369. Wesley is quoting Ephesians 4:13.

22. The index to the four volumes of sermons lists twenty-six uses of Hebrews 11:1. Of these, eight are explicit definitions of "faith." Volume 11 of the Bicentennial Edition of the *Works* includes the Appeals and related letters; of nine uses of Hebrews 11:1 in that volume, four are explicit definitions.

23. §II.1, *Works,* 2:160.

24. *A Farther Appeal, Part I,* §I.4, *Works,* 11:106-7. The quotations are from 2 Cor. 5:19 and Gal. 2:20.

25. §70, *Works,* 11:75. Wesley is referring to Acts 18:7 and Acts 19:9.

26. §I.8, *Works,* 2:160; (a) John 3:3; (b) cf. Rom. 8:13; (c) 1 Thess. 5:22; (d) Titus 2:14; (e) cf. Gal. 6:10; (f) cf. Luke 1:6; (g) see John 4:23, 24; (h) cf. Matt. 16:24.

27. I am indebted to Prof. John Deschner for this suggestion.

28. See Rex D. Matthews, "'Religion and Reason Joined': A Study in the Theology of John Wesley" (Ph.D. diss., Harvard University, 1986), chaps. 4 and 5.

29. Albert C. Outler, *Theology in the Wesleyan Spirit* (Nashville: Discipleship Resources-Tidings, 1975), 11.

30. January 6, 1756, Telford, 3:332.

31. §II.5 *Works,* 3:460.

32. *Notes,* Acts 21:20.

33. One could include in this category statements of Christian teaching from the early church and from the Church of England. However, Wesley explicitly acknowl-

edges the role played by these sources, and we will leave that discussion for another place. These sources are discussed in chapter 3 and their uses in chapter 6.

34. Timothy Ware, *The Orthodox Church* (Harmondsworth, U.K., and Baltimore, Md.: Penguin Books, 1963), 208-9.

35. They are as follows:

Ecclesiasticus 2:12—"The Circumcision of the Heart," §I.9, *Works*, 1:406.

Ecclesiasticus 2:18—*Earnest Appeal*, §63, *Works*, 11:71.

Ecclesiasticus 34:21—"The Use of Money," §I.4, *Works*, 2:272.

Ecclesiasticus 41:1-4—"Dives and Lazarus," §II.4, *Works*, 4:13.

Ecclesiasticus 44:1-7—"The Means of Grace," §I.4, *Works*, 1:379.

Wisdom 1:12—*Earnest Appeal*, §51, *Works*, 11:64; "Christian Perfection," §I.4, *Works*, 2:102; "Dives and Lazarus," §III.2, *Works*, 4:16; "On the Wedding Garment," §11, *Works*, 4:144.

Wisdom 1:13—"The New Creation," §17, *Works*, 2:509.

Wisdom 9:15—"The Image of God," §II.1, *Works*, 4:298.

36. To arrive at these numbers, I have relied on the "Scriptural Index" in volume 4 of the Bicentennial Edition. From this list I excluded footnotes where the text appeared only in the note, and those references where a canonical text was listed first as the most likely referent.

37. *Works*, 11:64; (a) cf. 2 Cor. 4:4; (b) cf. Wisdom 1:12.

38. §11, *Works*, 4:144; (a) Matt. 22:13; (b) Wisdom 1:12.

39. "The Circumcision of the Heart," §I.9, *Works*, 1:406; and "Christian Perfection," §I.4, *Works*, 2:102.

40. "Scriptural Christianity," §II.5, *Works*, 1:167.

41. *Works*, 2:130 n. 18.

42. *BCP*, [15]-[19].

43. F. F. Bruce, *The English Bible: A History of Translations* (New York: Oxford University Press, 1961), 110.

44. The Westminster Confession says that they "are no part of the Canon of the Scripture; and therefore are of no authority in the Church of God, nor to be any otherwise approved, or made use of, than other human writings" (chap. 1, §III, in John Leith, ed., *Creeds of the Churches: A Reader in Christian Doctrine from the Bible to the Present*, rev. ed. [Richmond: John Knox Press, 1973], 195).

45. John Wesley, *Lessons for Children* (London: Farley, 1746–54).

46. *Works*, 20:151.

47. His sources (in order of frequency within this sample) are John Milton, Charles Wesley, Virgil, Horace, Matthew Prior, Alexander Pope, Isaac Watts, Plato, Diogenes Laertius, George Herbert, Ovid, Quintillian, Thomas Otway, Cicero, Homer, Seneca, Hadrian, James Thomson, Samuel Wesley, Samuel Wesley, Jr., Suetonius, Lucretius, L. Annaeus Florus, and John Dryden.

48. The quotation is from *Paradise Lost*, i. 26; in §II.10, *Works*, 1:364-65.

49. "The Great Assize," §II.5, *Works*, 1:362, quoting Virgil, *Aeneid*, vi. 567-69. Outler's footnote 41 gives Wesley's own translation from another source, with the addition of the preceding line:

> O'er these drear realms stern Rhadamanthus reigns,
> Detects each artful villain, and constrains
> To own the crimes, long veiled from human sight:
> In vain! Now all stand forth in hated light.

50. Wesley gives a footnoted translation, "My friends, I have lost a day." The editors of the Bicentennial Edition cite Suetonius, *The Lives of the Caesars*, Book VIII, "The Deified Titus," §viii, quoted at *Works*, 11:52.

51. §II.1, *Works*, 2:593, quoting Milton, *Paradise Lost*, IV.677-78.

52. §10, *Works*, 11:48.

53. §II.11, *Works*, 2:182; (a) a paraphrase of Cicero, *De Officiis*, I.xxviii.99; (b) 2 Cor. 6:8, translation from *Notes*; (c) cf. Acts 22:22.

54. *Notes*.

55. "Free Grace," §5, *Works*, 3:545.

56. §20, *Works*, 3:552; (a) Rom. 9:13, quoting Mal. 1:2-3; (b) 1 John 4:16.

57. §26, *Works*, 3:556; (a) 1 Cor. 15:54; (b) Ps. 145:9.

58. §III.1, "The Witness of the Spirit, II" *Works*, 1:288.

59. "Christian Perfection," §II.20, *Works*, 2:116.

60. §III.1, *Works*, 1:384.

61. §V.4, *Works*, 1:395-97.

62. *Works*, 22:293.

63. *Works*, 22:352. Wesley refers to 1 John as "the deepest part of the Holy Scriptures" in *Journal*, July 18, 1765, *Works*, 22:13.

64. "On Charity," *Works*, 3:293, and *Journal*, March 30, 1789, Curnock, 7:483.

65. §II.2, Jackson, 10:72.

66. "Upon our Lord's Sermon on the Mount," §3, *Works*, 1:470.

67. Preface to 1 John, *Notes*.

68. §II.5, *Works*, 2:106-7.

69. §II.17, *Works*, 2:114. The argument summarized begins with §II.5, 106.

70. §II.20, *Works*, 2:116.

71. *Works*, 2:87-89.

72. §II.1, *Works*, 2:105; (a) Rom. 3:24; (b) Rom. 5:1; (c) Eph. 4:13.

73. §II.8, *Works*, 2:108; (a) cf. 2 Cor. 3:8-9; (b) Gal. 3:27; (c) cf. Matt. 22:29.

74. §II.14, *Works*, 2:111; (a) 1 Pet. 1:9-15.

75. *Works*, 4:651-87. John Vickers, the indexer, has relied upon the footnote Scripture references, those provided both by Wesley and by the editors. This index is of high quality with few errors or sources for confusion.

76. However, the designation for Matthew may really represent the Synoptic Gospels, since some of the Bicentennial Edition's footnotes would read like footnote 42, 2:88, "Matthew 7:21, etc." referring to other possible sources for the quote.

77. For the complete list, see appendix 2 in the present work.

78. Françoise Deconinck-Brossard, "L'Écriture dans la Prédication Anglaise," in Yvon Belaval and Dominique Bourel, eds., *Le siècle des Lumières et la Bible*, vol. 7 of *Bible de Tous les Temps* (Paris: Éditions Beauchesne, 1986), 532, remarks that Wesley's style: "se distinguent par l'absence presque totale de référence aux livres sapienti-aux, et par la très faible proportion de textes vétérotestamentaires. C'est une oeuvre essentiellement inspirée de l'Evangile, surtout de Matthieu, et de quelques épîtres pauliniennes, donc fort éloignée de l'équilibre caractéristique de John Sharp." Her analysis appears to be based on the texts for the "standard" sermons in Sugden. I would argue that it is more accurate to count the actual uses of texts in the sermons themselves, and not only their use as texts for sermons. Although her point about the relative infrequency of Old Testament references is overstated, Wesley's pref-erence for Gospel and Pauline texts is clear.

79. Timothy Smith, "John Wesley and the Wholeness of Scripture," *Interpretation* 39 (1985), agrees with this point.

80. §III.5, *Works*, 2:482.

81. "On Laying the Foundation of the New Chapel," §II.1, *Works*, 3:585, where he is quoting from the *Earnest Appeal*, §2, *Works*, 11:45.

Chapter 6: The Function of Other Authorities in Relation to Scripture

1. "The Case of Reason Impartially Considered," §I.2, *Works*, 2:590.

2. John Andrew Quenstedt, quoted in Heinrich Schmid, *The Doctrinal Theology of the Evangelical Lutheran Church*, trans. Charles A. Hay and Henry E. Jacobs, 3rd rev. ed. (Philadelphia: Augsburg Publishing House, 1899, repr.), 36.

3. "The Scripture Way of Salvation," §III.1, *Works*, 2:162.

4. §III.2, *Works*, 2:162-63.

5. §IV.3, *Works*, 1:391.

6. *Notes*, Rom. 3:20.

7. Cf. *Notes*, Matt. 22:12, where "implanted" is used for "imparted." In other places "imparted" is more common.

8. "The Circumcision of the Heart," §I.12, *Works*, 1:408.

9. *Notes*.

10. §II.14, *Works*, 2:112.

11. §II.1, *Works*, 4:297.

12. *Works*, 4:297 n. 19.

13. *Notes*.

14. §1, *Works*, 4:29.

15. *Works*, 4:29.

16. "Original Sin," §II.3, *Works*, 2:177.

17. He quotes Isaiah 41:21, "Bring forth your strong reasons," §I.1, *Works*, 2:589.

18. §I.2, *Works*, 2:590.

19. Rex D. Matthews, "'Religion and Reason Joined': A Study in the Theology of John Wesley" (Ph.D. diss., Harvard University, 1986), 157. See chap. 2, "Wesley's Consistent Concept of Reason," 121-83.

20. "Original Sin," §§2, 4, *Works*, 2:172-73.

21. "Christian Perfection," §II.2, *Works*, 2:105-6. Quotations are from Isa. 8:20 and Rom. 3:4.

22. E.g., *An Earnest Appeal*, §6, *Works*, 11:46.

23. Jackson, 11:484.

24. "Dives and Lazarus," §2, *Works*, 4:6.

25. *Earnest Appeal*, §14, *Works*, 11:49.

26. *Earnest Appeal*, §§19-22, *Works*, 11:51-52.

27. §32, *Works*, 11:56.

28. §35, *Works*, 11:57. For the quotation, cf. 1 Cor. 2:10.

29. "Dives and Lazarus," §III.7, *Works*, 4:18.

30. They are *Works*, §II.8, 1:384; §II.16, 2:113; §I.7, 2:159; §12, 2:490; §II.7, 2:529; §I.6, 2:592; §III.7, 3:208; §II.3, 3:586; §2, 4:6; §8, 4:33; §10, 4:33; §7, 4:90; §14, 4:94; and *Notes*, Matt. 18:18.

31. Ted Campbell has discussed these uses of Christian antiquity in chapter VI of "John Wesley's Conceptions and Uses of Christian Antiquity." He has grouped them under the headings of patterns for "Christian Teaching" (including warrants in arguments and interpretation of Scripture), "Individual Life," and "Corporate Life." I do not regard my analysis of Wesley's use of antiquity as differing in any material way from Campbell's.

32. "The Case of Reason Impartially Considered," §I.6, *Works*, 2:592.

33. "Dives and Lazarus," §2, *Works*, 4:6.

34. In the sermon "Christian Perfection" he gives this as the "literal" translation of 2 Cor. 12:7, §II.15, *Works*, 2:112. Note, however, that in *Notes* he uses "a thorn in

the flesh," following the AV. The *Notes* was published fourteen years after this sermon's publication.

35. §II.16, *Works*, 2:113. Outler notes that Wesley has in mind Tertullian's *De Pudicitia*, §13, Chrysostom's *Letters to Olympias*, 2, Cyprian's *Treatise*, IX.9, and Cyprian's *De Mortalitate*.

36. *Notes*, Matt. 18:18.

37. §I.7, *Works*, 2:159. Outler suggests that Macarius the Egyptian was not the author of the Homilies attributed to him in J. P. Migne, ed., *Patrologiae Cursus Completus, Series Graeca* (Paris, 1857–66), XXXIV.

38. §12, *Works*, 2:490. Wesley's only other use of this quotation in the sermons comes in §III.7 of the sermon, "On Working Out Our Own Salvation," *Works*, 3:208.

39. §14, *Works*, 4:94.

40. §8, *Works*, 4:33.

41. §10, *Works*, 4:33.

42. "The Means of Grace," §II.8, *Works*, 1:384.

43. "Dives and Lazarus," §2, *Works*, 4:6. Outler notes that this could be an inference from his *Ennaratio*, §§420-21 but that this phrase is not in Theophylact's text.

44. Wesley sometimes applies it to the Jews before Christ as "the ancient church of God," *A Farther Appeal, Part II*, §I.2, *Works*, 11:204.

45. E.g., "Such was Christianity in its rise. Such was a Christian in ancient days." "Scriptural Christianity," §I.10, *Works*, 1:165. See also Jackson, 10:141, 13:293, 14:270-71; Letter to James Hutton, 27 November, 1738; *Works*, 25:593; *A Letter to the Rev. Mr. Baily of Cork*, §II.15, *Works*, 9:305; and "On Sin in Believers," §I.2, *Works*, 1:317.

46. "Of Hell," §II.7, *Works*, 3:39.

47. §I.5, *Works*, 3:505-6.

48. "The Way to the Kingdom," §II.5, *Works*, 1:228.

49. "An Israelite Indeed," §II.2, *Works*, 3:284.

50. "On the Discoveries of Faith," §1, *Works*, 4:29. Outler notes that Thomas Aquinas discusses this at length.

51. *The Oxford Dictionary of the Christian Church*, s.v. "filioque," 512b.

52. See Wesley's *Letter to a Roman Catholic*, Jackson, 10:80-86. For Roman Catholic notice of its irenic spirit, see Augustin Cardinal Bea's Preface in *John Wesley's Letter to a Roman Catholic*, ed. Michael Hurley (London: Geoffrey Chapman; Belfast: Epworth House; Nashville/New York: Abingdon Press, 1968), 15-21.

53. §II.1, *Works*, 3:585.

54. §II.15, *Works*, 3:590.

55. §II.4, *Works*, 3:586. The last quotation is from the Collect for Purity in the Communion Liturgy of the *BCP*.

56. See reference to the letter to Dr. Horne, Telford, 4:175, in chap. 3.

57. *Farther Thoughts on Separation from the Church*, *Works*, 9:538.

58. "The Great Assize," §III.4, *Works*, 1:370.

59. Within the limited sample studied here, see also "Causes of the Inefficacy of Christianity," §§3-8, *Works*, 4:87-91, where even the Methodists are seen to fall short of the Christian standard.

60. §1, *Works*, 2:485.

61. §7, *Works*, 2:488.

62. §IV.2, *Works*, 1:428.

63. §65, *Works*, 11:72.

64. §99, *Works*, 11:89.

65. §32, *Works*, 11:374.

66. §11, *Works*, 3:548.
67. §13, *Works*, 3:549.
68. §18, *Works*, 3:550.
69. §19, *Works*, 3:551.
70. "The Case of Reason Impartially Considered," §1, *Works*, 2:587.
71. §II.1, *Works*, 2:593.
72. §II.2, *Works*, 2:176-77.
73. §II.5, *Works*, 4:299.
74. 1 John 4:7-8.
75. "Catholic Spirit," §3, *Works*, 2:82.
76. "The Use of Money," §II.5, *Works*, 2:275.
77. *Notes*, Rom. 3:10.
78. §46, *Works*, 11:62.
79. §61, *Works*, 11:70.
80. §4, *Works*, 4:30.
81. §7, *Works*, 4:31-32. (a) 1 John 5:7; (b) John 1:14; (c) Rom. 14:17.
82. §IV.2, *Works*, 1:293.
83. §II.2, *Works*, 2:105-6.

Chapter 7: Interpretation of Scripture

1. Preface to *Sermons on Several Occasions*, §5, *Works*, 1:105.
2. §1, *Works*, 3:579.
3. Preface, §6, *Notes*.
4. *Notes*, Matt. 16:24.
5. *Works*, 25:639-40. See also the account in the *Journal* for April 25-29, 1739, *Works*, 19:51-52.
6. *Works*, 19:387.
7. *Works*, 3:544.
8. See April 22, 1783, Curnock, 6:405, working on "The General Spread of the Gospel"; August 27, 1787, ibid., 7:319, working on "The Signs of the Times"; March 25, 1788, ibid., 7:366, working on "Dives and Lazarus"; June 11, 1788, ibid., 7:399, working on "On the Discoveries of Faith"; and July 2, 1789, ibid., 7:515, working on "Causes of the Inefficacy of Christianity."
9. Ibid., 8:54.
10. His translation of the New Testament for *Notes* makes a number of theologically significant points, e.g., his use of "happy" for μακάριοι in the Beatitudes.
11. E.g., the discussion about the Jewish tables in *Notes*, Matt. 1:1 and his quotations from Virgil, "The Great Assize," §II.5, *Works*, 1:362.
12. E.g., his familiarity with both Hutchinson and Newton on gravity, "On Spiritual Worship," §I.6, *Works*, 3:92-93.
13. E.g., his use of Augustine, "The General Spread of the Gospel," §12, *Works*, 2:490.
14. §I.2, Jackson, 10:482-84.
15. §55, *Works*, 11:66.
16. *A Letter to the Author of "The Enthusiasm of Methodists, etc.,"* §19, *Works*, 11:368.
17. James Strong, *The Exhaustive Concordance of the Bible* (Nashville: Abingdon Press, 1890, repr., 1980), s.v. "conversion," "convert," etc., 218.
18. §II.3, *Works*, 1:287.
19. The closing section of "Christian Perfection," §II.30, *Works*, 2:121, was discussed in chapter 5.

20. *Works*, 1:194, 405; 2:39, 160, 368, 593, 600; 3:492, 521; 4:30, and 188.

21. §II.1, *Works*, 2:160.

22. §II.1-2, *Works*, 2:161, Wesley's emphases.

23. *Notes*.

24. §IV.2, *Works*, 1:391.

25. Albert Outler categorized the sermon "The Great Assize" in this way. See his introduction, *Works*, 1:354.

26. §II.1, *Works*, 1:381.

27. §II.8, *Works*, 1:384.

28. Passim, §III.1-12, *Works*, 1:384-90.

29. §III.7, *Works*, 1:387.

30. Tyndale, the Great Bible, the Geneva Bible, the Bishops' Bible, the Rheims Bible, and the AV all read "Search the scriptures" with variants in spelling and capitalization. Luther A. Weigle, ed., *The New Testament Octapla: Eight English Versions of the New Testament in the Tyndale-King James Tradition* (New York: Thomas Nelson, n.d.).

31. Cf. also Wesley's interpretation of the "blasphemy against the Spirit" in *Notes*, Matt. 12:31: "And yet there is nothing plainer in all the Bible. It is neither more nor less, than the ascribing those miracles to the power of the devil, which Christ wrought by the power of the Holy Ghost." Such an interpretation has not been clear to everyone else!

32. The "Marks of the New Birth," §III.4, *Works*, 1:427. Such phrases occur frequently within Wesley's writings.

33. §I.5, *Works*, 1:420-21.

34. Cf. "Christian Perfection," §II.6, *Works*, 2:107; §II.9, *Works*, 109; and *Notes*, Rom. 8:9.

35. "Upon Our Lord's Sermon on the Mount, IV," §I.9, *Works*, 1:538.

36. §V.4, *Works*, 1:298.

37. "Christian Perfection," §I.6, *Works*, 2:102-3. Emphasis added.

38. §II.6, *Works*, 2:528-29.

39. *Notes*, Rom. 8:28.

40. In one place Wesley suggests that some interpret Ecclesiastes 3:18 "in a more literal sense than ever Solomon meant it." See "The Image of God," §[3], *Works*, 4:293.

41. Robin Scroggs, "John Wesley as Biblical Scholar," *Journal of Bible and Religion* 28 (1960): 419.

42. §17, *Works*, 2:509, quotation from Isaiah 11:6.

43. *Notes*, Matt. 2:18.

44. §II.4, *Works*, 2:526.

45. *Notes*.

46. §IV.5, *Works*, 1:392.

47. §1, *Works*, 2:266.

48. "The Means of Grace," *Works*, 1:378; "On Laying the Foundation of the New Chapel," *Works*, 3:579; and "Causes of the Inefficacy of Christianity," *Works*, 4:86.

49. §I.6, *Works*, 1:421.

50. *Notes*, Rom. 12:6.

51. §II.2, *Works*, 3:585; (a) cf. Deut. 6:5; Lev. 19:18; Matt. 22:37, 39, etc.; (b) cf. Rom. 13:10; (c) 1 Tim. 1:5.

52. For example, cf. "Upon Our Lord's Sermon on the Mount, IV," §III.4, *Works*, 1:544, where he quotes Habakkuk, Ephesians, Mark, and 1 John, followed by the conclusion which begins "Consequently. . . ."

53. *Notes.*

54. §III.13, *Works,* 2:167.

55. Harald Lindström, *Wesley and Sanctification: A Study in the Doctrine of Salvation* (London: Epworth Press, 1950), 124. For a longer discussion, see 198-218.

56. John Deschner, *Wesley's Christology: An Interpretation* (Dallas: Southern Methodist University Press, 1960), 178.

57. §II.2, *Works,* 3:204-5.

58. §I.8, *Works,* 1:537.

59. By this he means that it is not solitary, that it does require "living and conversing with other men" (§I.1, *Works,* 1:533-34), and that it should not be hidden. He does not have in mind what twentieth-century Christians have referred to as "social action."

60. §III.4, *Works,* 1:543-44.

61. *Notes.*

62. Preface to *Sermons on Several Occasions,* §5, *Works,* 1:106.

63. Albert C. Outler, "The Place of Wesley in the Christian Tradition" in *The Place of Wesley in the Christian Tradition,* ed. Kenneth E. Rowe (Metuchen, N.J.: Scarecrow, 1976), 14.

64. §69, *Works,* 11:74.

65. §IV.2, *Works,* 1:391.

66. §3, *Works,* 4:141.

67. *Notes.*

68. *Notes.*

69. *Notes.*

70. "The Marks of the New Birth," §II.5, *Works,* 1:424.

71. Cf. "The General Spread of the Gospel," §26, *Works,* 2:498. The passages quoted are Isaiah 11:9; 60:18, 19, 21; and 61:11.

72. "The General Spread of the Gospel," §10, *Works,* 2:489.

73. However, Weigle shows that Tyndale, the Great Bible, the Geneva Bible, and the Bishops Bible all agree with Wesley here.

74. *Notes,* Matt. 5:48. For the last Scripture quotation, cf. Jer. 31:33.

75. §2, *Works,* 1:103.

76. *Works.*

77. *Notes,* Rom. 1:13.

78. *Notes,* Rom. 4:4.

79. The wolf dwelling with the lamb in Isa. 11:6 "may be literally as well as figuratively understood," "The New Creation," §17, *Works,* 2:509.

80. "The Image of God," §[3], *Works,* 4:293.

81. *Notes,* Matt. 26:26.

82. *Notes,* Matt. 5:29.

83. *Notes,* Rom. 8:38.

84. *Notes,* Rom. 12:1. Wesley also finds this device in Rom. 4:24.

85. *Notes,* Matt. 6:3.

86. *Notes,* 1 John 5:8, quoted later.

87. *Notes,* Rom. 7:7.

88. *Notes,* James 3:1.

89. Eberhard Nestle and Erwin Nestle, et al., eds., *Novum Testamentum Graece,* 26th ed. (Stuttgart: Deutsche Bibelgessellschaft, 1979), 21.

90. *Notes,* Matt. 5:22.

91. *Notes,* 1 John 5:7-8.

92. First John 5:7 serves as the text for "On the Trinity." In §5, *Works*, 2:378-79, Wesley discusses its textual authenticity. He summarizes Bengel under three points: (1) It is found in many more copies than miss it, including those of the greatest authority; (2) it is cited by a "whole train of ancient writers from the time of St. John to that of Constantine"; and (3) Constantine's successor, the Arian emperor, would have sought to erase it.

93. *Notes*, Matt. 27:9.

94. §II.2, *Works*, 1:423.

95. In the Preface he writes, "In order to assist these in such a measure as I am able, I design, First, to set down the text itself, for the most part, in the common English translation, which is, in general, so far as I can judge, abundantly the best that I have seen. Yet I do not say it is incapable of being brought, in several places, nearer to the original. Neither will I affirm that the Greek copies from which this translation was made are always the most correct: and therefore I shall take the liberty, as occasion may require, to make here and there a small alteration." *Notes*, §4.

96. George Croft Cell, introduction to John Wesley, *John Wesley's New Testament* (Philadelphia: John C. Winston, 1938), xi; Scroggs, "John Wesley as Biblical Scholar," 416.

97. E.g., *Notes*, Matt. 8:21-22, 9:6, 9:12.

98. E.g., *Notes*, Rom. 9:30, 14:18.

99. E.g., *Notes*, Matt. 12:36.

100. E.g., *Notes*, Matt. 20:22.

101. See John Heylyn, *Theological Lectures at Westminster Abbey, with an Interpretation of the Four Gospels*, 2 vols. (London: J. and R. Tonson and S. Draper, 1749–61), where his translation does the same.

102. John Locke, *A Paraphrase and Notes on the Epistles of St. Paul to the Galatians, 1 and 2 Corinthians, Romans, Ephesians*, ed. Arthur W. Wainwright, 2 vols. (Oxford: Clarendon Press, 1987), 105.

103. The same translation is made at Matt. 24:46, Rom. 4:6-7, James 1:12, and James 1:25.

104. §II.3, *Works*, 2:177. The quote is from Eph. 2:12.

105. *Works*, 2:177 n. 30.

106. *Notes*, Eph. 2:12.

107. "The Scripture Way of Salvation," §I.1, *Works*, 2:156.

108. Scroggs, "John Wesley as Biblical Scholar," 417.

Conclusion

1. *Notes*, Rom. 12:6.

2. See his own account of this in the Journal, March 23, 1738, *Works*, 18:232, and May 24, 1738, *Works*, 18:248, §12.

3. "On Laying the Foundation of the New Chapel," §II.1, *Works*, 3:585.

Selected Bibliography

Aaron, Richard I. *John Locke.* 3rd ed. Oxford: Clarendon Press, 1971.

Allison, C. F. *The Rise of Moralism: The Proclamation of the Gospel from Hooker to Baxter.* New York: Seabury Press, 1966.

Arnett, William. "John Wesley—Man of One Book: An Investigation of the Centrality of the Bible in the Life and Works of John Wesley with Special Emphasis on His Labours as an Interpreter of the New Testament." Ph.D. diss., Drew University, 1954.

Baird, William. *History of New Testament Research. Volume One: From Deism to Tübingen.* Minneapolis: Fortress Press, 1992.

Baker, Frank. *John Wesley and the Church of England.* Nashville/New York: Abingdon Press, 1970.

_____. "John Wesley, Biblical Commentator." *Bulletin of the John Rylands Library* 71 (1989): 109-20.

Baxter, Richard. *The Saints' Everlasting Rest.* 7th rev. ed. London: Thomas Underhill and Francis Tyton, 1658.

Bengel, John Albert. *Gnomon of the New Testament.* Ed. M. Ernest Bengel and J. C. F. Steudel. Trans. James Bandinel, et al. 5 vols. 3rd ed. Philadelphia: Smith, English; and New York: Sheldon, 1860.

The Book of Common Prayer, and Administration of the Sacraments . . . According to the Use of the Church of England. Oxford: University Printers, 1710.

The Book of Discipline of The United Methodist Church, 1988. Nashville: United Methodist Publishing House, 1988.

Bozeman, Theodore Dwight. *To Live Ancient Lives: The Primitivist Dimension in Puritanism.* Chapel Hill and London: University of North Carolina Press, 1988.

Brantley, Richard E. *Locke, Wesley, and the Method of English Romanticism.* Gainesville: University of Florida, 1984.

Bruce, F. F. *The English Bible: A History of Translations.* New York: Oxford, 1961.

Burnet, Gilbert. *An Exposition of the Thirty-Nine Articles of the Church of England.* Rev. ed. James Page. New York: Appleton, 1842.

Burtner, Robert W., and Robert E. Chiles. *A Compend of Wesley's Theology.* Nashville/New York: Abingdon Press, 1954.

Buttrick, George Arthur, ed. *The Interpreter's Dictionary of the Bible*. Nashville/New York: Abingdon Press, 1962. S.v. "History of Biblical Criticism" by S. J. De Vries, 1:413-18.

Calvin, John. *Calvin: Institutes of the Christian Religion*. Ed. John T. McNeill. Trans. Ford Lewis Battles. Library of Christian Classics, vol. 20. Philadelphia: Westminster Press, 1960.

Campbell, Ted Allen. *John Wesley and Christian Antiquity: Religious Vision and Cultural Change*. Nashville: Kingswood Books, 1991.

_____. "John Wesley's Conceptions and Uses of Christian Antiquity." Ph.D. diss., Southern Methodist University, 1984.

_____. "The 'Wesleyan Quadrilateral': The Story of a Modern Methodist Myth" in *Doctrine and Theology in the United Methodist Church*, ed. Thomas A. Langford, 154-61. Nashville: Kingswood Books, 1991.

Cannon, William R. *The Theology of John Wesley, with Special Reference to the Doctrine of Justification*. Nashville/New York: Abingdon-Cokesbury Press, 1946.

Carpenter, Edward. "The Bible in the Eighteenth Century." In *The Church's Use of the Bible, Past and Present*, ed. D. E. Nineham, 89-124. London: S.P.C.K., 1963.

Casto, Robert Michael. "Exegetical Method in John Wesley's *Explanatory Notes upon the Old Testament*: A Description of His Approach, Use of Sources, and Practice." Ph.D. diss., Duke University, 1977.

Cell, George Croft. *The Rediscovery of John Wesley*. New York: Henry Holt, 1935.

Chillingworth, William. *The Religion of Protestants, a Safe Way to Salvation*. 3rd ed. London: J. Clark, 1664.

Clemons, James T. "John Wesley—Biblical Literalist?" *Religion in Life* 46 (1977): 332-42.

Clert-Rolland, Louis. "Jeremy Taylor et la Tolérance Religieuse au XVIIe Siècle." *Revue d'Histoire et de Philosophie Religieuse* 49 (1969): 257-64.

Collins, Anthony. *A Discourse of Free-Thinking, Occasion'd by the Rise and Growth of a Sect Call'd Free Thinkers*. London: n.p., 1713; repr., New York: Garland, 1984.

_____. *Discourse of the Grounds and Reasons of the Christian Religion*. London: n.p., 1724; repr. New York and London: Garland, 1976.

_____. *An Essay Concerning the Use of Reason in Propositions, the Evidence Whereof Depends upon Human Testimony*. London: n.p., 1707; repr., New York and London: Garland, 1984.

_____. *The Scheme of Literal Prophecy Considered; in a View of the Controversy, Occasioned by a late Book intitled "A Discourse of the Grounds and Reasons of the Christian Religion."* London: n.p., 1727.

The Compact Edition of the Oxford English Dictionary. 2 vols. Oxford: Oxford University Press, 1971.

Cragg, Gerald R. *From Puritanism to the Age of Reason.* Cambridge: Cambridge University Press, 1966.

_____. *Reason and Authority in the Eighteenth Century.* Cambridge: Cambridge University Press, 1964.

Cross, F. L., and E. A. Livingstone, eds. *The Oxford Dictionary of the Christian Church.* 2nd. ed. London: Oxford University Press, 1974.

Deconinck-Brossard, Françoise. "L'Écriture dans la Prédication Anglaise." In Yvon Belaval and Dominique Bourel, eds. *Le siècle des Lumières et la Bible.* Vol. 7 of *Bible de Tous les Temps.* Paris: Éditions Beauchesne, 1986, 523-43.

Deschner, John. *Wesley's Christology: An Interpretation.* Dallas: Southern Methodist University Press, 1960, 1985.

Downey, James. *The Eighteenth Century Pulpit: A Study of the Sermons of Butler, Berkeley, Secker, Sterne, Whitefield, and Wesley.* Oxford: Clarendon Press, 1969.

Dreyer, Frederick. "Faith and Experience in the Thought of John Wesley." *American Historical Review* 88 (1983): 12-30.

Farrar, Frederick W. *History of Interpretation.* New York: E. P. Dutton, 1886; repr., Grand Rapids, Mich.: Baker, 1961.

Ferguson, Duncan S. "John Wesley on Scripture: The Hermeneutics of Pietism." *Methodist History* 22 (1984): 234-45.

Frei, Hans W. *The Eclipse of Biblical Narrative: A Study in Eighteenth- and Nineteenth-Century Hermeneutics.* New Haven and London: Yale University Press, 1974.

Freiday, Dean. *The Bible—Its Criticism, Interpretation, and Use in Sixteenth- and Seventeenth-Century England.* Catholic and Quaker Studies Number 4. Pittsburgh: Catholic and Quaker Studies, 1979.

Gay, Peter. *Deism: An Anthology.* Princeton: Van Nostrand, 1968.

_____. *The Enlightenment: An Interpretation: The Rise of Modern Paganism.* New York: Alfred A. Knopf, 1966.

Gibson, Edgar C. S. *The Thirty-nine Articles of the Church of England.* 2nd rev. ed. London: Methuen, 1898.

Grant, Robert M. *A Short History of the Interpretation of the Bible.* Rev. ed. London: Adam and Charles Black, 1965.

Haller, William. *The Rise of Puritanism.* Philadelphia: University of Pennsylvania, 1938.

Hanson, R. P. C. *Allegory and Event: A Study of the Sources and Significance of Origen's Interpretation of Scripture.* Richmond, Va.: John Knox Press, 1959.

Heitzenrater, Richard P. *Mirror and Memory: Reflections on Early Methodism.* Nashville: Kingswood Books, 1989.

Heppe, Heinrich. *Reformed Dogmatics Set Out and Illustrated from the Sources.* Rev. ed. Ernst Bizer. Trans. G. T. Thomson. Grand Rapids, Mich.: Baker, 1978, repr.

Heylyn, John. *Theological Lectures at Westminster Abbey, with an Interpretation of the Four Gospels.* 2 vols. London: J. and R. Tonson and S. Draper, 1749–61.

Hirsch, Jr., E. D. *Cultural Literacy: What Every American Needs to Know.* Boston: Houghton Mifflin, 1987.

Hobbes, Thomas. *Leviathan.* New York: E. P. Dutton; and London: J. M. Dent, 1950.

Hughes, H. Trevor. *The Piety of Jeremy Taylor.* London: Macmillan; and New York: St. Martins, 1960.

Hume, David. *An Inquiry Concerning Human Understanding.* Ed. Charles W. Hendel. Library of Liberal Arts. Indianapolis, Ind.: Bobbs-Merrill, 1955.

Hurley, Michael, ed. *John Wesley's Letter to a Roman Catholic.* London: Geoffrey Chapman; Belfast: Epworth House; Nashville/New York: Abingdon Press, 1968.

Jedin, Hubert. *A History of the Council of Trent.* Trans. Dom Ernest Graf. 2 vols. London: Thomas Nelson and Sons, 1957.

Källstad, Thorvald. *John Wesley and the Bible: A Psychological Study.* Uppsala: Acta Universitatis Upsaliensis, 1974.

Keeble, N. H. *Richard Baxter: Puritan Man of Letters.* Oxford: Clarendon Press, 1982.

Kelsey, David H. *The Uses of Scripture in Recent Theology.* Philadelphia: Fortress Press, 1975.

Knott, John R., Jr. *The Sword of the Spirit: Puritan Responses to the Bible.* Chicago and London: University of Chicago, 1980.

Kümmel, Werner Georg. *The New Testament: The History of the Investigation of Its Problems.* Trans. S. McLean Gilmour and Howard C. Kee. Nashville/New York: Abingdon Press, 1972.

Langford, Thomas A., ed. *Doctrine and Theology in the United Methodist Church.* Nashville: Kingswood Books, 1991.

Lawton, George. *John Wesley's English: A Study of His Literary Style.* London: George Allen and Unwin, 1962.

Leith, John H., ed. *Creeds of the Churches: A Reader in Christian Doctrine from the Bible to the Present.* Rev. ed. Richmond, Va.: John Knox Press, 1973.

Lindström, Harald. *Wesley and Sanctification: A Study in the Doctrine of Salvation.* London: Epworth Press, 1950.

Locke, John. *An Essay Concerning Human Understanding.* ed. Peter H. Nidditch. Oxford: Clarendon Press, 1975.

_____. *A Paraphrase and Notes on the Epistles of St. Paul to the Galatians, 1 and 2 Corinthians, Romans, Ephesians.* Ed. Arthur W. Wainwright. 2 vols. Oxford: Clarendon Press, 1987.

_____. *The Reasonableness of Christianity.* Ed. and abr. I. T. Ramsey. Stanford, Calif.: Stanford University, 1958.

_____. *Two Treatises of Government.* Ed. Peter Laslett. Rev. ed. New York and Toronto: Mentor Books, 1960.

_____. *The Works of John Locke.* 10 vols. London: Tegg et al., 1823; repr. Germany: Scientia Verlag Aalen, 1963.

Locke, Louis G. *Tillotson: A Study in Seventeenth-Century Literature.* Anglistica vol. 4. Ed. Torsten Dahl, et al. Copenhagen: Rosenkilde and Bagger, 1954.

Lyons, George. "Hermeneutical Bases for Theology." *Wesleyan Theological Journal* 18 (1983): 63-78.

McAdoo, Henry R. *The Spirit of Anglicanism: A Survey of Anglican Theological Method in the Seventeenth Century.* New York: Scribner's, 1965.

McLachlan, H. *The Religious Opinions of Milton, Locke, and Newton.* New York: Russell and Russell, 1941; repr., 1972.

Maddox, Randy L., ed. *Aldersgate Reconsidered.* Nashville: Kingswood Books, 1990.

Margerie, Bertrand de. *Introduction à l'Histoire de l'Éxegèse.* Vol. 1 *Les Pères Grecs et Orientaux.* Paris: Editions du Cerf, 1980.

Marquardt, Manfred. *John Wesley's Social Ethics.* Trans. John E. Steely and W. Stephen Gunter. Nashville: Abingdon Press, 1992.

Martin, Hugh. *Puritanism and Richard Baxter.* London: S.C.M. Press, 1954.

Matthews, Rex Dale. "'Religion and Reason Joined': A Study in the Theology of John Wesley." Ph.D. diss., Harvard University, 1986.

Michaelson, Carl. "The Hermeneutics of Holiness in Wesley." In *The Heritage of Christian Thought: Essays in Honor of Robert Lowry Calhoun,* ed. Robert E. Cushman and Egil Grislis, 127-41. New York: Harper and Row, 1965.

Monk, Robert C. *John Wesley: His Puritan Heritage.* Nashville/New York: Abingdon Press, 1966.

More, Paul Elmer, and Frank Leslie Cross, eds. *Anglicanism: The Thought and Practice of the Church of England, Illustrated from the Religious Literature of the Seventeenth Century.* New York: Macmillan, 1957.

Mullen, Wilbur H. "John Wesley's Method of Biblical Interpretation." *Religion in Life* 47 (1978): 99-108.

Neil, W. "The Criticism and Theological Use of the Bible, 1700–1950." In *The Cambridge History of the Bible: The West from the Reformation to the Present Day*, ed. S. L. Greenslade, 238-93. Cambridge: University Press, 1963.

Nestle, Eberhard, and Erwin Nestle, et al., eds. *Novum Testamentum Graece*. 26th ed. Stuttgart: Deutsche Bibelgessellschaft, 1979.

Nuttall, Geoffrey F. *Richard Baxter*. London: Nelson, 1965.

_____. *Richard Baxter and Philip Doddridge: A Study in a Tradition*. Friends of Dr. Williams' Library Fifth Lecture. London: Oxford, 1951.

O'Higgins, James. *Anthony Collins: The Man and His Works*. The Hague: Martinus Nijhoff, 1970.

_____. "Archbishop Tillotson and the Religion of Nature." *Journal of Theological Studies* NS 24 (1973): 123-42.

Orr, Robert R. *Reason and Authority: The Thought of William Chillingworth*. Oxford: Clarendon Press, 1967.

Oswalt, John N. "Wesley's Use of the Old Testament in His Doctrinal Teachings." *Wesleyan Theological Journal* 12 (1977): 39-51.

Outler, Albert C. *John Wesley*. Library of Protestant Thought. New York: Oxford, 1964.

_____. "A New Future for Wesley Studies: An Agenda for 'Phase III'." In *The Future of the Methodist Theological Traditions*, ed. M. Douglas Meeks, 34-52. Nashville: Abingdon Press, 1985.

_____. "The Place of Wesley in the Christian Tradition." In *The Place of Wesley in the Christian Tradition*, ed. Kenneth E. Rowe, 11-38. Metuchen, N.J.: Scarecrow Press, 1976.

_____. *Theology in the Wesleyan Spirit*. Nashville: Discipleship Resources/Tidings, 1975.

_____. "The Wesleyan Quadrilateral—in John Wesley." In *Doctrine and Theology in the United Methodist Church*, ed. Thomas A. Langford, 75-88. Nashville: Kingswood Books, 1991.

Piette, Maximin. *John Wesley in the Evolution of Protestantism*. London: Sheed and Ward, 1937; repr., 1979.

Reedy, Gerard. *The Bible and Reason: Anglicans and Scripture in Seventeenth-Century England*. Philadelphia: University of Pennsylvania, 1985.

Reventlow, Henning Graf. *The Authority of the Bible and the Rise of the Modern World*. Trans. John Bowden. Philadelphia: Fortress Press, 1985.

Rowe, Kenneth E., ed. *The Place of Wesley in the Christian Tradition*. Metuchen, N.J.: Scarecrow Press, 1976, repr., 1980.

Rudé, George. *Hanoverian London, 1714–1808*. Berkeley and Los Angeles: University of California Press, 1971.

Runyon, Theodore H. "A New Look at Experience" *Drew Gateway* 57 (1987): 44-55.

Rupp, Gordon. *Religion in England, 1688–1791.* Oxford: Clarendon Press, 1986.

Schaff, Philip. *The Creeds of Christendom, with a History and Critical Notes.* 3 vols. New York: Harper & Bros., 1896.

Schmid, Heinrich. *The Doctrinal Theology of The Evangelical Lutheran Church.* Trans. Charles A. Hay and Henry E. Jacobs. 3rd rev. ed. Minneapolis: Augsburg, 1875; repr. 1961.

Schmidt, Martin. *John Wesley: A Theological Biography.* Trans. Norman P. Goldhawk and Dennis Inman. 2 vols. in 3. Nashville/New York: Abingdon Press, 1963–73.

Scholder, Klaus. *The Birth of Modern Critical Theology: Origins and Problems of Biblical Criticism in the Seventeenth Century.* Trans. John Bowden. London: S.C.M. Press, and Philadelphia: Trinity Press International, 1990.

Scroggs, Robin. "John Wesley as Biblical Scholar." *Journal of Bible and Religion* 28 (1960): 415-22.

Semmel, Bernard. *The Methodist Revolution.* New York: Basic Books, 1973.

Sergeant, John. *Sure Footing in Christianity, or, Rational Discourses on the rule of Faith. With . . . Animadversions on Dr. Pierce's Sermon.* London: n.p., 1665.

Shapiro, Barbara J. *Probability and Certainty in Seventeenth-Century England: A Study of the Relationships Between Natural Science, Religion, History, Law, and Literature.* Princeton: Princeton University Press, 1983.

Shelton, Larry. "John Wesley's Approach to Scripture in Historical Perspective." *Wesleyan Theological Journal* 16 (Spring 1981): 23-50.

Simon, Irene. *Three Restoration Divines: Barrow, South, Tillotson: Selected Sermons.* Bibliothèque de la Faculté de Philosophie et Lettres de l'Université de Liège Fascicule CLXXXI. 2 vols. in 3. Paris: Société d'Édition "Les Belles Lettres," 1967.

Smith, Timothy L. "John Wesley and the Wholeness of Scripture." *Interpretation* 39 (1985): 246-62.

Stephen, Leslie. *History of English Thought in the Eighteenth Century.* 3rd ed. 2 vols. 1902; repr., New York: Peter Smith, 1949.

Stranks, C. J. *The Life and Writings of Jeremy Taylor.* London: S.P.C.K., 1952.

Strong, James. *The Exhaustive Concordance of the Bible.* Nashville: Abingdon Press, 1890; repr., 1980.

Sullivan, Robert E. *John Toland and the Deist Controversy.* Cambridge, Mass., and London: Harvard University Press, 1982.

Sykes, Norman. "The Sermons of Archbishop Tillotson." *Theology* 58 (August 1955): 297-302.

_____. *From Sheldon to Secker: Aspects of English Church History, 1660–1768.* Cambridge: Cambridge University Press, 1959.

Taylor, Jeremy. *Holy Living and Holy Dying.* Vol. 2, *Holy Dying.* Ed. P. G. Stanwood. Oxford: Clarendon Press, 1989.

_____. *The Whole Works of the Right Rev. Jeremy Taylor.* Ed. Charles Eden and Reginald Heber. 10 vols. London: Longman Green, 1861–65.

Thorson, Donald A. D. *The Wesleyan Quadrilateral: Scripture, Tradition, Reason, and Experience as a Model of Evangelical Theology.* Grand Rapids, Mich.: Zondervan, 1990.

Tillotson, John. *The Works of the Most Reverend Dr. John Tillotson . . . Containing Fifty-four Sermons . . . together with the Rule of Faith.* 8th ed. London: T. Goodwin et al., 1720.

Trevor-Roper, Hugh. *Catholics, Anglicans, and Puritans: Seventeenth-Century Essays.* Chicago: University of Chicago, 1987.

Turner, George Allen. *The More Excellent Way: The Scriptural Basis of the Wesleyan Message.* Winona Lake, Ind.: Light and Life Press, 1952.

The United Methodist Hymnal: Book of United Methodist Worship. Nashville: United Methodist Publishing House, 1989.

Ware, Timothy. *The Orthodox Church.* Harmondsworth, U.K., and Baltimore, Md.: Penguin Books, 1963.

Weigle, Luther A. *The New Testament Octapla: Eight English Versions of the New Testament in the Tyndale–King James Tradition.* New York: Thomas Nelson, n.d.

Wesley, John. *Explanatory Notes upon the New Testament.* London: Wesleyan-Methodist Book Room, n.d.

_____. *John Wesley's New Testament.* Ed. George Croft Cell. Philadelphia: John C. Winston, 1938.

_____. *Lessons for Children.* London: Farley, 1746–54.

_____. *The Letters of John Wesley.* Ed. John Telford. 8 vols. London: Epworth Press, 1931.

_____. *The Sunday Service of the Methodists in North America with Other Occasional Services.* London, 1784. Reprinted as *John Wesley's Sunday Service of the Methodists in North America.* Quarterly Review Reprint Series. Nashville: United Methodist Publishing House and United Methodist Board of Higher Education and Ministry, 1984.

_____. *A Survey of the Wisdom of God in the Creation; Or, A Compendium of Natural Philosophy.* 2 vols. 1st ed. London, 1763.

_____. *The Works of John Wesley.* Ed. Frank Baker and Richard P. Heitzenrater. Vols. 7, 11, 25, and 26: The Oxford Edition, Oxford: Clarendon Press, 1975–83. All other vols.: Bicentennial Edition, Nashville: Abingdon Press, 1984–.

_____. *The Works of John Wesley, A.M.* Ed. Thomas Jackson. 14 vols. London: Wesleyan Conference Office, 1872. Repr., Grand Rapids, Mich.: Zondervan, 1958–59.

Wiener, Philip P. *Dictionary of the History of Ideas: Studies of Selected Pivotal Ideas.* New York: Scribner's, 1968–74. S.v. "Primitivism," by George Boas; "Primitivism in the Eighteenth Century," by A. Owen Aldridge.

Williams, Colin W. *John Wesley's Theology Today.* Nashville/New York: Abingdon Press, 1960.

Index